OUTLINE OF
BUSINESS LAW

by

O. J. ANDERSON

Associate Professor, Dept. of Business
Organization and Management
University of Nebraska

1978

LITTLEFIELD, ADAMS & CO.

Totowa, New Jersey

Library of Congress Catalog Number: 63-22777

Reprinted, 1966
Reprinted, 1970
Reprinted, 1975
Reprinted, 1978

PRINTED IN THE UNITED STATES OF AMERICA

PREFACE

An outline, properly prepared, serves as a guide to the mass of material available to the student in lectures, outside reading assignments and the prescribed textbook. Today's improved techniques of teaching, superior library facilities, and the general practice of making courses more significant by relating theory to everyday problems, make it more and more necessary to utilize to the best advantage, the limited time available.

By supplying the student with a skeleton or concise outline of the subject, the instructor is free to devote more of his time to the enrichment of the course through his lectures, and the student is free to devote more rapt attention. The printed page can never be a substitute for the insight and enthusiasm which a good lecturer can bring to a field of knowledge. Any device, therefore, that increases the opportunity of an instructor to share with his students the results of long experiences and research should be welcome.

The publisher welcomes all suggestions which will help to improve future editions of this book, either in content or format. Frequent revisions make it possible to include such changes promptly.

CONTENTS

INTRODUCTION

A. THE "LAW"

The purpose of teaching commercial law to laymen is to give them sufficient acquaintance with the elements of the law so they might know when to seek the aid of a lawyer. Businessmen will find they can save themselves many costly and time-consuming problems and procedures by obtaining legal advice in advance of, rather than after, taking action.

The "law" may be defined as a body of rules and regulations governing the conduct of human beings in their relationships with one another, and with society as a whole. As society becomes increasingly complex, so too must that body of written and unwritten rules which we call the law. Specifically, our law consists of:

(1) Constitutions—both Federal and State—provide broad general principles.
(2) Statutes—enacted by the Congress and State Legislatures—carry forward and make more specific these constitutional principles.
(3) Court Decisions—both Federal and State—add to our body of law rules concerning fields of activity not covered by statutory regulations. These court-made rules are designated as the "common law," and are established by the precedents of prior court decisions (*stare decisis*). Court decisions further contribute to the body of law by setting forth the interpretation of statutory and constitutional language, and thereby providing additional language and new meaning to the written law.

In the United States we have fifty-one sovereignties (Federal and fifty States), each having general law-making powers. The law is *not* uniform in each of these jurisdictions. Since a study of each of these one by one would be virtually impossible and entirely impractical, presentation, therefore, must be general.

The law may be broken down in several different ways:

(1) Criminal and Civil Actions—A criminal action is a proceeding by a government to enforce a public right by means of criminal penalties (fine or imprisonment), while a civil action is a proceeding brought by an individual or group of individuals to enforce a private right.

(2) Common and Code Law—The common law, which originated in England and was brought here by our ancestors, is court-made law as compared to code law (also referred to as Roman or civil law) which is wholly statutory and does not extend to situations not covered in the code.

(3) Substantive and Remedial Law—Substantive law provides us with our rights and obligations, and remedial law sets up the procedures necessary to enforce these rights and obligations.

(4) Law and Equity—Law, in contrast to equity, was a distinction originating in English legal history, and continuing to some extent to this day. Law, in the sense used here, comprised all the rules, rights, remedies, and procedures available in the law courts of England, which were originally the only courts. However, the proceedings in these courts became exceedingly formalized, and resulted in the law courts being unable to furnish any relief unless an injured party could fit his case into some particular "pigeonhole" in the court clerk's desk. The only recourse was an appeal to the King's chancellor, the "keeper of the King's conscience," who, if justice demanded, would grant relief in the name of the King himself by issuing a direct order to the other party. Gradually, appeal to the King's chancellor became the normal means of enforcing certain rights not protected by the law courts, and there developed a system of chancery or equity courts. Today, we have but one system of courts in most jurisdictions, but there still remains the distinction between legal and equitable remedies.

B. THE COURT SYSTEMS AND PROCEDURES

Although our major concern is with substantive law (rights and obligations) and not remedial law (procedures, etc.), a brushing acquaintance with some phases of remedial law is basic to a proper understanding of the substantive law.

The courts in the United States may be categorized by their major functions—trial or appellate. A trial court's function is to determine a controversy by listening to the evidence presented by the opposing parties, determining therefrom the "true" facts, and applying the law to these facts in order to reach a decision. An appellate court's function is to determine whether a trial court has correctly stated and applied the law. Most courts function at one time or another in both capacities, but they may be generally categorized as follows:

	STATE	FEDERAL
TRIAL COURTS	Justice of Peace Courts Municipal Courts County Courts District Courts	U.S. District Courts U.S. Court of Claims
APPELLATE COURTS	Court of Appeals Supreme Court	U.S. Court of Appeals U.S. Supreme Court

The District Courts are the principal trial courts, with other courts of limited jurisdiction available to provide simpler and speedier relief. The Supreme Courts (except in a few jurisdictions) are the final arbiters of the law and its application in each jurisdiction.

All major decisions of appellate courts are issued out in written reports which contain a summary of the facts involved, the judgment of the court, and the reasons and precedents used in reaching that judgment. Decisions of lesser import are issued in short, written reports (memoranda decisions) containing only the judgment of the court. The reports are first published in "advance sheet" form which appear each week. Later, these reports are compiled into conventional bound volumes, which form the permanent reports.

Each case has a title which contains the names of the opposing parties, and the name of the report, its number, and the page on which the case is to be found (e.g., *Doakes v. Doe,* 131 N.Y. 1012). Some older reports are named after the court reporter rather than the jurisdiction (e.g., 7 *Metcalf* 409).

As has been indicated, lawyers and courts look to previously decided cases to determine what rule of law is applicable to a given fact situation. They find such cases through elaborate indexes and digests especially designed for that purpose. Once found, the cases must be read and analyzed with reference to the current problem. The most helpful "tool" for analyzing and preserving for future use those cases pertinent to the problem is the brief, which, as the name indicates, is a short statement of the case and the decision. The brief is usually in five parts, as follows:

PART	EXAMPLE
1. Title	Doakes v. Doe, 131 N.Y. 1012 (1955)
2. Facts	Doakes, working on a construction gang, said he would give $100 for an ice-cold drink. Doe, hearing this, jumped into his car and brought him one. Doakes wouldn't pay. Trial court found he must pay the $100 to Doe.
3. Judgment (Court's order)	Reversed. Judgment for defendant Doakes.
4. Rule (The legal precedent established)	An offer made in jest or without seriousness cannot be accepted by a knowing party and turned into an enforceable contract.
5. Decision (The reasoning of the court)	Parties to a contract must intend to enter into such, and an offer not intended to be seriously taken cannot be snapped up by another party. There would be no contract, for there would be no intention of such.

Trial procedures and the applicable terms are best illustrated by example:

John Black was riding in an elevator in a building owned by Bill White. Black was on his way to see his dentist. The elevator cable broke, and the elevator, along with Black, crashed to the bottom of the shaft, resulting in serious injury to Black. Several months later, Black has recovered and proceeds to see White in order to be reimbursed for his medical and hospital expenses, as well as the wages lost from absence at his job. Black believed the elevator accident was the result of White's negligent failure to keep it in repair. However, White disclaimed any responsibility and merely said, "Tough, old boy; accidents will happen, you know. Why, you are lucky to be alive."

Black, not considering himself the luckiest man on earth, went to see a lawyer. The lawyer, after careful questioning of Black and further investigation, decided that Black had a good negligence case. The lawyer then drew up a petition (complaint), which is a statement in simple and concise language of the facts constituting the reason for court action.

A verification of the petition was made by the plaintiff (Black), said verification being a written statement signed under oath (affidavit) that the allegations contained in the petition are true, to the best of his knowledge.

A filing of the petition was made in the office of the clerk of the proper court, whereupon a docket number was assigned to the case and stamped on all documents pertaining thereto.

The defendant (White) must then be brought into the case by means of a summons. Black has submitted himself and his case to the jurisdiction of the court by filing the complaint. To submit White to the jurisdiction of the court, White must be properly notified. This method of notification is called "service of process" and in nearly all cases is carried out by the clerk of the court issuing, under seal, a document known as the summons. The summons is addressed to the defendant and informs him that he is being sued and must, therefore, answer within a specified time or be defaulted. The law requires that the defendant get the best possible notification, so, if at all possible, this summons must be personally served upon White, i.e., must be handed to the defendant along with a copy of the complaint. If the defendant refuses to take the summons, merely touching him with it and dropping it to the ground will suffice.

After service, the process server (a sheriff or marshal) prepared a return, which is an affidavit to the effect that the defendant has been served. This return was filed with the clerk of the court.

The summons that White has received informs him that he must make an appearance on a certain date, or submit an answer within a certain time-period, or be in default. This means a judgment will be entered by the court against White unless he takes steps to prepare an answer or defense.

White should go immediately to his lawyer, whereupon the latter will scrutinize the complaint and White's story. White's attorney will either prepare an answer, which is the defendant's counterpart to the plaintiff's petition, denying in part or in whole the plaintiff's allegations, or file with the court a demurrer on the grounds that the petition does not state a cause of action. The demurrer places into issue questions of law as to whether the complaint sets out facts, even if all are true, sufficient to allow the plaintiff to win. The demurrer is argued before the judge by the attorneys. If the judge sustains the demurrer, the plaintiff may amend his petition to correct the defects, but failing to do this, or if the amended petition is still deficient, the court will dismiss the case on the grounds that there is no valid cause of action. If, however, the judge overrules the demurrer, the defendant's attorney must file an answer.

These preliminary pleadings are but steps to pinpoint the legal and factual issues that the court and the jury must decide. When these issues are shaped, the case is taken to trial.

On the appointed day, both parties appeared in court with their attorneys and witnesses. The first step in the trial is the selection of a jury, if a jury is to be used. Equity cases are tried before a judge sitting without a jury, and the jury in law cases may be waived by consent of both parties.

For one reason or another, Black's attorney felt that a jury would be more favorable to his client. Therefore, both attorneys proceeded to pick a jury from a group initially selected by the court. Each attorney examined the individuals to assure impartiality on their part. An unlimited number of potential jurors may be removed (challenged) for cause, if the judge agrees, and a limited number may be removed without cause by means of peremptory challenges.

After the jury has been selected, the trial goes forward with the presentation of evidence, which includes documents and the testimony of witnesses. It is important to remember that the most difficult task for the attorney, and of prime importance, is the preparation of the case for trial, and not the trial itself. The effectiveness of counsel at trial is the result of his preparation beforehand.

At the close of the presentation of evidence, and any summary arguments of fact, the jury was presented with instructions by the judge as to the law applicable to the case. The jury is to decide only questions of fact, and, therefore, must be instructed by the judge as to the law so that they might reach a verdict. The verdict in this case, if for the plaintiff Black, will state the sum of money he is to recover from White.

Either party may appeal the decision of the Trial Court through his attorney if he feels serious errors of law were committed during the course of the trial affecting his rights. The Appellate Court will consider only errors of law, and normally it will not consider any information not contained in the record, i.e., all documents and exhibits filed in the case plus a stenographic transcript of everything said at the trial. The Appellate Court may either reverse the judgment, dismissing the case or calling for a new trial, or may affirm the judgment of the Trial Court. If the judgment is affirmed, the appellant (the party taking the appeal) may go on to a higher court, if available, or accept the judgment of the Trial Court. If the case is reversed, the appellee has the same choice of actions.

Thus are the procedures of the law in court actions. But only a small portion of our legal system or law involves court action. The major function of our legal system, that which most affects our daily lives, is yet to be presented.

Chapter 1

CONTRACTS

A. INTRODUCTION

A contract may be defined as follows: "A contract is an agreement to do or to refrain from doing a certain thing which the law will enforce." You may ask why it is necessary to add the last clause to this definition. Well, suppose *A* asks *B* to dinner and *B* accepts and then fails to appear. Can *A* sue *B* for breach of contract? Obviously not, although *B* has broken his "agreement to do a certain thing." Therefore, we must add to the definition the condition that the law will enforce the agreement.

Contracts may be broken down into several, but not parallel, classifications as follows:

(1) Express and Implied Contracts—A contract is an agreement, but an agreement is a concept, not a tangible object. It is a state of mind. There may be evidences of that state of mind which are perceptible to our senses, e.g., words on a piece of paper, telephone calls, documents under seal, etc., but the contract is still the intangible concept—the state of mind. An express contract is one in which this state of mind is reduced to words, written or spoken, or even both. An implied contract is reached without any spoken words; the state of mind being indicated by the actions of the parties, as for example, stockbrokers who in a day may make contracts totalling thousands of dollars without a word being spoken. Thus, contracts are created by both words and actions.

(2) Executory and Executed Contracts—In an executory contract, the obligations of the parties have yet to be fulfilled. Thus, if *A* promises to pay to *B* $500 for his car next Thursday, and *B* promises to deliver the car that day, at the time the agreement is entered into it is an executory contract. On Thursday, when the car has been

delivered and the money has been paid, the contract is said to have been executed.

(3) Contracts and Quasi-Contracts—As we have previously seen, contracts may be created by either words or actions of the parties. In addition, contracts may be created by operation of law. Thus, while a contract is the result of a voluntary and intentional assent to an obligation, a quasi-contract is an obligation imposed by law. Thus, if one man has profited at the expense of another under circumstances that in justice call for a readjustment of rights, the law will impose a contract obligation on the man unjustly enriched in order to reimburse the injured party.

(4) Bilateral and Unilateral Contracts—A bilateral contract is an exchange of promises—a promise for a promise. For example, a bilateral contract would be evident where *A* promises to sell *B* his watch for $50, and *B* promises to pay *A* $50 therefor. A unilateral contract is an exchange of a promise for an act. The classic example of this type of contract is an offer of reward. Thus, *C* offers a $25 reward for the return of his lost watch—a promise on C's part only. Now if *D* finds and returns the watch, *C*'s promise becomes enforceable by *D*. *D*'s act has ripened *C*'s offer into a unilateral contract. *C*'s offer can only be accepted by an act, not by a promise. In the case of the bilateral contract offer, *A*'s offer can only be accepted by another promise.

(5) Void and Voidable Contracts—A void contract is not a contract at all, so it is, in a sense, a misnomer. A void contract is an agreement that has all the trappings of a contract but is not enforceable at law. Thus, if Murder, Inc. offers *A* $5,000 to kill *B*, and *A* complies, the illegal purpose of the agreement makes it impossible for *A* to enforce the agreement in court. Thus, the "contract" is void. A voidable contract is one by which certain shortcomings in the agreement provide to one of the contracting parties the option to either cancel or enforce the contract. For example, if *C* pays $25 down to a store to have a suit, falsely represented to be made of wool, laid away until he pays another $25, *C* may either pay the $25 and enforce the store's obligation to deliver the suit or may repudiate the contract and recover his $25

because of the fraudulent representation.

(6) Formal and Informal Contracts—A formal contract is precisely that which its terms indicate. It is a contract in which terms have been set out in a written instrument, normally prepared by an attorney. An informal contract need not even be in writing.

(7) Joint and Several Contracts—Most contracts are between two parties only. However, if other parties are introduced, the law apportions rights and duties according to the category of the multi-party contract. Assume *A* and *B* agree to pay *C* $1,000 for a piano. In a several contract, both *A* and *B* are individually responsible to *C* for payment of the full purchase price. In a joint contract, each is responsible only for a pro rata share. A joint and several contract combines features of both of the preceding types. In most jurisdictions, multi-party contracts are, in the absence of words to the contrary, presumed to be joint and several.

B. ELEMENTS OF THE CONTRACT

As we have seen, a contract is an agreement which the law will enforce. This definition raises the question as to what agreements the law will enforce. Well, the law will enforce agreements which are composed and will meet the requirements of the following elements:

(1) Mutual Agreement—It must be a mutual agreement reached through offer and acceptance, and free from fraud, duress, undue influence, or mistake.

(2) Capacity—The parties to the contract must be competent to enter into enforceable agreements.

(3) Legality—The purpose of the agreement, or the subject matter involved, must be lawful.

(4) Consideration—A contract must be supported by consideration on both sides.

We shall now proceed to examine these elements in detail.

I. Mutual Agreement

a. MEETING OF THE MINDS

An agreement exists when the minds of two or more persons

have "met." How can we tell when this occurs? Since it is of course impossible to read another's mind, we obviously have to look to the outward evidences of the parties' states of mind. It is impossible to know with certainty what a party is thinking merely from the outward evidence—words, gestures, behavior, etc.—but it is not impossible to make a pretty shrewd guess.

In order for two or more parties to reach a meeting of the minds, it is necessary that each intends to enter into a contract. This presents a sticky problem in many circumstances, as is illustrated in the following four examples:

(1) Suppose *A* promises to sell his car to *B* for $500, and *B* agrees to buy. *B* then tenders *A* $500, but *A* refuses to deliver the car, stating that he did not mean what he said, that he never intended to sell.

(2) Suppose *A* offers to sell *B* the Brooklyn Bridge and all rights to the tolls in exchange for $8,000, and *B* accepts. *B* pays and, now that he has not received title to the bridge, seeks damages equaling the amount of profit he would have made on tolls for the life of the bridge.

(3) *A,* enraged over the robbery of a flashlight from his car, offers a $100 reward for the return of the flashlight, the value of which is, at most, $15. *B* finds the flashlight and returns it. *A* tenders him only $5 as a reward.

(4) Suppose *A* takes his car into *B*'s garage and tells the mechanic to oil and grease the car and to fix the windshield wiper. *A,* on leaving, adds, "Do whatever else you feel is necessary." When *A* returns, the garage has put a new motor in his car, repainted the body, and added tail-fins "to stabilize the highway travel." *A* won't pay, but the *B* garage insists that he pay, that they felt the things done were necessary, and that *A* agreed to pay for them.

In example (1), *A* must deliver the car. Whether he intended to sell or not is irrelevant, so long as his actions cause *B* to reasonably believe that he, *A,* intended to sell the car. This, then, is the test used: Do the outward evidences of a party's intent make another person reasonably believe that the party intends to enter into a contract? The person who is or is not reasonably led to believe the intent of the party may be either the other party to the contract or an independent, reasonable, third party, depending upon the jurisdiction. Applying this test to the remaining examples, we are likely to find that there are no contracts in numbers (2), (3), and (4) because the intention of entering upon a contract is lacking. In number (2), *B* may recover his money but he cannot recover the lost profits, for no reasonable person could really believe *A*'s offer. In number (3), *B* could not recover the full award for the same reason as in (2). The circumstances showed an offer by *A* that no reasonable person could believe he meant to fulfill. In number (4), we call upon our experience to tell us that *A* did not intend to make a contract as broad as the meaning of his words. Of course, there would be additional circumstances and evidence to consider in these cases upon an actual happening. The important point at present is the test to be used.

A problem concerning the meeting of minds arises when a contract is made combining elements both express and implied; when the terms of the contract are express and the acceptance of the terms is implied by inaction.

For example, suppose *A* telephones his insurance broker and asks him to send out a fire insurance policy on *A*'s new house. *A* receives his policy, glances through it but does not read the provisions, and pays the first premium. The house burns down, and *A* puts in a claim. The insurance company replies that it does not consider itself liable, as this particular loss was caused by a hazard not covered by the policy. To this, *A* replies, "I did not read the policy, and I am not bound by all of that fine print!" Who prevails? Well, if the insurance company's contention is substantively correct, they prevail, for *A* is bound by his acquiescence. *A* knew, or reasonably should have known, that the policy contained binding terms, and his ignorance was unjustified.

Suppose again that *B*, an orange grower, prepares to ship his fruit to the East from California. When the railroad takes custody of his shipment, it presents *B* with a bill of lading. *B* does not read the terms on the bill. *B* is nevertheless bound by those terms, for he should have known that the bill of lading contains binding terms.

But suppose that *C* checks his suitcase at a baggage stand and is given a claim check by the attendant. When C returns to claim his bag, it is discovered to be missing. *C* is dismayed, for the suitcase and its contents are worth $500. However, when he demands reimbursement from the check-stand, he is told that they will pay no more than $25; that these were the terms of the agreement, and that these terms appeared on the back of *C*'s claim check. *C* replies that he did not know of the terms and that it was the check-stand's business to see that no luggage disappeared. This time, *C* will prevail, for it is to be reasonably believed by a party checking his baggage that the claim check is for identification purposes only. However, had the terms of the contract been called to the attention of *C* by the check-stand attendant, then *C* would be bound.

These cases are referred to in order to show that, while it is generally stated that the law requires an actual meeting of the minds, this requirement should not be taken in its strict, literal sense.

b. Offer and Acceptance

1. In General

The student will remember that manifested intent is necessary to the creation of a contract. This unanimity of intent is reached through the machinery of offer and acceptance. For instance, *A* offers, "I will sell you my watch for $50," and *B* accepts, "O.K., it's a deal." The parties have now agreed; there has been a meeting of the minds through offer and acceptance.

It is important to remember that the person making the offer (called the offeror) may phrase his offer in any manner that he so desires. It is his offer, and he may interpose any terms and conditions that he desires, however absurd or outlandish.

In the simple illustration above of an offer and acceptance, the offer disclosed an intent, directed toward a person who was asked to consider the proposal, and which proposal concerned matters specifically stated.

Suppose someone wrote another party, "I have about 1,800 bushels of millet seed. I want $2.25 per cwt. for this seed." Is this an offer? Well, the Supreme Court of Nebraska has ruled that it is not, for it did not disclose willingness to bear the legal consequences of a proposal. Such is the situation for most advertisements, circulars sent to trade customers, and the like. The courts generally find these not to be offers but instead are invitations for offers. Suppose *A* sells men's clothing. *B*, walking down the street, sees an overcoat in *A*'s window marked $75. *B* walks into the store, hands the clerk $75, saying, "I'll take that coat in the window." The clerk takes the coat out of the window, examines it, and then tells *B* that there has been a mistake, that the price of the coat is actually $90. *B* protests, but, if we were present, we could tell him that his only hope would be to appeal to *A*'s goodwill—that he would be unsuccessful in a court of law. Again, the courts do not consider the marking in the store window to be an offer. An incidental note to the above that will later be developed further, is that had the clerk accepted the $75, only to discover later the actual price, no extra charge can be made to *B*. There has been a "professed meeting of the minds."

Who is the offeror at an auction? Surprisingly, it is the bidder, and the auctioneer is the acceptor when he drops his hammer indicating acceptance. It will be seen later that the bidder may withdraw his bid at any point before the auctioneer's "knock down" of the item.

You must not presume from the foregoing that it is impossible to make an offer by advertisement, as it is—provided it is clear that the author intends the ad to be an offer. In a reported case, a company advertised it would pay a $100 reward to anyone who used their smoke ball and contracted influenza. One user contracted influenza and brought proceedings in court to recover after the company refused payment. The court held the advertisement to be a valid contract, finding that the company intended such to be an offer.

An offer that is met by an unqualified acceptance ripens immediately into an agreement. Thus, upon acceptance, the offer disappears, and the agreement (which is usually a contract) comes to life. Only the person to whom an offer has been directed may accept the offer. This is true since a contract is a voluntary proposal and the offeror can select with whom he cares to deal and with whom he is to be reasonable. This statement includes in its meaning that the offer has, in fact, been communicated to the offeree by the offeror or his authorized agent. If the offeree learns of the offeror's intention from some outside source, no offer results. The city council of a town near Jersey City passed a resolution authorizing its mayor to execute a contract with Jersey City for a water supply. Jersey City, learning of this resolution, drew up a contract meeting the specifications set out in the resolution. Then the council repealed the resolution. Jersey City sued for breach of contract. Judgment was for the defendant, as there was no offer because none was communicated. *Mayor, etc. of Jersey City v. Town of Harrison,* 72 N.J.L. 185.

Following this reasoning, an offer for a reward is effective to give rise to a unilateral contract only if the act is performed with knowledge of the reward promised.

2. Duration of an Offer

As has been noted, an offer which has been accepted is immediately extinguished, becoming merged into the contract. Likewise, an offer that has not been accepted does not continue indefinitely, but has a limited existence and may be destroyed or removed in several ways. These are:

(1) Revocation
(2) Rejection
(3) Counteroffer
(4) Lapse of stated or reasonable time.

Revocation of the offer may be made by the offeror at any time prior to an acceptance, but this revocation must be communicated to the offeree in order to be effective. Revocation is usually accomplished by express words, but the law will also imply that the offeror has revoked if he dies or becomes insane. Remember, we have discussed a basic requirement of a contract —a meeting of the minds—and there obviously can be no meeting of the minds if one of the parties is dead or insane.

An offer of a reward which is published in a newspaper presents a special problem. These offers may be revoked by publishing a revocation, which will thus be of the same character as the original offer. Such published revocations are effective even as to those who do not actually read the revocation. The Secretary of War at one time caused to be published in the newspapers an offer of reward for the apprehension of a certain person. *H. M.* apprehended the person being sought, and claimed the offered reward. However, five months before this apprehension, a revocation was published, given the same circulation as the offer, although *H. M.* did not actually see the revocation. *H. M.* was paid a portion of the amount offered as a reward, and brought court proceedings to recover the remainder. However, the court held that regardless of his lack of knowledge of the revocation, it was effective and he could not recover. See *Shuey, Executor v. United States,* 92 U.S. 73 (1875).

At this point, it should be noted that the power of revocation may be stayed by the offeree by means of an option. An option may be defined as a contract entered into for the purpose of preventing revocation of an offer, this offer being for another contract. The holder of the option has given something of value for the right to delay decision on the offer, without the possibility that it will be revoked. Without the giving of something of value, called consideration, as discussed later, the offeror may revoke his offer at any time prior to acceptance by the offeree. Thus, if *A* offers to sell his house to *B* and says, "I'll give you ten days to think it over," *A* is not legally prevented from revoking his offer before the ten days have elapsed. However, if *B* is quite interested in *A*'s offer, but must sell his own house before agreeing to buy that of *A, B* would be wise to "take an option," by giving *A* a sum of money to insure that *B* may not revoke his offer. A contract has now arisen, in which *A*'s promise not to revoke his offer is exchanged for *B's* money. Thus, where *S* paid *R* a sum of money for an option on *R*'s services for a year, and later discovered that *R* would not perform these services according to the terms of the option, *S* was able to successfully bring a court proceeding to prevent *R* from selling these services under option from being rendered to another party. The terms of the option were thereby enforced, and revocation was prevented.

Rejection of an offer causes it to pass out of existence. Thus, if *A* offers to sell his watch to *B* for $50 and *B* refuses to buy, rejecting the offer, *B* cannot later change his mind and bind *A* to the original offer to sell.

A counteroffer has the same effect as a rejection, as it is a form of rejection. Thus, if *B,* in the example above, had said, "No, but I'll give you $35," the offer is still extinguished and *B* cannot go back to the original offer and accept it. A counteroffer rejects the offer by varying the terms of it. This must be distinguished from a "mere inquiry," however. Thus, if *B* had asked, "Would you accept $35?," this would be a mere inquiry, and not a counteroffer. In this instance the original offer is still open for acceptance.

Lapse of the stated or reasonable time may also cause an offer to expire. If no time is stated during which the offer will remain open, it will be considered to be open for a reasonable time. The offeror may specify any time limit for the offer to be open that he chooses, and this will limit the time during which the offeree may effectively accept. Lacking this specified time, a reasonable time will limit the period during which the offeree may accept, as determined by consideration of (1) method of communication (mail or telegraph); (2) nature of the subject matter of the offer (as bricks compared to fresh fruit, or corporate stocks compared to real estate); and (3) any special circumstances known to the offeror and offeree. Common sense is the usual guide in these situations. The examples used may be explained by considering that for corporate stocks, a short time would be considered reasonable because the offeror does not want the offeree to speculate at the risk of the offeror; whereas, for a building (real estate), a longer time would be reasonable because of the time necessary to arrange for financing, examining the title to the property, and so forth.

The method of communication is very important, as most business today is conducted at a distance. In the situations presented earlier, the parties have always been together when the offer was made. When the offer is made from a distance, and the acceptance must be communicated at a distance also, the method of communication may become very significant. The acceptance is considered to be communicated between the parties forming a contract when the offeree accepting the offer places his acceptance in the mail or other method of communication and the acceptance starts on the way to the offeror. Thus, if *A,* in New York, writes to *B,* in Chicago, offering to sell his house for $10,000, and *B* places his acceptance in the mailbox several days after receiving the offer, the acceptance is legally effective at the moment it is dropped into the mailbox in Chicago.

A complication arises when *B*'s letter, properly addressed and stamped, does not reach *A*. *A,* because he has not received the acceptance from *B,* and thinking that *B* is not going to accept, makes an offer to sell his house to *C*. *A* has allowed a reasonable time to elapse. *C* immediately accepts *A*'s offer. Under the rule above, *B*'s acceptance is legally effective, and *C*'s immediate acceptance is also legally effective, thus leaving *A* in the position of being legally bound to two contracts of sale. *A* must obviously breach one of these two valid contracts. *A* could easily have avoided this dilemma by merely including in his letter to *B* the words "No acceptance shall be effective unless and until received by me." As you can see, someone must accept the risk of time delay, and this is usually the offeror, but he may shift the risk of loss during the communication by the method indicated here.

3. Means of Acceptance

The offeror may specify the means by which his offer must be accepted. Unless this is done, the offeree may use any reasonable means of communicating his acceptance to the offeror. Usually this indicates that the offeree may use the same means of accepting as the offeror has used in communicating the offer. If any standard method is used, the acceptance ripens into a contract when the acceptance is deposited with the carrier. Thus, if *B* receives *A's* letter offering to sell his house, and *B* is so anxious to buy that he telegraphs his acceptance immediately, the acceptance is effective when *B* gives the message to the telegraph company. However, because *A* used the mails, thus implying a request that *B* also use the mails, *B* should have written a letter. By using a different means of communication than impliedly authorized, *B* takes the risk of delay, missent messages, and such. Therefore, the safest procedure is always to employ the means of communication used, and thus impliedly authorized, by the offeror.

Revocations, rejections, and counteroffers are not effective until received or communicated. To illustrate, *A*, in New York, offers by mail to sell his house to *B*, in Chicago. *B* accepts by mailing a letter on Tuesday. *A*, however, has changed his mind and decided not to sell, so on the prior Monday had mailed a letter of revocation which did not reach *B* until after the letter of acceptance was in the mail. The revocation is not effective, and *A* is legally bound to sell his house to *B*. However, if *B* knows that *A* has already sold the house to *C*, regardless of how *B* gains this information, this is sufficient to make the revocation effective. This act, known to *B*, shows clearly the intent to revoke, and *B* may not validly accept after learning of this intent.

In the case of a unilateral contract, the rules are somewhat different. Although generally an offer may be revoked at any time prior to acceptance, the law will not permit revocation of an offer to form a unilateral contract after part performance in good faith by the offeree. Assume that *A* says to *B*, an artist, "I'll give you $500 if you will paint my portrait," and *B* immediately starts to work. Before the portrait is completed, *A* states, "*B*, I have changed my mind and do not want my portrait painted, so I hereby revoke my offer." *B* will recover, the court either construing this as a bilateral contract, or under one of the following theories:

(1) Once the offeree begins to accept the offer, he has the time stated or a reasonable time to complete the act, during which time the offer may not be revoked; or

(2) The offer may be revoked, but *B* will recover in quasi-contract for the value of the services which he has rendered, not to exceed the contract price. The law simply enforces the duty to pay as though a promise, or contract, in fact exists, in order to achieve justice. The duty to "mitigate damages" will be discussed later, which may conflict with (1) above, and mere preparation to accept is not sufficient to prevent the revocation or withdrawal of the offer.

The acceptance may be prescribed by the offeror to be made by an unequivocal act of the offeree. Thus, *A* may offer to sell his piano to B, saying, "*B,* if you want to accept this offer, you must wear to class next Monday a straw hat covered with roses." As *B* would probably not wear such a hat for any reason other than to accept, this act when done constitutes a valid acceptance. However, if *A* had said, "*B,* if you want to accept this offer, you must wear a white shirt to class next Monday," this is an equivocal act, and if *B* wears a white shirt he must also tell *A* that he intends by doing so to signify his acceptance to have a valid acceptance. *B*'s wearing of the white shirt has no independent significance, as *B* would very possibly wear a white shirt even had *A* not mentioned such an act, and the mere wearing of the shirt will not constitute a valid acceptance.

An important exception to the rule that the offeror may specify means of acceptance is that the offeror cannot require the offeree to take positive action to reject the offer. He cannot specify that the silence of the offeree shall constitute acceptance. There are situations where this exception does not apply, as:

(1) Silence may create acceptance where the property is received and used knowing that it is not intended to be a gift. This is termed a contract implied in fact, and arises when a person accepts the benefits of the goods without protest under such circumstances that he knows no gift was intended. Thus, if *A* is at home, and watches *B* repair the roof on *A*'s house without protest, even though *A* did not request such work, *A* may be forced to pay for the work. However, if *A* is out of town and finds a new roof on his house, due to a mistake on the part of the repairman, *A*'s silence will not constitute acceptance.

(2) When one solicits orders subject to the seller's approval, notice within a reasonable time of its rejection is required. Silence will operate as acceptance. Thus, when an agent took an order for a seeder, subject to approval of the home office, and the office neither approved nor notified the buyer of rejec-

tion of the order, silence was considered by the court to be acceptance, and the buyer recovered his damages due to the non-delivery of the machinery.

(3) Prior dealings between the parties may make silence constitute acceptance, by creating a duty to speak. Thus, where a salesman takes an order, and continues to see the buyer every week without mentioning the order, while the price of the goods greatly increases, the silence has been held by the court to be acceptance. The seller is not permitted to remain silent, to choose at his leisure whether to accept or reject the order, to the detriment of the buyer.

(4) When the offeree stands under some legal duty to the offeror and the latter orders the offeree to discharge the duty or accept a reasonable alternative, acceptance will be implied by the offeree's silence or refusal to act. This implied contract has been held by a court to arise when the plaintiff published a notice in a newspaper warning trespassers on his pasturage to remove their cattle or pay 50 cents per day, per head for grazing. Defendant read the notice, but failed to remove his animals, and plaintiff recovered.

4. Illusory Contracts

Although illusory contracts actually properly fall under the material dealing with consideration, discussed later, they also pertain to the points of offer and acceptance, so they will be mentioned here briefly. The term "illusory contracts," like the term "void contracts," is actually a misnomer, because there is no contract at all. These "contracts" are merely agreements not enforceable at law due to no consideration. The only consideration which might be found is actually an illusion. However, the purported contract may be an offer for a contract.

Thus, assume that *A* owns a fleet of taxicabs, and *B* is the proprietor of a service station. *B* promises to supply all of the gasoline that *A* wants for one year, and *A*, in return, agrees to buy from *B* all the gasoline that he, *A*, wants during the year. After purchasing all his gasoline from *B* for several months, *A* suddenly begins buying from *C*, who is selling at a greater discount. Can *B* sue *A* and recover? No, because this is an illusory contract. The term "wants" is illusory, meaning that *A* had not promised to buy all of his gasoline from *B*, but has only promised to buy gasoline from *B* if he feels inclined to do so. If *A* had promised to buy from *B* all of the gasoline that he needed, *B* could sue *A* and recover if *A* purchased from someone else, indicating that *A* had definite needs, and that the contract, therefore, was not illusory.

Illustrating the earlier statement that the illusory contract may be an offer, consider the example above, and assume that the parties carried out their agreement for several months. *A* then telephones *B* and places an order for 500 gallons of gasoline. *B* refuses to deliver this amount, claiming that this is merely an illusory contract, and not enforceable. *A* may sue and recover from *B*, for the law will declare that by the terms of the agreement, *B* has offered to sell gasoline to *A* at the given price, and that each order which *A* makes is an acceptance of the continuing offer. After the delivery of the 500 gallons, *B* may rescind his offer.

c. Reality of Consent (Intent)

An acceptance of an offer does not give rise to a contract when that acceptance does not possess what is called reality of consent (intent). For purposes of this discussion, the two terms above will be considered interchangeable. We have already discussed the meeting of the minds as one of the necessary elements of a contract. If the manifest intent of the parties is present, one portion of this requirement is satisfied. In addition, however, there must be real intent. The difference may be seen in the following examples:

(1) *A* offers to sell to *B* a piano for $450, and *B* accepts. There is both manifest intent and real intent in this case, and a binding contract is formed.

(2) *A* offers to sell to *B* the same piano, for the same price, but represents that this piano is a Steinway, only 14 months old, whereas actually the piano is not a Steinway, and is 10 years old. *B* believes *A*'s representations, and accepts the offer. Manifest intent is clearly present because *B* accepted the offer with the intent to form a binding contract, but real intent is lacking. *B*'s real intent is not to buy this piano, but a 14-month-old Steinway, as described by *A*. *B*'s intent here is a "manufactured intent" rather than a real intent, manufactured by *A*'s fraud and misrepresentations, and not real or genuine.

The law requires that the consent of the parties to a contract be free, mutual, and communicated by each to the other. An apparent consent is not free (or real) if it is obtained through fraud, duress, undue influence, or mistake, and the consent so obtained may be rescinded. The agreement thus obtained may be voided at the option of the defrauded party, or the contract may be void if mutual mistake is shown, meaning that no contract ever arose from the transaction.

II. Capacity

Because by our definition of a contract the agreement must be one which the law will enforce, our discussion must now turn to another element of the problem of what will constitute an enforceable agreement. This element consists of the limitations placed by the law upon the capacity of certain classes of persons to contract. These limitations make certain persons incapable of giving a binding assent to enter into a contract. Because all persons are presumed to have the capacity to contract, the burden of proof is upon the party attempting to avoid a contract on the basis of incapacity to contract to prove this incapacity. Following, we will consider some of these limitations.

a. Corporations

Although we are not at this time interested in the law concerning corporations or partnerships, we must consider them briefly, due to limitations upon their capacity to contract. Corporations are given power to do certain acts by their charter. Anyone contracting with a corporation is presumed to know what powers it has, because this charter is a matter of public record. Therefore, before entering into a contract with a corporation, one should investigate its charter to ensure that by entering into this contract the corporate powers are not being exceeded. If the contract is not within the charter powers of the corporation, it is termed *ultra vires*, meaning "beyond the powers granted." These acts may be challenged by the stockholders of the corporation.

Another problem is the power of agents to bind the corporation, because the corporation can only act through agents, such as the board of directors, officers, and employees. For an important contract, the safest procedure is to demand that a certified copy of the resolution authorizing the officers to enter into the contract be executed and affixed to the contract. The contract must be signed in the name of the corporation, by the officers authorized to do so, and stamped with the corporate seal.

In partnerships, each partner can bind the partnership to a contract which is within the scope of the partnership business. If any doubt exists as to whether the contract is within the scope of the partnership business, it is best to have the contract signed by all of the partners.

b. Minors

Most states have statutes which specify at what age a person reaches his majority and thereby becomes competent to enter into a valid contract. A typical example of such a statute would be: "All persons under the age of 21 years are declared to be minors, but in case a female marries under the age of 21 years, her minority ends." In the case of the female who marries prior to reaching age 21, this statute is usually interpreted not to apply to all situations—for example, she cannot buy alcoholic beverages, and she cannot vote, where the lawful age for both these activities is 21 years. However, she may enter into contracts which are not voidable on the grounds of incapacity due to age.

The general rule is that all natural persons may make any type of lawful agreement. For their own protection, the law limits the power of some classes of persons to contract, such as minors, insane persons, drunkards, and aliens. A minor may make an enforceable contract just as an adult may, subject, however, to disaffirmance by the minor. Disaffirmance is the right "to get out of the contract." Contracts made by minors fall into two classes:

(1) Contracts, other than for necessities, which the minor may make subject to the power of disaffirmance. To disaffirm this type, the minor need pay nothing, but must return the consideration which he received or what is left of it at the time of the disaffirmance. Thus, when a minor purchases a car, not necessary for business, he may return it at any time, or what is left of it, and demand return of his purchase money. In former years, this has also been held true for a purchase by a minor of a horse and buggy, not used except for pleasure, even though the horse was shot. See *McGuckian v. Carpenter*, 43 R.I. 94, 110 Atl. 402 (1920).

(2) Contracts for necessities made by a minor, not under the care of a parent or guardian, for such items as food and clothing, which the minor may disaffirm, but for which he must pay the reasonable value of the goods (not the contract price). To determine what are necessities, the following points must be considered:

(a) The nature of the item, i.e., food, clothing, lodging, medical care, education.

(b) The quality of the goods, i.e., according to his station in life. A minor with a large estate could be expected to require expensive clothing, whereas one with no estate would only require inexpensive clothing.

(c) Quantity of the item, i.e., some might justify four overcoats, whereas others would only require one.

(d) That the item is not being supplied elsewhere, as from parents, guardian, etc.

(e) That the items were actually furnished to him. Thus, a minor must pay a reasonable value for rent if the lodgings were actually furnished for his use, but not if he had moved out and was no longer occupying the rooms.

It may readily be seen that if this power of disaffirmance were not limited, a minor alone in the world could not induce merchants to sell him necessary food or clothing because of their fear that they would suffer a loss when he exercised his power of disaffirmance. For this reason, the law states that a minor may disaffirm a contract for things necessary for his support, but must pay the reasonable value of these items. Thus, the law implies an agreement by the minor to pay the reasonable value of necessities, allowing the other party to the contract to recover in quasi-contract, as discussed elsewhere. If the contract price is reasonable, disaffirmance has no effect, but if the contract price is higher than would be reasonable, the power of disaffirmance operates to deduct only the amount above the reasonable price.

The right of disaffirmance, to avoid the contract, is personal to the minor, and may only be exercised by him. Thus, a car dealer may not cancel a contract of sale to a minor because of his minority; only the minor may assert this fact to cancel the contract.

Generally, a minor may disaffirm his contracts either before or after becoming of age, except that:

(1) He cannot avoid a conveyance of land until he reaches majority;

(2) He cannot avoid any agreement after the lapse of a reasonable time after reaching his majority;

(3) After reaching majority and ratifying, or confirming, his contract by showing an unequivocal intent to be

bound by it, he cannot later change his mind and elect to avoid the contract.

If the minor elects to avoid the contract, he must do so wholly, not in part. If he so elects, he must return the consideration which is still in his possession. However, if he has squandered the goods or for other reasons no longer has them in his possession, this will not prevent disaffirmance and recovery of that which he has given. Thus, a college student of moderate means may disaffirm a contract for the purchase of elaborate food items, even though they have been consumed already; and the minor, in an example above, could recover the amount paid for a horse, although the horse had been shot.

A minor may not disaffirm his torts (a civil wrong), and therefore may be guilty of fraud if he intentionally misrepresents his age or improperly exercises dominion over the goods of another, termed conversion. Even here the minor, or infant, may avoid the contract, but he must pay for any injury resulting to the property acquired through his fraud. Thus, in case of an accident which seriously damages an automobile purchased by a minor, the minor may disaffirm and recover his purchase money, but must pay for the cost of replacing the auto in the condition in which he bought it, if he has misrepresented his age as 24. See *Myers v. Hurley Motor Co.*, 273 U.S. 18 (1927).

c. Others

Due to the requirement for a meeting of the minds to form a valid contract, certain other persons are not considered capable of making valid contracts. These include (1) persons without understanding, or adjudged insane; (2) persons not adjudged insane and not completely without understanding, but mentally incompetent; and (3) a person so drunk that he cannot understand the nature of his acts.

(1) Persons completely without understanding, or adjudged insane, cannot make any contracts at all. Any attempted contract is void. However, they must pay the reasonable value of necessities furnished to them or their family.

(2) Those not completely without understanding may contract, but subject to disaffirmance, as with minors. Disaffirmance here is conditioned upon their restoring the consideration which they received, or paying its equivalent, unless they can show that the other party knowingly took advantage of their status.

Insanity cannot be based merely upon mental weakness. There must be a mental defect or disease which renders the person incapable of understanding the nature and consequences of his act. Even one who is insane under this definition may have lucid, or rational intervals, and may make valid contracts during these periods.

(3) A person so drunk that he does not know the nature and consequences of his actions is treated as a person under (2) above. He could not logically be held to a contract as, under this condition, he lacks the necessary understanding for a meeting of the minds.

Aside from these limitations, there are others, both historically and for current situations.

Under the common law rules, married women could not contract. This situation has now been abolished by statute, and all states tend to give a married woman rights equal to those possessed by her husband.

During conflict, an enemy alien cannot enforce existing contracts or enter into new contracts, but if sued he may defend himself. An alien is one owing allegiance to a country other than that of his residence, and an enemy alien is one owing allegiance to a country which is at war with the country of his residence.

Persons convicted of felonies, including treason, once forfeited all of their worldly possessions to the crown and were considered civilly dead. Today, these persons are under very little, if any, disability in regards to their ability to contract.

III. Legality of Subject Matter

An agreement which results from mutual assent by parties capable of contracting, and which meets all the requirements of a valid contract, will still be unenforceable if it falls into the class of illegal contracts. Any agreement is illegal if its formation or performance is criminal, tortious, or otherwise opposed to public policy under the common law or the statutes.

a. Types of Illegal Subject Matter Contracts

Examples of contracts where the subject matter is illegal because statutes declare them to be void are contracts entered into or to be performed on Sunday (in many states), and contracts calling for a usurious rate of interest. Contracts which violate the common law or are contrary to public policy as defined by the common law or statutes, or both, include contracts in restraint of trade or marriage, contracts to influence public officials or to compound a crime, and contracts which purport to limit the liability for negligence by one who offers his services to the general public, such as common carriers and public warehouses.

1. Restraints of Trade

The common law declared monopolies contrary to public policy because they restrained competition, and the early view was that all contracts which had restraint of trade as their objective were illegal. As trade and competition increased, this stringent rule was modified, and contracts in restraint of trade were held to be illegal only if they were unreasonable. The reasonableness rule still exists today, based upon consideration of the length of time and area involved. Assuming that there is no statute involved, a contract which provides that one of the parties will refrain from doing a certain type of work for a reasonable length of time and within a reasonable area is not illegal when it is made a part of the contract for the sale of a business for the purpose of protecting the vendee's goodwill, which he has paid for in the purchase price.

The California Civil Code provides generally that all contracts in restraint of trade are unlawful except:

(1) Where the goodwill of a business is sold, and the seller promises not to engage in the same business at any place in the same county for as long as the purchaser continues to own the business. These are valid. The basis of this exception is that the personality of the seller is an important factor in the success of a business. Since the purchaser usually pays a substantial sum for the goodwill, the law should aid him in realizing on it by preventing the seller from competing with him if such is their agreement.

(2) Where upon the dissolution of a partnership, the partners have agreed that some of them shall not engage in a similar business within the same city in which the partnership business was transacted, founded upon the same theory.

When a code or statute describes how far a restraint may extend in time and area, our problem is easy, but if no such measure of reasonableness is provided, then each case must be decided upon its own merits. Generally, the proper area depends upon how extensive the business operations are (i.e., local retail store vs. national manufacturing plant) and what is reasonably required to protect the purchaser, partnership (from the retiring partner), vendor (as to property which he retains), or employer (from former employee). These are determined to be valid because the restraint is reasonably necessary as being incidental to another contract.

If the restraint exceeds the limits of the code, or the limits of reasonableness, some courts say that they are void only as to the extent to which they exceed these limits. Other courts in such cases consider the entire agreement void. The latter rule seems best, as it puts pressure on the one being protected by such an agreement to be reasonable, and also eliminates the need for the courts to determine the valid extent of the agreement when it attempts to be too broad.

Today, the Sherman Antitrust Act, the Clayton Act, the Robinson-Patman Act, and the Federal Trade Commission Act reinforce the common law by levying criminal penalties and creating rights of action for civil damages for the injured parties made victims of monopolistic agreements, such as conspiricies in restraint of trade (for the purpose of eliminating competition), price discrimination, unfair methods in commerce (as misbranding and boycotts), and unfair and deceptive practices (as false advertising).

A discussion of retail price maintenance shows how public policy, or socially desirable things, may vary greatly over a period of time or between areas. Price maintenance agreements were once held to be illegal restraint of trade because they robbed society of the forces of competition which tended to keep prices low. Then, during the depression years, ruinous price wars caused the states and federal government to pass fair trade laws and the Miller-Tydings Act. However, the states included "non-signor" clauses in their statutes, and the Supreme Court of the United States declared these acts to be illegal, a burden on interstate commerce, and therefore unconstitutional. Congress passed the McGuire Act which, in effect, said that the mere effect of these laws burdening interstate commerce should not be considered an infringement of the power of the federal government.

2. Limitations of Liability

An agreement between two parties may ordinarily assign the respective liabilities as they wish, but an attempt to limit liability from negligence by a quasi-public institution (one offering to deal with the public in general for a particular service which is an everyday necessity, such as a bus company) is contrary to public policy and therefore void.

Thus, if a transportation company made every passenger, before he paid his fare, sign a card limiting or exempting the company from liability for any injuries incurred through the negligence of the company or its agents, the exemption would not be enforceable. The same policy holds true for railroads, public warehousers, and airlines. The basis for such holdings is that the public is compelled to deal with these businesses if they want their services and thus, there is no equality of bargaining. Thus, to protect the public, the courts hold such provisions to be void.

The same basic reasoning applies to prevent a railroad from issuing a bill of lading which states, "All goods are shipped at shipper's risk," and enforcing the clause to exempt the railroad from liability for a loss caused by the negligence of the railroad. However, a railroad may issue a bill of lading stating, "In consideration of the reduced rate herein granted, in case of loss it is agreed that the maximum liability of the railroad for the goods shipped shall be $100." This is merely a liquidated damage clause which is proper because the rate is based upon weight, bulk, and value, and by declaring a reduced value the shipper's rate covers a loss of limited value only.

Contracts fixing the amount of damages to be paid in the event of a breach are void, but only as to the provision for such liquidated damage. The exceptions to this rule are those contracts in which the nature of the subject matter renders it impracticable or very difficult to compute the actual damages resulting from a breach, such as where the promised performance is unique and has a peculiar value to the person to whom it is due. To illustrate the distinction:

(1) *A* agrees to buy from *B* a certain quantity of cement for a certain price. If *B* refuses to deliver the cement when it is due, *A* has the right to buy the cement elsewhere and to sue *B* for breach of contract. The measure of damages will be the difference between the contract price and the amount that *A* paid in the open market. A provision in the contract that $100 is to represent the amount of damage suffered in the event of a breach would almost inevitably fail to represent accurately the loss suffered. If liquidated damage clauses were permitted, *A* would be entitled to the liquidated damages

even though he paid less in the market; and if he paid $1,000 more than the contract price, he would still be entitled only to $100.

(2) Assume that *A* promised to buy a rare portrait from *B* for a stipulated price, and the agreement contained a provision for liquidated damages in the amount of $10,000 in the event of a breach of the contract by the seller. Such a provision as this would come within the class of exceptions to the rule, because a rare portrait has a peculiar and unique value, and it would be impracticable to attempt to ascertain the loss suffered by one who has been deprived of the right to buy a rare portrait.

3. Others

Wagers create new risks and for this reason are considered anti-social and therefore void, as they offend the public policy which is against the creating of risks. A sale of grain futures could be a wager if the parties never intended to do anything other than make a cash settlement. However, because these sales are beneficial to business, courts hold them to be valid if so drawn that delivery must be accepted if tendered. If the agreement is so drawn that it shows no intent to make a sale, but merely to create a wager, or cash settlement, it is void.

Insurance policies are valid if the insured has an insurable interest so that the policy merely shifts the risks rather than creating a new risk.

Usury is strictly statutory, not being known at common law, and consists of charging interest in excess of that permitted by law. There is usually a maximum, or control rate set, and also a legal rate supplied which applies where the rate is not fixed by the parties and yet interest shall be allowed. The statutes usually impose penalties for those who violate the usury law, and these vary from causing forfeiture only of the excess interest to forfeiture of all interest and principal. The basis of these statutes is to protect needy borrowers, and therefore corporations are usually not included. Loans to a corporation may usually be made at any rate desired, without conflicting with usury laws. Often small loan companies are permitted to charge a higher rate of interest than for major loans. Discount, or interest paid in advance, is valid, not being considered usury. When discounting business paper, this is regarded as merely selling it for what it is worth, not the payment of interest.

In some states, contracts to be performed or entered into on a Sunday are void, by statute.

Contracts to refrain from prosecuting criminal acts are illegal and void, and may also be a crime, called compounding a felony.

A promise by a legislator to vote for a certain measure is unlawful and, in addition, a flagrant breach of trust. Contracts tending to interfere with the proper performance of the duties of a public officer are contrary to public policy and void.

Promises by persons to be witnesses at a trial are not unlawful. Expert witnesses are frequently hired by legal contestants and paid large fees for their testimony. This is valid, if the fee is not contingent upon the success of the employing party. This contingency would offer an inducement to perjury and would tend to prevent the administration of justice, and is therefore void.

4. Some Examples

(1) *X* promises to steal *Y*'s car for *Z*, and *Z* promises to pay *X* $200 for this act. Being a contract to perform a criminal act, it is not enforceable.

(2) An unlicensed doctor operates on you and sues for his fee. The object of the license is to protect the public from unqualified doctors. The doctor cannot recover, because the courts feel that such unqualified doctors should not be aided in violating the law.

(3) *A*, without procuring a peddler's license, sells to *B* a ring and now sues for the price. The object of this license is to gain revenue. Merely a violation of a revenue measure, the contract is enforceable. If, however, the purpose of the license was to protect the public from unsuitable persons engaging in business, same result as in (2) would be reached.

b. Effect of Illegal Contract

Generally, the courts will not aid either party to an executory illegal contract (one which has not been performed) to enforce it, nor will they give any relief (as recision) if the contract is executed in part or in full. There are at least four exceptions:

(1) If the law is to protect the public. Under many usury

statutes a person may recover the excess interest which he has paid, because the purpose of the statute is to protect needy borrowers. Also, if a bank lends more money to a customer than the law permits, the best interest of the public is to enforce the illegal contract. The basis for this is that to refuse to grant relief has the indirect effect of enforcing the illegal contract.

(2) If the guilt of the parties is not equal. In such a case, the less guilty party may seek and be granted relief.

(3) When consideration is paid for an illegal act not yet performed. Thus, if a person wagers $5 on the outcome of a football game but before the game is played he repudiates the agreement and requests the return of his money, he should recover. Not to permit relief would put an obstacle in the way of the repentant.

(4) A party who performs an illegal contract in ignorance of the fact that it is illegal because certain important facts are not known by or revealed to him. This would apply where a trucking firm believes that it is transporting groceries while in reality, unknown to the firm, it is transporting liquor in an area where the law makes such transportation illegal. The trucking company could collect the contracted price for transportation.

A contract for telephone service was held enforceable when the telephone company tried to cancel the services due to a letter from the state attorney-general to the effect that the purchaser of the services was part of an illegal "book-making" operation. Mere knowledge of the intended illegal purpose of the services does not make the contract, otherwise lawful, illegal and unenforceable. The telephone company could have enforced its claim against the purchaser of the services, because no illegal purpose was part of the contract itself. See *People v. Brophy*, 49 Cal. App. 2d 15, 120 P.2d 946 (1942).

IV. Consideration

A contract is an agreement to do or not to do a certain thing which the law will enforce. The agreement must result from a meeting of the minds through the medium of offer and acceptance; there must be a real intent; the parties must have capacity; the object of the contract must be legal; and, finally, there must be consideration. We have explored all the elements but the last listed above, and now will discuss this last element of consideration necessary to form a binding contract.

a. IN GENERAL

Consideration might briefly be defined by stating that a contract will be enforced only when it has been paid for, or purchased. Consideration is that which is bargained for and given in exchange for a promise. A more formal definition would be that it is any benefit conferred, or agreed to be suffered, by such person other than such as he is at the time of consent lawfully bound to suffer, as an inducement to the promisor. Do not be alarmed if you did not quite follow the preceding sentence, for the remainder of this section is primarily devoted to clarifying it.

Note that the promisor is the party who has promised to do something, and that the promisee can enforce this only if the promise is supported by consideration. There must be mutuality of consideration, with each party doing or agreeing to do something they were not legally bound to do or refraining from doing something they had a legal right to do. This is sometimes referred to in a shorthand manner as the "benefit or detriment" idea of consideration. In the development of contract law in medieval days, a promise was enforceable only when the parties intended their promises to be taken seriously. This seriousness of intent that the agreement was to have legal binding effect was evidenced by a seal placed upon the written agreement. As contracts became more numerous in a trading economy, the present day doctrine of consideration supplanted the seal, and made it possible for oral contracts to supplant the old sealed instruments. Now let us see some examples.

In the usual sales transaction there is a benefit and a detriment on both sides. If *A* sells goods to *B* for a certain price, *A* confers a benefit upon *B* by giving *B* ownership of the goods, and suffers a detriment by giving up his legal right to keep the goods. On the other hand, *B* confers a benefit upon *A* by giving *A* the purchase money, and suffers a detriment by transferring the money to *A*. The promise on each side, in a contract of this sort, results in both parties bestowing a benefit and both suffering a detriment. It is not essential that there be both a benefit and a detriment on each side. As long as there is either a benefit or a detriment supporting each promise, there is sufficient consideration.

Although consideration is a necessary element of an enforceable agreement, the amount of the consideration on each side is not important. For example, if *A* agreed to sell *B* a textbook for $1,000, the consideration exchanged, each for the other, would be entirely out of proportion, but there would be an enforceable contract. There need not be equality of consideration. The theory underlying this rule is that different things have different values to different people, and the law will not undertake to set absolute values. Nominal consideration may be valid. One exception to this rule is when the contract is for the exchange of money or fungible goods for these items have an exact value to everyone, and the law will not enforce a contract to exchange $1 for $5, or one bushel of Grade A wheat for 5 bushels of Grade A wheat. This exception obviously would not apply where the money on one side has value as a collector's item.

Returning to the "benefit-detriment" doctrine of consideration, assume that an uncle tells his nephew, "If you will promise not to smoke for one year, I will give you $100." The nephew accepts the offer. There is good consideration in the detriment suffered by the nephew in foregoing the exercise of his lawful right to smoke. The promise of the nephew is supported by the benefit conferred by the uncle in promising to pay the money. The nephew has promised to refrain from doing that which he has a legal right to do and this is as much consideration as promising to do that which you are not legally bound to do. See *Hamer v. Sidway,* 124 N.Y. 538, 27 N.W. 256 (1891). However, if the agreement had been for the nephew to obey all the traffic laws for one year, there would not have been an enforceable contract; the nephew could not suffer any legal detriment by performing the promise because he was legally obligated to obey the traffic laws regardless of the uncle's promise.

Other examples of "no consideration" are (1) where a sheriff arrests a person who committed a crime and claims an offered reward (doing only what he was legally bound to do); (2) promising to be a witness at a trial when an obligation is already imposed by statute; and (3) promising to do that which you are already legally bound by contract to do. This third example poses some additional problems in that if unforeseen difficulties are encountered after the original contract is entered into, a promise to pay an additional amount for the completion of the contract is generally deemed to be binding. See *Linz v.*

Schuck, 106 Md. 220, 67 Atl. 286 (1907), where an encountering of unforeseeable swamp land was sufficient to justify enforcing additional payments on a contract to dig a basement. The courts reason and conclude that the original agreement was subject to recision due to a mutual mistake as to a material factor (the condition of the land) which induced the original contract, and that the making of the new agreement rescinded the original one by implication. Only unusual and extraordinary difficulties justify such results. For this reason, price changes, shortages in material, and such circumstances that are foreseeable do not qualify. A comparable problem arose in *Leggett v. Vinson,* 155 Miss. 411, 124 So. 472 (1929), where a promise to pay additional money to a contractor for building a house when the contractor ran out of money was held not to be enforceable. Here it would have been best to rescind the original contract expressly and enter into a new contract when such a situation arose. Also, under this example, if the parties had added some new and different consideration, such as promising to complete the contract at an earlier date or in a different manner, the contract would be binding because of the new consideration.

b. NO FORMAL CONSIDERATION NECESSARY

Past consideration is not sufficient to support a promise. If the performance in return for which the promise is given has already been executed, and the person benefiting from that performance is under no legal obligation to perform his promise, there is no consideration. For example, *A* returns home to discover his house is on fire. He offers *B* $50 to run in and get a valuable oil painting, and *B* does so. Here there is good consideration for the promise to pay the $50. But, if *B* saved the painting before *A* returned home and *A*, being overjoyed and grateful, promised to pay *B* the sum of $50, this would not be enforceable. The obligation out of which the promise arose was only moral, and not legal, and therefore is not sufficient consideration. As a general rule, a moral obligation will not support a promise. There is one exception to this rule, as follows:

If *A* owes *B* $500 and the claim becomes barred by the statute of limitations, or *A* is discharged through bankruptcy, *A* is no longer legally obligated to pay *B*. He is of course morally obligated to pay. If *A* subsequently gives *B* a note for this same debt, there is sufficient consideration for the note because the obligation, although only a moral obligation (after the running of the statute of limitations or the discharge in bankruptcy) arose out of a legal obligation, and is, therefore, a good consideration to the extent of the pre-existing obligation. Other cases merely say that this is a situation in which no consideration is necessary, and some others say that the obligation always existed and *A* has merely waived his statutory protection on the old debt, and thereby restored its effective status. Many courts require such a promise to be in writing since it would be easy to allege such a promise and yet so difficult to prove.

Another possibility that is perhaps an exception to the general rule would be a charitable subscription, i.e., pledges to churches, schools, and other charitable institutions, which are enforced under various theories. These are:

(1) Some courts say that such contracts (subscriptions) are an exception and do not require any consideration to be enforceable. That such promises should always be enforced merely as a matter of public policy is the basis of this group of cases.

(2) Another view is that a subscription is an offer for a unilateral contract, one which is accepted when the institution does an act, i.e., creates liabilities or makes expenditures. Thus, both the promisee and promisor have suffered a detriment, giving rise to consideration on both sides and a valid contract. The detriment to the promisee is the incurred expenditure, and to the promisor the promise to donate.

(3) A third method used to enforce these subscriptions is by use of a third party beneficiary theory. This is discussed later in the text here.

(4) Another method is by use of the estoppel theory, by which the defense of no consideration may not be raised due to the justifiable reliance upon the promise by the promisee to his detriment.

Illustrations of these rules in regard to subscriptions are:

(a) If the individual subscription merely says, "I agree to subscribe $5 for a class scholarship," no enforceable contract is created because the promisee has not agreed to confer a benefit or suffer a detriment, and there is, therefore, no consideration for the promisee to subscribe. This is enforceable under (1) above.

(b) If the subscription states, "I agree to subscribe $5 to the class scholarship in consideration of the other members of the class agreeing to subscribe a similar amount," an enforceable contract is created, the detriment suffered by each member of the class being the consideration supporting the subscription of every other member. This is enforceable under either (1) or (3) above.

(c) If, however, in the type of subscription described in (a) above, the class committee, in reliance upon the representation that the subscriber will pay the subscription, makes a contract with another party for something necessary to the venture, and becomes obligated under such a contract, then the purported subscribers will not be allowed to raise the defense of no consideration, as under (4) above. The defense of no consideration in theory would still exist, but the party who had made the representation by the subscription would not be allowed (would be estopped) to raise the defense.

c. LIQUIDATED VS. NON-LIQUIDATED CLAIMS

It becomes of importance to know whether a debt is liquidated or unliquidated in order to determine whether a release of a claim or a compromise of a claim is legally binding, because we have already found that doing that or promising to do that which you are already legally bound to do is not valid consideration.

For an unliquidated debt: Assume that *A* renders services to *B* and sends *B* a bill for $1,000. *B* thinks that this amount is exorbitant and tells *A* that he considers the services to be worth $500 and no more. Following this good faith dispute, *A* and *B* compromise, agreeing upon $750 as the fee for the services. This agreement of compromise is supported by a benefit and a detriment on both sides, and therefore is enforceable. *A* has given up his right to sue and *B* has promised to pay *A* a "sum certain" and given up his right to dispute the reasonableness of *A*'s charge. The basis of this rule is a good faith (bona fide) dispute as to the amount of the original debt.

For a liquidated debt: Assume that *B* admits that he owes *A* $1,000, but *B* is a miser and forces *A* to accept $750 in full settlement by threatening not to pay at all until sued, unless *A* will settle for $750. *B* has not suffered a detriment or bestowed a benefit on *A*. Therefore, there is no consideration and *A* can sue and recover the remaining $250. *A*, by accepting the $750, has promised he will not collect the balance, but since *B* is only doing part of that which he is legally bound to do—and therefore has not suffered a legal detriment—there is no consideration for *A*'s promise.

Some states have the Uniform Written Obligations Act, which provides (even under our second illustration) that if *A* gives *B* a written release that the $750 is accepted in full payment, *A* cannot collect the balance. Even without the aid of the statute, some courts say that the written receipt is evidence of a valid executed gift, and an executed gift needs no consideration. Other courts strain to find adequate consideration. The policy or basis of the Uniform Act is to prevent creditors from luring debtors into a false sense of security.

Assume that *A* owes *B, C, D,* and *E* each $100. *A* is financially almost bankrupt, so that *B, C, D,* and *E* agree that if *A* pays each of them $50 they will consider this as payment in full. *A* pays each $50 and now *C* sues *A* for the remaining $50 still due him. Can *C* collect? No, for this is termed a composition of creditors, and enforceable.

The acceptance of the offer to pay less than the amount owed is supported by a sufficient consideration, and thus forms a valid contract. These compositions of creditors are an exception to the general rule that an agreement to discharge a debt by the payment of a lesser sum is not supported by consideration. This exception is based upon the theory that the consideration flows between the creditors, each agreeing to accept less in consideration for the others also agreeing to accept less, for the benefit of the debtor. This type of an agreement is called a "third party beneficiary" contract, and may be enforced by the party for whose benefit it was made, even though he has given no consideration for the promise. The most common example of a third party beneficiary contract is a life insurance policy made between a husband and the insurance company for the benefit of the wife. Upon the death of the husband, the wife may enforce the contract, though she has given no consideration therefore.

The recital of a consideration, "for value received," or "in consideration of $100 in hand paid," etc., in a contract is not essential to its validity in spite of this common practice. Such a recital is actually meaningless because if there actually is no consideration, this may be shown in court, and if there is consideration, the presumption of such consideration arises from the fact that the contract is in writing, not from the recital contained in the writing.

d. SUMMARY AND REVIEW

Some examples to use in reviewing this portion:

(1) Uncle promises nephew $500 on his 21st birthday. Is this a valid contract? No, for this is merely a promise to make a gift, and unenforceable because there is not consideration on the part of the nephew.

(2) *A* agrees to pay interest on a note two days early if *B* will extend the note's maturity date sixty days. Enforceable? Yes, for valid payment of the interest two days early is good consideration for the promise to extend the note.

(3) a. *G* agrees to build a house according to plans and specifications for $18,000. Later he refuses to go on, because of price increases in materials, unless the owner agrees to pay an additional $1,500, and the owner does so agree. Can *G* collect $1,500 on completion of the house? No, for he was already obligated to complete the house, and there is no consideration for the promised additional payment.

b. *G,* upon excavating the basement ran into bedrock, otherwise the same as above. Some courts say no, that *G,* by the original contract, agreed to build the house for $18,000 and thereby assumed all risks incidental to the job, and his subsequent agreement gave the owner nothing that he was not already entitled to under the existing contract. Therefore, there is no consideration, and *G* could get only $18,000. Other courts follow the unforeseen difficulties and implied recision theory, and would allow *G* to recover $19,500.

(4) *A* has a tort claim against *B* which *A* thinks is valid, and *B* offers to settle for an amount of $500 which *A* considers smaller than adequate. *A*'s acceptance makes a binding contract because the claim was unliquidated.

A had given up the right to sue, and *B* has promised payment of a sum certain.

(5) *A* sells his business to *B* for $10,000. Two weeks later, *A* agrees not to enter the same business for two years in the same town. There is no valid contract because there is no consideration for the second promise.

(6) *A*'s wife is about to leave him and go home to Mother. *A* promises his wife $5,000 if she will stay with him and take care of things as she always had for another six months. Wife does this, and now sues for $5,000. Will she recover? No, she is merely doing what she was already legally bound to do as *A*'s wife.

(7) *A* has a liquidated (undisputed amount of claim) against *B* for $1,000. *A* agrees to settle (a) for *B's* car worth $500; (b) for payment of $600 by *B*. Can *A* recover the balance? (a) No. (b) Yes. See *Herman v. Schlesinger,* 114 Wis. 382, 90 N.W. 460 (1902) where by giving absolute title to goods formerly only used as security an agreement was upheld in court compromising a debt.

(8) Under (4) above—*B* finds that *A's* claim is invalid and therefore refuses to pay. *A* sues for the $500 and *A* wins. Good consideration exists, and therefore a valid contract was formed. Another reason is that the law favors compromise of doubtful claims.

(9) *A* sends *B* a bill for dental services in the amount of $1,000. *B* goes to *A*'s office and they dispute the correctness of the charge, which was unliquidated. *B* later sends *A* a check for $750 marked "payment in full," (called an accord), and *A* cashes the check (called satisfaction). The debt is completely discharged. The sending of the check was an offer of a compromise settlement of a good faith dispute. The money was to become *A*'s only if he took it according to the terms of the offer. By cashing the check, *A* showed that he accepted the offer of the accord, and satisfaction of the obligation took place when he cashed the check.

Summary of the rules concerning consideration:

1. Consideration may be an act which one is under no legal duty to perform; a forbearance, i.e., a promise to refrain from doing that which you have a legal right to do; or a return prom-

ise (promise to pay in return for a promise to sell).

2. We must distinguish between liquidated and unliquidated debts to determine the validity of a compromise settlement. A bona fide promise to compromise a disputed claim in good faith is valid, and it does not matter whether a suit would be successful or not.

3. It does not matter to whom the consideration goes or from whom it moves, as in composition agreements.

4. Past consideration, a moral obligation, or illusory contracts all constitute no valid consideration, and do not serve as the basis for valid contracts.

5. A contract not only includes what the parties said, but also what is necessarily implied from what they do.

6. Some promises are enforceable without consideration, as:

a. Charitable subscriptions. (Remember, there is some conflict on the applicable law; but they are usually enforced as a matter of public policy.)

b. Goods and/or services which are furnished with the expectation to receive payment, and not to make a gift.

c. Past legal obligations now barred by the statute of limitations or bankruptcy.

d. Infant's affirmance after reaching majority. c. and d. require a new promise if they are to be enforceable, and some courts require such a new promise to be in writing.

C. FRAUD AND MISREPRESENTATION

Fraud and misrepresentation are practically identical, with the exception that in misrepresentation there is no intent to deceive, called "innocent misrepresentation," as in fraud. However, the remedies afforded to the injured party are not the same. For misrepresentation, the remedy is limited to recision. Other remedies are available for fraud, which will be discussed later.

I. Elements of Fraud

(1) Misrepresentation of a material fact. Representations of opinion are not, as a general rule, fraudulent. It is, therefore, important to distinguish carefully between representations of fact and of opinion.

A says that the weather yesterday was sunny and clear. This is a representation of fact. However, if *A* says that the weather tomorrow will be sunny and clear, he is representing opinion only, because tomorrow's weather is something *A* cannot possibly know as a fact.

"Puffing" statements are representations of opinion only. For example, if an auto salesman says a Ford is the best car in the lower price group, he is merely representing that it is the best in his opinion. Also, the representation must be as to a material fact, material in the sense of being important in determining the injured party's choice of conduct in the transaction.

(2) Knowledge of the statement to be false or made recklessly with disregard as to its truth or falsity. This is not innocent misrepresentation. This includes statements made without reasonable grounds for believing them to be true, and includes also a person speaking as though he had knowledge when he actually has no knowledge.

(3) Intent to induce the other party to do or to refrain from doing some act, or intent to mislead him. The statement must be made with the intent to have the other party act upon it, or under such conditions that the person making the statement cannot help but realize that the other party will act upon it.

(4) Reliance by the other party. The other party must be actually misled by it. If the person does not believe it, or knows the statement is false, then there is no justifiable reliance and therefore no fraud. In some cases the party does not know the representation is false, but nevertheless makes his own investigation and then buys. The question then becomes one of reliance. If there was no reliance upon the fraudulent statement, there is no cause of action. Thus, when a person after being told that the bricks were first-class, looked into the kiln himself to see the bricks, he could not later recover damages when the bricks turned out to be defective, because the defect was one which his investigation should have revealed to him, eliminating the reliance upon the statements of the seller. See *Meickley v. Persons,* 66 Iowa 63, 23 N. W. 265, 55 Am. Rep. 261 (1885).

(5) Injury or damage. Injury must have been suffered by the party acting upon the representation, believing it to be true. Unless the party is injured by the fraud, he cannot successfully complain in court.

(6) Promptness. When the injured party finds out about the fraud, he must act with reasonable promptness if he desires to rescind the contract.

The absence of any of the above elements is usually fatal to an action for damages for fraud or deceit.

Although ordinarily a seller's opinion of the value of the property is merely opinion, not fact, and the purchaser is not entitled to rely upon this opinion as to the value of the property, there is an exception when the statement of value is made as an affirmation of a fact and with the intent that it should be understood as fact and not opinion. However, if *A* offers to *B* some corporation stock, stating that, "This stock is worth $200 per share," and *B* accepts the offer, finding out later that it is only worth $175 per share, *B* cannot rescind. The reason is that *B* cannot justifiably rely when the only act needed to check this statement is to read the market report in the morning paper. People are expected to be sufficiently wary to look up the market price before buying.

Assume that the seller of a farm says, "This is the best farm in this entire area." Is this merely puffing? Yes. However, if he had said, "This is a fertile farm and a real money-maker," this would not be classified as puffing.

We must distinguish between fraud in the inducement and fraud in the execution of a contract.

(1) If *A* is persuaded to sign a contract which he is led to believe is not a contract, but only an autograph album, there is fraud in the execution, i.e., the deceit lies in the obtaining of the signature to the contract. This makes the contract void completely.

(2) If *A* signs a contract with the full realization that he is signing a contract, but signs because he has been fraudulently misled concerning the quality of the consideration that he is to receive, the fraud is in the inducement of the contract, and the contract is merely voidable, not completely void. Unless *A* rescinds the contract, it is valid and enforceable.

II. Actual and Constructive Fraud

a. Actual Fraud

The situations discussed previously have all dealt with actual fraud, i.e., an act performed with intent to deceive another, or to induce him to enter into a contract. The act may take any of the following forms:

(1) The suggestion, as a fact, of that which is not true, by one who does not believe it to be true. *A* tells *B* that the piano which he is offering for sale is a new Steinway. The piano is really an old Baldwin. *A* makes the state-

ment knowing that it is false, for the purpose of inducing *B* to buy the piano.

(2) The positive assertion, in a manner not warranted by the information of the person making it, of that which is not true, even though the person making the assertion believes it to be true. *A* tells *B* that the piano is a new Steinway, although *A* has never seen the piano. *A* believes that the piano is a new Steinway, because the person from whom he purchased it told him that it was.

(3) The suppression of a fact which is true, by one having knowledge of, or belief in, the fact. *A* tells *B* that the piano is in perfect playing condition, when he is practically certain that three of the keys are missing.

(4) A promise made without any intention to perform it. *A* promises that he will see to it that the piano is properly tuned before it is delivered to *B*. As a matter of fact, *A* does not intend to have the piano tuned before delivery. The misrepresentation in this case is of the fact of *A*'s intention.

b. CONSTRUCTIVE FRAUD

Constructive fraud is any act that, although not actually fraudulent, is a breach of duty which gains an advantage for the person so acting by misleading another to his prejudice; or any act or omission declared by the law to be fraudulent but not actually fraudulent. Most cases of constructive fraud arise out of confidential relationships where the law implies a duty to speak and the party who has this duty remains silent.

Normally there is no duty to speak, but if a party elects to speak, he must speak the whole truth and not just half-truths. The following exceptions to the rule of no duty to speak will illustrate when "silence may constitute fraud."

(1) Where there is a fiduciary relationship, there is a duty to disclose all information. *A* knows there is a mine on the land of *B*'s, which B knows nothing about. *A* seeks to purchase it as farm land and at farm land prices, and does so. If *B* finds out about the mine, can he rescind? No, for you need not inform one with whom you are dealing. But if *A* was *B*'s manager of the farm, a fiduciary relationship (a relationship of trust and confidence), when *A* had a duty to speak, and his failure will be

fraud. See *Guaranty Co. v. Liebold,* 207 Pa. 339, 56 Atl. 951 (1904).

(2) Latent defects must be disclosed if known to the seller. This includes such things as termites in the basement of a house which may not be observed by the buyer, but are known to the seller. Physical concealment of the facts is fraud, as when a defective wagon tongue was so altered and painted as to conceal its weakness. See *Kuelling v. Roderick Lean Mfg. Co.,* 183 N.Y. 78, N.E. 1098 (1905).

(3) Where one party has special knowledge inaccessible to the other party, this cannot be concealed. This may be shown where one agent of a company does not know of arrangements made by another agent, but a third party does, to get a ship towed to port. Therefore, the third party, taking advantage of knowledge of the actions of the second agent, contracts with the first agent by concealing knowledge of the actions of the second agent. This contract, by concealment of the special knowledge, is not enforceable. See The *Clandeboye,* 70 Fed. 631 (1895).

As mentioned, a contract fraudulently induced does not mean that the contract is void; it is merely voidable, and the injured party may:

(1) Rescind the contract by restoring the consideration received and ask to be put in a position that he was in before entering the contract.
(2) Affirm the contract and sue in torts for the fraud.
(3) Waive the fraud and continue the contract just as though no fraud existed.
(4) Set up fraud in diminution of the purchase price, when he is sued for this price.

III. Duress

Duress consists of the unlawful confinement of the party or a close relative of the party, or unlawful detention of his property, to prevent the free exercise of his own will. It includes coercion by actual or threatened injury or restraint which is sufficient to prevent the party from exercising his free will. Therefore, as a contract resulting from duress is not formed by the exercise of the free will of the party, there is no genuine consent, and such a contract is voidable.

IV. Undue Influence

Undue influence consists of using the confidence of a party, or authority over a party for the purpose of obtaining an unfair advantage over this person who relies upon the confidence, or is subject to the authority. It also includes the taking advantage of the weakness of the mind of another. It is a form of mental coercion which destroys the free will of a party, and constrains him to do that which is against his will. Undue influence is not of great importance in contract cases, being found more frequently in will contest cases, for obvious reasons. However, when it does appear in a contract case, it renders the contract resulting from it voidable.

V. Mistake

While "mistake" does not properly fall beneath the heading of fraud and misrepresentation, it is included here as the last sub-part of fraud because of the similarities between the two. As a general rule, a person cannot escape from the obligations of a contract merely by showing that he made a mistake. A unilateral mistake, or one-sided error as to value, quantity, or quality, unless made a condition to the contract, usually does not affect the agreement.

(1) *A* sells *B* a coat for $20. *B* thinks that the coat is worth $30, whereas it actually is only worth $10. This is a mistake as to value, and the contract is valid. This also applies where a stone is sold as a topaz, price $1,000, believed to be such by both parties, and is later discovered to be an uncut diamond worth between $700 and $1,000. The sale was valid, as held by the court in *Wood v. Boynton,* 64 Wis. 265, N.W. 42 (1885).

(2) *A* sells *B* a farm. *B* looks it over and thinks that there are 200 acres, whereas actually it only contains 175 acres. This mistake as to quantity will not affect the contract. However, if both parties mistake the quantity, as in *Newton v. Tolles,* 66 N.H. 136, 19 Atl. 1092, 9 L.R.A. 50, 49 AmSt. Rep. 593 (1890), the contract may be rescinded. This mutual mistake is discussed more fully later.

(3) *A* sells a note to *B* for a debt owed by *C*. Later, *A* and

B discover C to have been insolvent at the time the note was sold. Assuming that there was no fraud, (*A* did not know of the insolvency) *B* is the owner of the note, the contract of sale being valid.

There is one more example of a case which will not affect the validity of a contract, even though it is a mistake. This is the case of an error of computation, for example quoting of a lower price than intended on a building contract, if not caused by or known to the other party. This does not furnish grounds for recision. See *Steinmeyer v. Schroeppel,* 226 Ill. 9, 80 N.E. 564, 10 L.R.A., N.S. 114 (1907).

There is an exception to this rule. If the mistake is made without negligence, and is so glaring and obvious to the party not making the error that he is warned of the probable mistake (such as a bid on a construction project) to the extent that he could not have acted in good faith, no contract results even though the error is claimed to be unilateral. It must, however, be so obvious that the party could not help but to suspect that an error had been made.

There are some differences in the results of these cases from different courts. This is because some courts place emphasis upon the stability of commercial transactions, whereas others desire to avoid the great hardships and unjust advantages which would result from a unilateral mistake.

A bilateral mistake makes the consent unreal, by preventing mutuality of consent, and therefore no contract results. Both parties have not assented to the same agreement. The contract is void, but only in two instances does the bilateral mistake doctrine apply.

(1) Mutual mistake as to the identity of the subject matter. *A* offers to sell his car to *B* for $500. *B* accepts, thinking that *A* meant car *X*, but actually *A* meant car *Y*. The offer is ambiguous in that it has two meanings and, therefore, no contract results as each is mistaken though neither realizes that his promise has been misunderstood by the other party. See *Raffles v. Wichelhaus,* 2 H. & C. Rep. (Eng.) 906 (1864).

(2) Non-existence of the subject matter of the contract, not known to the parties. *A* offers to sell *B* his car for $500, and *B* accepts. Later, both discover that the car had

burned before the contract was made, yet neither was aware of this fact. The contract is void. (See also *Uniform Sales Act,* section 7.)

Of course, they could contract in such a fashion that the contract is not dependent upon the existence of the subject matter, but this must be specified in the contract. This was done in former Marine Insurance Policies by the phrase "lost or not lost."

Now consider this situation: *P* and *D* entered into a contract for the sale of a cow which both *P* and *D* thought was barren and would not breed. When it came time to deliver the cow, *D* found out that the cow was with calf, and therefore instructed his agent not to deliver it. The sale price was $80, and the value of the cow not barren was $1,000. Is this a mutual mistake? In *Sherwood v. Walker,* 66 Mich. 563, 33 N.W. 919 (1887) it was held yes, that this was a mutual mistake as to the existence of the subject matter, a mistake as to material fact, material as to the inducement to the formation of the contract. The item sold, a barren cow, had no existence. The item actually contracted for was a beef creature, whereas only a valuable breeding cow existed. The court was not unanimous. Some of the members of the court decided that there was no mistake as each party was aware of the risk taken; *D* that the cow could be bred, and *P* that the cow could not be bred. This may be distinguished from the case of *Wood v. Boynton,* discussed under unilateral mistakes earlier, in that in the Wood case involved a change in the value or quality of the thing bargained for and the value did not go to the root of the contract, while here the problem was not only value but in addition the actual subject-matter being bargained.

D. RIGHTS OF A THIRD PARTY

A third party is just what is implied—a party other than the original two who first entered into a contract. He can become involved, or shall we say legally interested, in the contract made by the other two in two differing ways—by assignment and by being a third party beneficiary.

I. Assignments

a. IN DETAIL

Assignments deal with certain concepts which are fundamental to the law of contracts and indispensable to an understanding thereof. An assignment of a contractual obligation occurs when one person transfers all his rights under a contract to another person. An assignment may be made in the same manner as a simple contract. It is to be noted that only rights under a contract may be assigned.

The rights one has under a contract are his property and he may assign them to whomever he pleases, but his duties under the contract may not be assigned or delegated. The person who makes an assignment is called an assignor, and the person to whom an assignment is made is called an assignee. Let us take an assignment of a simple bilateral contract and see what happens to the respective rights and duties of the parties.

> *A* agrees to deliver to *B* a certain amount of iron for a certain price. *A* has the right to the purchase money, and the duty to deliver the iron. *B* has the right to receive the iron, and the duty to pay the money. *B* assigns to *C*. *A* is told of the assignment.
>
> *C* now has the right to the iron. *B* still has the duty to pay the purchase price, since it cannot be assigned, but take note: *C* also has the duty to pay the purchase price. In accepting the rights under the contract, *C* must also accept the duties unless *C* and *A* have agreed otherwise, in which case there would be, not a true assignment, but merely a sale of the iron by *B* to *C*. Thus, we see that an assignment vests all the rights and all the duties of the assignor, *B*, in the assignee, *C*, but the duties under the contract also remain in the assignor, *B*. He cannot relieve himself of the burdens under the contract by assigning it. It would not be fair to *A* to allow *B* to force *A* to rely upon a stranger to the contract for the performance of the duty owed to *A*. So *C* now has the exclusive right to the iron, and *B* and *C* both have the duty to pay the money to *A*.
>
> If *C* does not notify *A* of the assignment, and *A* delivers the iron to *B* in good faith, *C* has no right of action against *A*, because *A* is merely performing the contract according to its terms as he knows them. *C* does have a right as against *B*, because an assignor impliedly warrants that he will not do anything to impair the value of the assignment. If *A* delivers the iron to *B* after he has been notified of the assignment to *C*, then *C* has a right of action against both *B* and *A*. (The moral is thus: always notify the obligor of the assignment of the contract if you are an assignee, because until he is

notified of the assignment he has the right to proceed as though there were no assignment.)

An assignee takes an assignment of a contract right subject to all defenses that the obligor may have against the assignor at the time of assignment, and subject to any defenses that may accrue prior to notice of the assignment. Example:

> *A* buys goods from *B* for $500. The goods are defective and *A* promptly offers to return them. *B* refuses to take back the goods, and assigns the account to *C*, who sues *A* for $500. *A* may set up as a defense against *C* the defective character of the goods. Thus, it is said that the assignee stands in the shoes of the assignor. A subsequent assignment to *D* would not change the situation. *A's* defense would be good against all assignees of *B*, not just against the immediate assignee.

The effect of this rule is to make a prospective assignee rather cautious in accepting an assignment, and tends to impair the saleability of a contract right.

Some contracts are not assignable. Where assignment is expressly prohibited by a clause in the contract, the rights under the contract may not be assigned. Certain types of contracts, because of the nature of their subject matter, are not assignable. This occurs when the nature of the duties to be performed depend for their value upon the personal skill of the party contracting to perform them. Example:

> *A*, a famous portrait painter, contracts with *B* to paint a portrait of *B*'s wife. *A* cannot assign the contract to C, because that would amount to imposing upon B an entirely different contract.

Contracts involving the personal confidence of the parties or the personal relationships of the work or subject matter are also of such a nature that they cannot be assigned. (e.g., a valet, or the recipient of a scholarship.)

Partial assignments, or assignments of only a part of the contract ($1,000 debt to 1000 people), change the nature of the original promise, and courts may not require the original party to accept such even when given notice and, therefore, the assignee may lose out.

The assignor impliedly warrants, when he assigns, the following:

(1) That he has title which has no defects, i.e., contract is genuine (obligor has no defenses to claim) and he hasn't made a prior assignment.

(2) That he will do nothing to defeat assignor's right, i.e., make a subsequent assignment or breach contract with obligor.

(3) That he has no knowledge of facts which would impair the validity of the contract or render it valueless, i.e., not that rights assigned will be realized, but that he knows of nothing that will indicate this.

Only present rights may be assigned. The right need not be due at the time of the assignment, but it must arise out of a present contract. Examples:

(1) If I'm employed, may I assign next month's wages? Yes. Wages which are to accrue under an existing contract of employment are assignable even though the period of employment and the amount of wages are uncertain.

(2) If I'm unemployed, may I assign next month's wages? I have been promised a job. No, a mere expectation and, therefore, no vested rights to assign.

(3) Can I assign any rights to property I might acquire upon my Mother's death? Generally no, for reason given in (2) above. A few courts of equity will enforce if consideration is adequate.

(4) If my Mother is dead at time of assignment? Yes, if you will acquire something.

b. SUMMARY

As we have seen, one may assign all of one's rights under a contract, unless the contract expressly prohibits assignment, or unless the nature of the subject matter of the contract is such that an assignment would materially prejudice the other party. When an assignment takes place, the assignee steps into the shoes of the assignor, and any defense that the obligor had as against the assignor may be asserted as against the assignee. The obligor may be compelled to perform for the assignee only after he has been given notice of the assignment, and the assignee must assume the duties of the contract if he accepts the benefits.

II. Novation

A novation takes place when the original parties to a contract agree that a third party shall take the place of one of them, and the third party assents to such an agreement. The party whose position in the contract has been taken then drops out of the picture entirely. A novation is, in effect, a new contract.

III. Third Party Beneficiary Contracts

Where a promise is made to *A* by *B* for the benefit of *C*, *C*, for whose benefit the promise is made, may bring an action for its breach.

A third party benefiting from a contract may fall into one of three classes of beneficiary: incidental, donee, or creditor. It depends upon the classification a beneficiary falls in when determining whether he has a right to enforce the contract, and also whether the original contracting parties may rescind their agreement without the consent of the beneficiary. Illustrations:

(1) City contracts with Construction Co. to pave *X* street. *B* lives on *X* street and tries to sue Construction Co. because of harm caused him by their delay and failure to complete the paving according to the terms of the contract.

B is a mere incidental beneficiary and has no rights under the contract. Any benefits accruing to *B* would be merely incidental as the contract was not made directly for his benefit. For this reason, the contract may be rescinded without *B*'s consent, and *B* cannot enforce its terms or recover damages for its breach.

(2) *A* sells wheat to *C* and *C* agrees to pay purchase price to *B*. *A* has no obligations to *B*, but merely wants to bestow a gift on *B*. *B* is a donee beneficiary and may sue *C* if *C* fails to pay as the contract was made expressly for his benefit.

A and *C* may not rescind this agreement without *B*'s consent even if *B* did not know of the agreement. Acceptance of a gift is presumed and, therefore, benefits accrue to *B* as soon as contract is made. But if *A* and *C* reserved the right to rescind the contract when the agreement was made, then they could do so even over *B*'s objection. This right to change beneficiaries is generally reserved in insurance contracts.

(3) *A* owns a house mortgaged to *B*. C buys and agrees to pay *A*'s debt (mortgage) to *B*.

B is a creditor beneficiary and may sue *C* if *C* fails to pay, and unless *B* agreed to look to *C* only, *B* may also hold *A* (no novation) as one cannot get rid of his obligations by making an assignment.

Courts hold that no benefits are created to a creditor beneficiary until he is informed and indicates his acquiescence. For this reason, the original parties (*A* and *C*) may rescind their agreement anytime prior to *B*'s "acceptance" and if they rescind prior to *B*'s acceptance, *B* would not acquire any rights under the contract as against *C*.

This now completes third party rights. One note of caution—rights of third parties under contracts and under negotiable instruments differ vastly. So onward!

E. EVIDENCE OF THE CONTRACT

I. Introduction

An oral contract made between two honest men may frequently result in a dispute as to its terms, which dispute will have to be settled by the courts. Now, if the oral contract is made between two men, one of whom is dishonest, the likelihood of a dispute arising is much greater and, since the terms of the agreement are not capable of any proof other than the memory of the contracting parties, the dishonest party has almost as much a chance of establishing non-existent terms and conditions as has the honest party of proving the actual terms of the contract. If the dishonest party is successful, he has made use of the courts in order to perpetrate a fraud on the other party. Frauds of this type may be prevented if the terms of the contract are set down in some permanent form which may later be used as evidence of the contract, and its terms and conditions. In order to accomplish this result, a set of rules has been drawn up requiring certain contracts to be set down in writing. This set of rules is known as the Statute of Frauds and Perjuries.

Now, what we commonly speak of as contracts are really only the evidences of contracts. A contract is invisible and intangible. Written instruments, spoken words, acts and various combinations of these merely give rise to contracts and evince that a contract exists, but are not the contract itself. Such evidence tends to show the existence of a meeting of the minds of the parties and the terms and provisions resulting from this meeting of the minds. Written instruments undoubtedly furnish the best evidence of the existence and terms of such meeting of the minds, and so the Statute of Frauds requires that certain agreements be evidenced by a writing. All contracts may be oral except those that are required to be in writing. It might be said that all contracts may be oral, but because certain oral contracts cannot be enforced due to the Statute of Frauds requirements of writing, they are not really contracts at all as they are not agreements "which the law will enforce."

II. The Statute of Frauds

By the provisions of the Statute of Frauds, certain types of agreements are invalid unless they are (1) in writing, and (2) signed by the party to be charged. The party to be charged merely describes the person against whom a contract is sought to be enforced. Thus, if the contract is one which the Statute of Frauds requires to be in writing, then the party who is to be sued for failure to perform must have signed the contract.

The following types of contracts with accompanying illustrations are commonly within the purview of the Statute of Frauds (i.e., invalid unless in writing and subscribed to by the party to be charged):

a. An agreement which by its terms is not to be completely performed within one year from the making of the contract. The essence of this rule is that the terms of the agreement prevent a completion of the performance of the contract within a year of its making.

Illustrations:

1. On 1/1/59, *A* promises to sell and deliver to *B* one African lion, on or before 2/1/60. Must this be in writing? No! A performance required to be rendered "on or before" a certain date is not within this rule, even though the date is more than a year later than the date on which the contract was made.
2. *A* agrees to build *B* a house. Eighteen months later *A* completes it, but *B* is happy with his trailer home and refuses to take or pay for the house. *A* sues, and *B* raises the defense of the Statute of Frauds. Is this a good defense? Again, no. Since the home is capable of being built within one year, the rule above is inapplicable.
3. *A* puts a new roof *on B*'s house, which *B* had to take. *A* orally guarantees the roof for five years. *B*, having learned a little law from his past experiences, insists that *A* put it in writing. Did *B* have to insist on this? No, for the contingency (the roof coming apart) upon which

liability for the guarantee is to accrue may happen within one year, which would cause the contract of guarantee to come to an end in less than the rule's one year.

4. *C* agrees to work for *D* all of his life. Again, the rule is inapplicable as *C* may die within a year, bringing the contract to an end.
5. If *C* agrees to work for *D* for two years, the contract must be in writing to be enforced, as death here would be only an excuse for non-performance. The contract cannot possibly be fully performed within one year.
6. *C* borrows $1,000 from *D* and promises to repay it with 6% interest within two years. The Statute of Frauds is inapplicable since *C* may repay it with interest before even a year elapses.
7. On December 1, *C* agrees to work for *D* for 51 weeks beginning January 1. Although here the actual performance of the contract will be for a period of time less than a year, the contract must be in writing for it cannot be fully performed within one year from the "making thereof."

You can see from the above illustrations that the crucial issue is generally whether the agreement is at all possible of completion within one year from the making of it, and, if so, no writing is required even though actual completion takes more than a year. See *Chase v. Hinkley*, 126 Wis. Rep. 75, 105 N.W. 230 (1905); *Warner v. Texas & Pacific R.R. Co.*, 164 U.S. 418 (1896).

b. A special promise to answer for the debt, default, or miscarriage of another, including the promise by an executor of a will to pay the debts of the decedent from the executor's own estate. This type of agreement is commonly called a guaranty and a few illustrations should suffice to clarify this second type of contract which must be in writing.

Illustrations:

1. If a store owner calls *A* on the telephone and asks if *A* will guarantee the payment of all charges made by *B*, even though *A* answers yes, the owner cannot enforce *A*'s promise, as it is not in writing.

2. Similarly, if *B* had given the name of *A* as a credit reference and charged goods at the store on the same day, a subsequent written guarantee by *A* for *B's* debts cannot be enforced as against those purchases, although it is effective for any future purposes.
3. *B* goes to the store without money or a charge account and asks if he might make some purchases with *A* taking care of the payment. The store owner calls *A*, and *A* tells him to go ahead and give the goods to *B*, and that he will pay for them. Here, *A* is bound by his oral contract and it can be enforced against him as he is primarily liable—he promised to pay directly for the purchases, not merely to pay if *B* did not. *Sanders v. Hodges,* 109 Fla. 391, 147 So. 571 (1933).
4. *A* orally agrees to pay a doctor for medical services rendered to *B*, an employee of *A*, if *B* did not pay. *B* had been injured while in A's employ and they had settled outside of court, *A* agreeing to pay all of the medical expenses of *B*. The doctor now sues *A* for his services. *A* pleads the Statute of Frauds in defense. Who wins? Well, the doctor does, for he is not suing on *A*'s promise to him, but instead on *A*'s promise to *B* wherein the doctor was a third party beneficiary, and under this agreement *A* became primarily liable to the doctor.

As you should note from the last two illustrations, if the agreement is so worded as to make the promisor primarily liable, no writing is required because the promise is an original one. On the other hand, if the wording is such that the promisor is only secondarily or collaterally liable, then the person receiving the promise must make sure he gets it in writing if he wishes to be able to enforce the agreement.

c. An agreement made upon consideration of marriage other than a mutual promise to marry. A suit by a party because of a breach of a contract to marry can be successful without that party producing a written contract agreeing to marriage, but a suit upon an agreement stating, "Marry me and I will give you one-half of my farm," will be unsuccessful unless a writing is produced because the promise to marry was the consideration given to support the promise of one-half of the farm. In other words, there must be a writing only when the marriage is the consideration to support a promise other than one of marriage.

d. Contracts for the sale of land or any interest therein. Although this only requires that the promise to sell be in writing, and requires nothing of the purchaser, the requirements of mutuality force the seller to demand a writing of purchaser's promise to pay, even though the purchaser promises only to pay money.

Illustrations:

1. *A* leases some real estate for one year. This must be in writing, for a lease for one year or more is considered an interest in land. It might be noted, though, that leases for a period shorter than one year are exempt from the requirements of the Statute of Frauds by statute in many states. Otherwise, most leases and rentals are required to be in writing to be enforced.
2. *A,* relying on an oral 10 year lease, gives up another lease, and enters the new premises in order to prepare them for his business. He expends $1,000 in preparation of the premises. *B,* the lessor, then tells *A* that he required a higher rent, and, if *A* does not pay, then *B* will remove him. We know here that for *A* to enforce the contract in a court of law he must produce a writing, but *A* here charges that the whole thing was a fraudulent scheme. *A,* in a court of equity, could sustain his lease by proving this to be true, as the Statute of Frauds cannot be used to perpetrate any fraud.
3. *A* pays *B* $100 as down payment for a building on *B*'s land. *A* agrees to remove the building and pay the balance within 60 days. *B* changes his mind after about 20 days, and tenders back the $100. *A* sues *B* in order to have the contract enforced, and *B* argues the Statute of Frauds. The court in *Wetopsky v. New Haven Gas Light Co.,* 88 Conn. 1, 90 Atl. 30 (1914) held that no writing was necessary as this was not a sale of an interest in land, but instead a sale of personal property.

This last illustration leads us into the next rule.

e. Contracts for the sale of personal property of a value in excess of $500 (this amount varies in different states) unless (1) there has been a down payment, or (2) a delivery and acceptance of part of the goods, or (3) the goods have been especially manufactured for the buyer and are not readily salable in the seller's usual course of business. This provision requiring contracts for the sale of personal property to be in writing was originally Section 17 under the Statute of Frauds. Today, this is covered in the Uniform Sales Act. Because of the importance of this provision and its numerous applications, it is set out in full below:

> "(1) A contract to sell or a sale of any goods or choses in action of the value of $500 or upwards shall not be enforceable by action unless the buyer shall accept part of the goods or choses in action so contracted to be sold or sold, and actually receive the same, or give something in earnest to bind the contract, or in part payment, or unless some note or memorandum in writing of the contract or sale be signed by the party to be charged or his agent in that behalf.
>
> "(2) The provisions of this section apply to every such contract or sale, notwithstanding that the goods may be intended to be delivered at some future time or may not at the time of such contract or sale be actually made, procured, or provided, or fit or ready for delivery, or some act may be requisite for the making or completing thereof, or rendering the same fit for delivery; but if the goods are to be manufactured by the seller especially for the buyer and are not suitable for sale to others in the ordinary course of the seller's business, the provisions of this section shall not apply.
>
> "(3) There is an acceptance of goods within the meaning of this section when the buyer, either before or after delivery of the goods, expresses by words or conduct his assent to becoming the owner of those specific goods."

This section dealing with the sale of goods is less stringent than the previously mentioned sections in that the previous sections require a writing and nothing else will suffice. But in the sale of goods, part performance, down payment, or the manufacture of special goods for the buyer will satisfy the statute in addition and instead of a writing.

Because of the different rules applicable to real property and personal property, some knotty problems arise over things which have properties of both realty and personalty. Such is especially true of growing crops and standing timber. The courts have become so confused as to the determination of the correct solution that a Georgia Court was led to conclude: "We are free to confess that the only deduction we have been able to draw from a review of the cases is that a growing crop is a sort of legal species of chameleon, constantly changing colors to meet the emergency of each case in which the question arises whether it is considered personalty or realty."

You can readily see why the question gains importance when you consider a sale of $300 worth of real property requires a writing, whereas if it were personal property no writing would be required, and even if the amount exceeded $500 a down payment or an acceptance of part of the goods would equally suffice for personal property. Some of the court conclusions on this problem of growing crops have been:

1. It is realty until matured and ready for harvest (e.g., green apples vs. ripe apples).
2. If the parties to the dispute are landlord and tenant, the tenant is favored by calling the crops personalty, if at all possible; if the parties are vendor and vendee, the vendee is favored and the crops are called realty, unless specified to the contrary in the contract.
3. If title to the crops or timber is to pass before they are severed from the land, it is real property, and if title is to pass after severance, it is personal property.

When it is known that a contract must be in writing and signed by the party to be charged to be enforceable under the Statute of Frauds, the question then arises as to how much of a writing is required to satisfy the Statute. The written evidence necessary to satisfy the Statute may be a letter, telegram, receipt, memo of sale, or even a check. The whole contract need not be contained in a single writing as long as the signed writings refer to the unsigned and link them all together. The test is whether or not it can be seen from the writing or writings (1) who the parties to the contract are, (2) what the subject of the contract is, and (3) what the terms of the contract are. Thus, a memo agreeing to sell "40 acres of land" would not be enforceable because from the memo itself it would not be possible to determine exactly what land was being agreed to be sold.

The written evidence may be supplied at any time prior to the commencement of an action to enforce the contract, and it need be signed only by "the party to be charged." The following hypothetical situation illustrates these points: *A* has an oral contract to sell *B* \$600 worth of goods. *B* decides to back out of the agreement. *A* sends him a letter stating the terms, the subject matter, and so forth, and states that the agreed price was to be \$800. *B* then writes back, "The agreement referred to in your letter is unenforceable because it was not put in writing by us, and anyway, the agreed price was \$600." Well, if *B* signs his letter, *A* has him.

III. The Parol Evidence Rule

Parol evidence nowadays refers merely to oral evidence, although it once referred to oral evidence and written evidence not under seal. The rule in reference to it is that this evidence may not be used to vary the terms of a written contract when that written contract is complete in itself. If the writing is not complete (i.e., partly written and partly oral), then parol evidence is admissible to establish the terms and subject matter of the contract. We have seen that some contracts are required to be in writing, but any contract may be in writing. Any written, integrated contract supersedes all previous understandings and negotiations. This is on the theory that all the terms of the contract have been drawn together and set forth in the writing. For this reason, parol evidence is not admissible to enlarge, diminish, alter, modify, or in any other manner change the terms of the written contract.

There are two important exceptions to the parol evidence rule. The first exception comes into play when the terms of the agreement are ambiguous, or if trade terms having special meanings have been used. Oral evidence is then admissible to clarify and resolve the ambiguity. The second exception is applicable at any time, and in substance permits the use of oral evidence to show fraud, duress, mutual mistake, or no consideration because this evidence is not for the purpose of varying the terms of the contract but, instead, to show that no contract in fact existed.

F. INTERPRETATION AND PERFORMANCE OF CONTRACTS

I. In General

Before it is possible to determine whether there has been a full performance of a contract and no breach thereto, it is necessary to interpret the contract so as to determine its meaning. The courts will generally seek to enforce that which the parties have expressed as their agreement, giving the ordinary meaning to words as evidenced by the conditions surrounding the making of it. Thus, words are given their ordinary meanings unless they have acquired a special meaning by usage in a "trade" or have been specially defined in the contract. This is merely to say that the "intent of the parties" controls.

Obviously, from our discussion of the parol evidence rule, a written statement will be honored supreme over an alleged oral statement. Printing on letterheads, sales invoices, etc., are not a part of the contract unless incorporated therein by reference. Obvious mistakes in grammar will be corrected and, in cases of conflict, written words will prevail over words in print. The courts strive to interpret words in a manner similar to that which the party who did not write the contract would reasonably understand their meaning to be. In other words, the language used will be construed most strongly against the party using it, but nevertheless reasonably rather than unreasonably.

II. Conditions

A condition in a contract is a promise or a statement to the effect that the acquirement of any contractual rights or duties is contingent upon some event other than the mere lapse of time. Depending upon the time sequence of the conditions, duties, and rights, a condition is denominated either a condition precedent, condition concurrent, or condition subsequent. Failure to live up to any condition is a material breach of the contract wherein the injured party may rescind and refuse to perform his part of the agreement, and, in addition, sue for any damages. Minor or technical breaches of conditions entitle the injured party only to a suit for damages without allowing him to escape performances. However, a "condition" generally indicates that upon breach the other party may rescind. There are also conditions which occurrence or non-occurrence is outside the control of the parties, and their failure to occur does not entitle any party to damages but merely terminates the contract as to both parties. For example, *A* promises to wash *B*'s car on Monday if the sun is shining that day. If the sun does not shine on Monday (a failure of the condition), then the contract merely terminates.

a. Conditions Precedent

A condition precedent is a condition which is to take place before some right dependent thereon accrues, or before some act dependent thereon is performed. For example: *A* agrees to paint *B*'s house, and *B* agrees to furnish *A* adequate housing while he works and pay him $300 for the job. Now, *B's* right to expect *A* to carry out his promise to paint is dependent upon *B*'s securing *A* adequate housing (a condition precedent), and *A*'s right to be paid $300 is dependent upon his painting the house first (another condition precedent).

1. Time as a Condition Precedent

If no time is mentioned in a contract, the parties have a reasonable time in which to perform, and this reasonable time is determined by all the surrounding circumstances. But assuming that the time for performance is mentioned in the contract, the question then becomes whether completion within the time indicated is a condition precedent. The answer to this question depends upon the subject matter involved, the importance of time, and whether the breach was so great as to justify the remedy of recision.

Illustrations:

(1) *A* agrees to build a garage for *B* for $300, and have it completed by September 1. *A* does not complete the garage until September 15. *B* is entitled only to damages that may have resulted from the 15-day delay, but he cannot refuse to pay the $300 as the breach was not so great as to justify the remedy of recision. The date of completion constitutes a term of the contract but not a condition precedent to the carrying out of *B*'s promise.

(2) *A* agrees to deliver to *B* the deed to some land on January 1, but fails to deliver until January 5. Again, the date of delivery is not a condition precedent.

(3) *A* agrees to deliver certain goods to *B* on March 1. In this case, the question whether the delivery date is a condition precedent depends upon the character of the goods. If the goods are highly perishable, are of unstable value, or have only a seasonable demand, then the time of delivery is a condition precedent.

In all contracts, time may be made a condition precedent by agreement, and this is generally done by inserting a clause in the contract to the effect that "time is of the essence." However, even though such a clause is inserted, some courts will not hold time as a condition precedent if the result would be manifestly unjust.

2. Special Approvals as Conditions Precedent

In many contracts, an approval by one of the parties or by a third party to the performance of the other party to the contract is required. Is the securing of this approval a condition precedent to the performance (usually payment) of the one party? This is best answered by illustration:

(1) A building contract provides that the builder must secure an architect's certificate of approval prior to his being entitled to receive payment. Condition precedent? Well, the mere failure to secure the certificate will not preclude the builder from bringing suit, and if it is shown that the certificate is being withheld without good cause, the court will render a judgment for the builder even though he has been issued no certificate. In other words, performance of the condition is excused if the architect dies, becomes insane, or arbitrarily, fraudulently, or whimsically refuses to give the certificate. In these latter cases, the question to be considered by the jury is whether a reasonable man would be satisfied with the performance. After all, the performance of a building contract relates to something desired for its commercial value, upon which ordinary men may pass.

(2) *A* secures *B* to paint an oil portrait of *A*, payment to be made of $1,000 if *A* approves of the result. Here the approval does constitute a condition precedent. The courts are reluctant to substitute their judgment for that of the recipient, regardless of how arbitrarily it appears his approval is being withheld. The distinction is that in this illustration the performance relates to one's taste, sensibility, or fancy, and even though experts may testify that the portrait is a great work of art, no recovery of the fee may be had by *B* without *A*'s approval. Other contracts of this type are contracts for personal services, such as contracting for a maid or a cook, and contracts for personal objects, such as contracting for a tailored suit.

b. CONDITIONS CONCURRENT

Conditions concurrent are often referred to as mutual conditions precedent. They are conditions mutually dependent and to be performed at the same time. Both parties have the obligation to perform before either can be held in default. The typical example of the application of these conditions is the exchange of money for goods in any retail store. Taking another example for better illustration, suppose *A* promises to sell his car to *B* for $1,500, and *B* promises to buy the car. The conditions here are concurrent as the obligations of the parties arise simultaneously. The transfer of the title is dependent upon payment by the other party, and the payment is dependent upon transfer of the title. However, it would be both silly and unjust to require *B* to pay the $1,500 before he can declare *A* to be in default if *A* has decided not to go through with the delivery of the title to the car. Thus, the law requires of *B* only a tender of performance. Tender of performance requires *B* to show he is ready, willing, and able to perform his side of the bargain in the exact manner, place, and time called for in the contract. Once *B* tenders performance and *A* refuses to make good his side of the contract, *B* is discharged from his obligation and is entitled to rescind the contract and sue for damages. There is one exception to this last statement. If *B*'s obligation to pay money arose from an existing debt, the tender of the amount due and *A*'s refusal to accept will not discharge the obligation. It will, however, cut off any interest that might accrue in the future, entitle *B* to recover any security held by *A* (e.g., a mortgage), and, in the event *A* later sues to collect the debt, he must furnish both parties' "costs." For further problems in this area, see *Moore v. Norman,* 52 Minn. 83, 53 N.W. 809 (1892).

c. CONDITIONS SUBSEQUENT

Conditions subsequent refers to a future event upon the happening of which the obligation no longer becomes binding upon the other party if he so chooses, or it may make certain additional rights accrue under the contract. It is a condition which terminates the obligations which are being fully performed and would continue to be unless the condition occurs.

Illustrations:

(1) *A* rents or sells property to *B* so long as *B* does not use the property for the sale of alcoholic beverages. The condition subsequent here, if it occurs, will revert the property back to *A* and terminate the contract.

(2) Father promises to give Son an allowance of $75 a

month for as long as Son maintains a B average in school. If Son's average falls below a B, the condition subsequent will discharge Father's liability.

Many goods are sold on a basis of "sale or return." Such a sale passes title to the buyer, but he has the option to return the goods if they do not meet his approval. This option is a condition subsequent. It differs from "special approvals" in that the title has passed to the buyer, and the obligations have been performed on both sides. The buyer, however, is given the option to return both parties to the same status which existed prior to the making of the contract.

d. Doctrine of Substantial Performance

At common law, strict performance of all the conditions and terms of the contract was required in order to recover from the promisor for services rendered to him. The courts gradually accepted what is now called the doctrine of substantial performance in order to avoid grave injustices which would occur where one in good faith attempted to perform his contract and did so substantially, although there would be some slight deviation or technical and unimportant defect or omission. Substantial performance is a relative test, and no precise rule may be laid down as to what is substantial, and what insubstantial. See *Boljen v. Ellegaard*, 43 N.Y.S. 2nd 527 (1943).

The doctrine of substantial performance is often applied to building contracts. Thus, before the contractor can collect anything, substantial performance is a condition precedent. In other words, a contractor who has not substantially performed can recover none of the promised payments except for the cost of materials and labor, if the non-performance was not willful; while, on the other hand, if he meets the test of substantial performance, even though omitting some details, he may recover the contract price less the damages resulting from his omissions.

One illustration of substantial performance: *A* had a contract to haul all the wood off *B's* property. *A* was to be paid 85¢ a cord for the job, with *B* withholding 25¢ per cord until the contract was completed. *A* hauls off 8,345 cords, but *B* finds that *A* omitted 7½ cords, and refuses to pay the 25¢ per cord that has been withheld. In this actual case, the court required *B* to pay all the contract price, finding that *A* had substantially performed his part of the contract. *Drew et al. v. Goodhue*, 74 Vt. 436, 52 Atl. 971 (1902).

III. Entire and Divisible Contracts

A divisible contract is one in which fractional performance by one party is the equivalent of a corresponding fractional performance by the other party, and where the contract calls for several distinct performances and counter performances, set off against each other and regarded by the parties as the exact equivalents of each other. The distinguishing mark of a divisible contract is that it admits of an apportionment of the consideration on either side so as to correspond to the unascertained consideration on the other side. In other words, is the contract in reality several individual, distinct contracts that are independent of each other, or is the contract a necessary, indivisible whole which is inseparable?

It is important to determine whether a contract is entire or divisible for the following reasons, which are merely the different effects of each:

(1) If the contract is entire, there is only one cause of action, while if the contract is divisible, there are several.
(2) If the contract is entire, the one party must perform all of the promises before being entitled to payments, while if the contract is divisible, the one party is entitled to partial payments as each promise (or separate contract) is performed.
(3) Most important, if the contract is entire, any breach of any installment allows the other party to rescind as to any future, unperformed part of the contract, while if the contract is divisible, the other party may only rescind the portion actually breached.

Whether a contract is entire or divisible depends upon many factors, and may turn on what may be considered an insignificant part of the agreement. For example: *A* contracts to sell to *B* twelve "gifts-of-the-month" for $24. The question, of course, is whether this is one contract or twelve separate ones. If *B* is to pay $2 for each gift as he receives it, the contract would most likely be considered divisible and thus actually be twelve contracts, while if *B* is to pay $24 at the end of the year, the contract would most likely be considered entire.

IV. Nonperformance of the Contract

The failure of a party to perform his part of the contract, under proper circumstances, will not always result in barring that party from recovering on a contract, or, on the other hand, necessarily mean that such party will lose a suit if he is sued for the nonperformance of the contract. Nonperformance of a contract may be excused under the following circumstances:

(1) Anticipatory breach
(2) Prevention of performance
(3) Waiver of performance
(4) Impossibility of performance

These justifications for non-performance will now be discussed in some detail.

a. ANTICIPATORY BREACH

An anticipatory breach occurs when one party to a contract is justifiably led by the other party to believe that performance by the other party will not be forthcoming at the time when due under the contract. This anticipatory breach by the other party occurs when that other party unequivocally renounces the contract (e.g., the other party sells a house which is under contract to be sold to a third party). Upon the occurrence of an anticipatory breach, the injured party is excused from performance of his part of the contract, and may treat the contract as ended, and immediately bring a cause of action for damages without even tendering performance to the other party. It must be noted that the injured party must take immediate steps to mitigate the damages.

Some cases seem to conclude that this doctrine applies only where the contract is wholly executory, and if one party has wholly performed and the other refuses, the injured party has no right of action until there has been an actual breach of the contract. For example, suppose *A* agrees to sell goods to *B*, allowing *B* 90-days credit. Now, if *A* delivered and *B* says that he will not pay, there is no anticipatory breach by the above reasoning. But, if *B* says he will not pay before *A* delivers, such is an anticipatory breach. Under the first possibility, there exists no anticipatory breach because *B*'s only duty is to pay money 90 days hence, and *A*, having already delivered the goods to *B*, can take no steps to mitigate his damages. Under the second possibility, however, *A* may prefer to ship the goods elsewhere and not incur the expense of shipping the goods to *B* in order only to put *B* in actual default (i.e., by tendering performance).

In either of the above examples, and in all cases of anticipatory breaches, *B* may retract his renunciation of the contract anytime before *A* has elected to treat the contract as ended. *A*, to excuse himself from performance, must end the contract by either notifying *B* that he rescinds, or by suing *B* for damages, or by changing his position in any other fashion (e.g., selling or contracting to sell the goods to others) in reliance upon the breach.

b. PREVENTION OF PERFORMANCE

The law will not allow anyone to benefit by his own dereliction. In every contract there is an implied promise on the part of each party that he will not do anything to render performance impossible. The party attempting to perform is excused and may bring an immediate action for damages against any party that so interferes. For example, *B* promised to buy from *A* land which *A* intended to buy at an auction. Then *B* appeared at the auction and consistently outbid *A*, finally receiving the property for less than the amount he had agreed to pay *A*. *A* sued and recovered damages for the profit he would have made under the contract had not *B* interfered. See *Patterson v. Meyerhofer*, 204 N.Y. 96, 97 N.E. 472 (1912).

c. WAIVER OF PERFORMANCE

Waiver of performance may be clearly expressed or may be implied from conduct. In either case, nonperformance is excused. A waiver is an intentional relinquishment of a known right by one party, excusing the other party from performance of that right. For example, if *A* accepts a suit knowing the tailor did not comply with the contract as to the material and wears this suit for several weeks, *A* has waived his right to say that the tailor did not perform his part of the contract and therefore *A* will have to pay. As you see, the tailor's nonperformance is excused by *A*'s waiver.

d. IMPOSSIBILITY OF PERFORMANCE

In the chapter on consideration, we mentioned recision of the contract by implication, and concluded this would occur only when unusual and extraordinary difficulties which could not be reasonably foreseen were encountered. We mentioned that price changes, shortages of materials, strikes, fires, and various so-called acts of God did not qualify, even though they may make performance much more difficult. These are circumstances that are considered foreseeable and therefore should have been provided for in the contract. Even if performance becomes impossible because of one of these happenings, the nonperforming party is not excused and will be liable for his nonperformance. However, when impossibility of performance results from the destruction of the subject-matter of the contract, a change in the law, or the death of a party, we have some exceptional circumstances wherein the law excuses nonperformance.

1. Impossibility Due to Destruction of the Subject Matter

Impossibility here is best explained by illustrations:

(1) Rancher Jones contracts to deliver to feeder Smith 1,000 bales of hay. Jones' hay crop is a failure. However, Jones must go out and buy the hay from someone else or pay damages, for his performance is not excused.

(2) Rancher Jones contracts to deliver to feeder Smith 1,000 bales of hay "out of my current year's crop." Jones' hay crop is a failure. This time, Jones does not have to perform or pay damages, for the subject matter of the contract was destroyed.

(3) *A* contracts to paint *B*'s house. *A*'s paint and equipment is destroyed in a fire. However, *A* is not excused. The job may be more difficult or costly, but it is not impossible.

(4) *A* contracts to paint *B*'s house. *B*'s house is destroyed by fire. Here both parties are excused from performance, for it has become impossible due to the destruction of the subject matter.

The above illustrations are distinguished in that one is not excused merely because the contract becomes more difficult to perform or because he might suffer an unanticipated financial loss from performance, while the others are excused because the very nature of the thing promised has been destroyed. What the law is doing is merely reading into the contract what the parties would probably have included had they anticipated these occurrences.

2. Impossibility Due to a Change of Law

One illustration should suffice here: *A* contracts to sell to *B* 30 cases of whiskey, delivery in 90 days. Within the 90-day period, the 18th Amendment to the Federal Constitution comes into effect. Both parties are excused. Many other examples of this rule occurred during war times, when the government put into effect many economic restrictions.

3. Impossibility Due to Death or Illness

Here, nonperformance is excused because of death or illness if the contract called for personal services, but is not excused if the acts could be performed by others. For instance, the death of an artist contracted to paint a portrait of *A* excuses the deceased one's personal representative, but death of a building contractor hired to build *A*'s house does not excuse the personal representative, who must carry out the contract or pay damages.

In all of these cases of impossibility, if there has been a partial performance by one party and further performance becomes impossible and is excused, the other party must pay a pro rata share of the contract price for the goods actually received or for the benefit he would have received had impossibility not arisen. Thus, if *B*'s house burns after *A* has applied one coat of paint, *B* must pay *A* for such. It should be noted that if performance becomes impossible because of some willful act by one party, after that party has partially performed, the recipient of the benefit from this partial performance must return the goods (if that is what is involved) or pay for them, as in the case of impossibility not due to a willful act; but if the benefit received is something which cannot be returned (a coat of paint), the recipient need not pay anything.

G. DISCHARGE OF CONTRACTS AND REMEDIES OF PARTIES

I. Discharge

Contractual obligations may be discharged by performance (including substantial performance), by operation of law, by mutual agreement, and by impossibility. Nearly all contracts are discharged, of course, by performance. Once a contract has been fully performed by both parties, it is no longer in existence. Since discharge by performance, by impossibility, and, in the cases of mistake, fraud, duress, undue influence, and incapacity, by operation of law have already been discussed, only additional methods of discharging contracts will be treated separately at this time.

a. Discharge by Operation of Law

The law will, in addition to previously discussed circumstances, discharge a contractual obligation in the following cases:

(1) Statute of Limitations
(2) Bankruptcy
(3) Merger
(4) Material Alteration

1. Statute of Limitations
If a party fails to enforce his contract rights within the time specified by the statutory law, the obligation of the other party becomes discharged. The object of the statute of limitations is to encourage persons to enforce their claims before they become stale—before witnesses die, move, or forget the facts. The statute of limitations, in effect, bars any recovery in a court by a party after a certain lapse of time from an accrual of a contract right by that party.
2. Bankruptcy
By certain court proceedings, a person falling within certain statutory requirements may be declared bankrupt. After such declaration, the court strives to pay as much as possible on all contractual obligations of the bankrupt party. After the available assets of the bankrupt have been expended, the bankrupt is discharged from any further obligation on these contracts. The object of the bankruptcy laws is to aid in preventing a hopelessly indebted person from becoming a "bum" because of his lack of possibility, and therefore incentive, to ever accumulate wealth.
3. Merger
Whenever a party accepts a superior right to an inferior one, this inferior right is discharged by its merger into the superior. Thus, when you sue on a note for $500 and get a judgment for $500, the lesser rights involved in the note are merged into the more superior rights accrued in the judgment.
4. Material Alteration
Whenever a material alteration of a written contract is made intentionally by a party to the agreement without the consent of the other party, the contractual obligations

of the other party are discharged. A material alteration is an alteration which changes the nature of the obligation. Thus, if *A* agrees to sell goods to *B* on 30-days credit, and *A* later changes the contract to C.O.D., *B* may refuse to accept and pay for the goods.

b. Discharge by Mutual Agreement

The original contract may provide that it is to terminate upon a condition subsequent or that disputes over the provisions and performance of the contract are to be settled by arbitration. Such mutual agreement provisions are valid and useful in avoiding costly law suits. In the case of arbitration, once the arbitrator makes an award, the parties must abide by it as if it were a part of the original contract. Actually, the original contract merges into the award, and a subsequent lawsuit would be on the award and not the original contract.

In addition to mutual agreements for discharge appearing in the original contract, a contract may be discharged by agreement subsequent to the making. These subsequent agreements take different forms, as follows:

(1) Recision by Mutual Agreement
(2) Substitution
(3) Novation
(4) Accord and Satisfaction

1. Recision by Mutual Agreement

This is merely an agreement by the parties to a contract to the discharge of all obligations under that contract. However, this agreement is and must be a contract itself, and therefore must conform to all rules applicable to contracts. In the case of wholly executory contracts, the agreement to discharge all obligations is a binding contract supported by good consideration as it releases both parties from doing something they might otherwise be required to do. However, if one party has already performed his part of the original contract, the other party must give something in return for being released from his obligation, or otherwise the mutual agreement to discharge would not be a binding contract because of lack of consideration.

2. Substitution

This is merely the recision of an old contract and the

entering into a new one by the parties. The consideration for the contract to discharge the old contract is the entering into the new one. This, then, is known as a discharge of an old contract by substitution.

3. Novation
Novation is also a discharge by substitution, but, instead of a substitution of the terms of the contract by the same parties, it is a substitution of the parties to the old contract. Thus, if *A* and *B* have a contract, and *A*, *B*, and *C* agree that *C* is obligated to *A* instead of *B*, *A* has a valid claim against *C* only, and *B* is discharged by novation.

4. Accord and Satisfaction
An accord is a new agreement and, like all contracts, requires satisfaction. The satisfaction is the performance of the new agreement which discharges the original obligation as well as the accord. It takes *both* the accord and satisfaction to discharge the old obligation, unless the new obligation (the accord) expressly states that it is being substituted for the old contract. In this case, the discharge is really by substitution and not by accord and satisfaction. To illustrate accord and satisfaction, suppose *A* buys a horse from *B*, agreeing to pay *B* $150 in 60 days. *A* fails to pay. *A* and *B* then reach an accord that if *A* delivers to *B* 150 bushels of corn, *B* will be satisfied. In other words, they make a new contract which exchanges a horse for 150 bushels of corn. But the old contract of a horse for $150 is not discharged until *A* delivers the 150 bushels of corn. Anytime before *A* delivers the corn, *B* may sue on the original contract for $150. Only after *A* delivers the corn (satisfaction) is the original contract discharged.

II. Remedies

A party injured as a result of a breach of a contract may seek his remedy in a law court, as distinguished from a court of equity, if all he desires is money damages. However, if money damages are inadequate so that the injured party is entitled to more in the way of specific performance, injunction, or recision of the contract, he may seek the aid of a court of equity. The only remedy granted by law courts is money damages.

a. MONEY DAMAGES

Money damages may be awarded whenever a contract is breached. The amount of the award should equal the injured party's loss resulting directly from the failure of the other party to perform. The court may allow nominal, compensatory, or exemplary damages.

For every breach of contract, regardless of how technical, the party not in default may bring an action for damages. In the event the jury, after proper instructions from the court, concludes that no damages have been sustained, the plaintiff would be awarded $1, more or less, as nominal damages. If, on the other hand, the jury concluded that the damages suffered were $1,000, these damages would be termed compensatory damages. Compensatory damages are supposed to total the amount necessary to put the injured party in the same position in which he would have been had there been no breach of the contract —to the extent money damages are capable of doing this.

Exemplary damages are like a fine. They are a penalty inflicted to teach the defaulting party a lesson. As a general rule, exemplary damages are not awarded for breach of contract actions.

The party who loses the lawsuit must generally pay the court costs. An exception is frequently made by assessing these costs to the plaintiff if he gets merely nominal damages. The object, in this case, is to deter the trial of lawsuits for technical or unimportant breaches of contract. Generally, each party, win or lose, pays his own attorney's fees.

To illustrate:

(1) *A* has a contract to sell 100 tons of paper to *B* at $80 per ton. *A* breaches the contract, forcing *B* to buy elsewhere at $90 per ton. *B* can get $1,000 damages. *A* must pay the court costs.

(2) Same contract, same breach. However, *B* either is able to or does actually obtain 100 tons at $80 per ton. *B* is only entitled to $1 nominal damages.

1. Liquidated Money Damages

Now, in either of the above illustrations, if in their contract *A* and *B* had agreed that, in the event of a breach the damages would be $500, they would then have a provision in their contract known as a liquidated damage clause. Would this provision be recognized by the courts? Probably not. It has been discussed elsewhere that when the subject-matter of a contract is of such a nature that damages would be difficult to determine, it is proper that these damages be agreed upon in advance. This, then, is the only occasion for the use of a liquidated damage clause.

However, even in these circumstances, the clause will not be enforced if it is unreasonable or acts to penalize rather than compensate. To summarize, the parties to a contract may insert a liquidated damage clause if the damages in case of a breach would otherwise be uncertain and difficult to judge, and they set the liquidated damages at a figure reached from a bona fide pre-estimate of possible resulting damages.

2. Mitigation of Money Damages

Mitigation of money damages is a duty imposed by the law upon the injured party to keep the damages as low as reasonably possible. The injured party cannot sit idly by and expect to recover all losses which his inaction may entail, but must, instead, be reasonably diligent in recouping his loss. So states the law. To illustrate: *B* refuses to accept goods he was obligated to buy from *A*. If the goods are perishable, *A* must resell the goods if at all possible rather than let them spoil. Whether *A* resells or not, he can collect only the loss he would have suffered had he resold the goods.

3. Collection of Money Damages

Once the injured party has won his cause of action, he still must get the judgment awarded him satisfied. Normally, the defendant pays. If, however, he fails, there are various so-called "writs" available to obtain a satisfaction of the judgment. The judgment creditor may get a writ of execution issued by the court, which authorizes the sheriff to seize any exempt property owned by the judgment debtor and sell it at a public auction, the proceeds of which go to pay off the judgment creditor and the surplus in excess of the amount of the judgment to return to the debtor.

In the event the property of the judgment debtor is in someone else's possession, the property is reached in a similar fashion by what is know as a writ of garnishment. This method is used to secure payment out of a debtor's bank account or out of the wages to be paid by the debtor's employer.

If prior to the trial of a suit for breach of contract, the

defendant is a non-resident of the State, or a resident who is about to remove his property from the State in order to delay or defeat his creditors, the plaintiff may prevent this by obtaining a writ of attachment issued at the start of the suit. However, the plaintiff must post a bond in such case in order to cover any loss the defendant would incur in the event the plaintiff failed in his cause of action. This latter requirement prevents the abusive use of this writ.

b. EQUITABLE REMEDIES

The courts of equity grant the following remedies, but only when money damages are inadequate.

1. Recision

   Recision is a means of backing out of the contract and returning the parties to their original positions. As previously discussed, this remedy may be granted for mutual mistake, fraud, undue influence, duress, incapacity, and breach of a contract.

   To be entitled to recision for a breach of a contract, the breach must be a material breach, going to the essence of the contract, or be a willful breach.

   The election to rescind must be exercised promptly upon discovering the facts upon which the right is based, and is conditioned upon the injured party returning or tendering the return of the consideration received by him under the contract, to the extent such is possible.

2. Specific Performance

   Specific performance is a means of compelling a party to a contract to carry out the terms of the contract. If the court would find it difficult to supervise the carrying out of its order, this remedy will be denied.

   Specific performance will be granted for all contracts to sell land, for land parcels are considered unique and money damages would not enable the purchase of another identical parcel. On the other hand, contracts to sell personal property will not be specifically enforced unless the chattel is so unique that it cannot be readily obtained in the market (e.g., an original painting, an old or rare edition of a book, etc.). Contracts of employment will not be specifically enforced because of the difficulty of supervision by the court as well as the fact that it would violate the constitutional prohibition of involuntary servitude.

3. Injunctive Relief

Injunctive relief is a means of preventing the commission of an injury. Law courts cannot prevent a commission of an injury. They can only award damages after an injury has been sustained. But through injunctions, a court of equity is able to prevent the commission of a wrong and thus prevent irreparable injury.

When the court orders specific performance or issues an injunction, it enforces its order by subjecting a non-complying party to a fine or imprisonment for contempt of court.

This completes the chapter on contracts. Although you may feel the law is detailed, you have seen only a smattering of the law on this subject. As you may have realized in the study of this chapter, there is no such thing as a contract but only the law of contracts. Without becoming too abstruse, the law of contracts is but a means of achieving fair play in the dynamics of economics, and, to be effective, it is necessarily as complex as is our economy and as is our concept of justice.

Chapter 2

SALES AND BAILMENTS

A. INTRODUCTION

"A sale of goods is an agreement whereby the seller transfers the property (title) in the goods to the buyer for a consideration called the price." "Goods" means "all chattels personal other than things in action and money. The term includes emblements, industrial growing crops, and things attached to or forming part of the land which are agreed to be severed before sale or under the contract to sell." These quotations have been taken from the Uniform Sales Act, specifically Sections 1 and 76, which is a proposed uniform act codifying all the rules pertaining to "sales," and which has actually been adopted by almost all of the States. The purpose of codifying these rules was to aid in making the law of the various states applicable to sales as uniform as possible.

From the definition of "goods" quoted above, it is apparent that the law of sales does not concern real property or negotiable instruments. However, quasi-negotiable instruments—documents of title such as bills of lading and warehouse receipts—will be given special treatment in this section as they effect the sales of goods.

The law of sales obviously concerns contracts. A "sale of goods" involves a contract. Instead of a sale, there may be an agreement to transfer title to goods, called a contract to sell goods. Neither of these contracts requires a special form nor must they be in writing—unless the Statute of Frauds is applicable. (See Contracts.) The law of sales concerns itself with this specialized area of contract law as well as the transference of title to goods. It is within this area that this chapter will be devoted.

I. Contract of Sale and Contract to Sell

The distinction between a contract of sale and contract to sell has already been noted, but it is set out here separately for emphasis. "A contract to sell goods is a contract whereby the seller agrees to transfer the property (title) in the goods to the buyer for a consideration called the price." (U.S.A., § 1 (1)). "A sale of goods is an agreement whereby the seller transfers the property (title) in the goods to the buyer for a consideration called the price." (U.S.A., § 1 (2)). As may be seen, if title passes to the buyer immediately, such transaction is designated as a contract of sale, whereas if title is to pass at some future time, the transaction is called a contract to sell. These two different types of transactions should be kept in mind at all times, and their differences noted.

One reason for noting the differences is that a person can contract to sell anything he desires, even if he does not own it when he so contracts, but a contract of sale indicates a present transfer of title, and thus is dependent upon the ownership of existing goods. Thus, goods not in existence can be the subject-matter only of contracts to sell, not contracts of sale.

II. Time When Title Passes

In considering when title to goods passes from the seller to the buyer, we will become acquainted with the most important aspects of the law of sales and, additionally, will become acquainted with new terms and sub-rules applicable to sales. First, however, we will discover why it is important to know just when title passes.

1. If title has passed and the seller defaults, the buyer may sue for breach of contract or for possession of the goods. This is because the buyer is the owner. If title has not yet passed, the buyer's remedy is limited to a suit for breach of contract. Supposing the seller is insolvent, the availability of remedies takes on practical significance, for in the case where the title has passed, the buyer may get the goods while, in the case where the title has not passed, the buyer only has a suit for money against the seller who may owe twenty other creditors and own only those goods he contracted to sell.
2. Only the person holding title may convey good title to another. A buyer then could not resell goods if title has not yet passed to him.
3. The general rule (there are exceptions) is that risk of loss follows the title. Thus, if the goods are destroyed without fault on the part of either the buyer or the seller, the loss

may fall on either the buyer or the seller depending upon whether title has or has not passed.

Now that we know why it is important to determine when title passes, we turn to the question again of just when title does pass. The answer to this appears simple—title passes according to the intent of the parties. It is simple if the parties expressed their intent of when title is to pass in the agreement, but is less simple if no intent has been expressed. Turning to that question later, we must qualify the rule that title passes when intended. Regardless of expressed intent, title cannot pass until the goods to which title is to pass are in existence and properly identified. We have already seen that they must be in existence, but, in addition to this requirement, goods must also be properly identified or ascertained. Ascertained goods (or specific goods) means the exact items to which title is to pass must have been separated, marked, or otherwise designated.

a. Fixing Intent

When does title pass in the absence of express intent? The answer to this question is set forth in various sections of the Uniform Sales Act. Here are two:

Rule 1. "When there is an unconditional contract to sell specific goods, in a deliverable state, the property in the goods passes to the buyer when the contract is made and it is immaterial whether the time of payment, or the time of delivery, or both, be postponed."

Rule 2. "Where there is a contract to sell specific goods and the seller is bound to do something to the goods, for the purpose of putting them into a deliverable state, the property does not pass until such thing be done."

As may be seen, the seller must put the specific goods into a deliverable condition before title passes to the buyer, and once the goods are in such condition, the title passes automatically. "Goods are in a deliverable state when they are in such a state that the buyer would, under the contract, be bound to take delivery of them." (Uniform Sales Act, § 76). To illustrate: *B* agrees to buy a hog from *A* if *A* agrees to fatten it. Title will not pass until the specific hog is fattened. This illustration is easy, as are cases where the seller must repair or finish the goods. Other situations, not worthwhile to go into here, present harder questions as to whether and when goods are in a deliverable state.

We have been talking up to now about specific goods. Now let us take the case of fungible goods. "Fungible goods means goods of which any unit is from its nature or by mercantile usage treated as the equivalent of any other unit." (U.S.A. § 76). In other words, a bushel of wheat, a bucket of bolts, etc.

"In the case of fungible goods, there may be a sale of an individual share of a specific mass, though the seller purports to sell and the buyer to buy a definite number, weight, or measure of the goods in the mass, and the number, weight, or measure of the goods in the mass is undetermined. By such a sale the buyer becomes an owner in common of such a share of the mass as the number, weight, or measure bought, bears to the number, weight, or measure of the mass. If the mass contains less than the number, weight, or measure bought, the buyer becomes the owner of the whole mass and the seller is bound to make good the deficiency from similar goods unless a contrary intent appears." (U.S.A. Sec. 5 (2)).

From this section of the Sales Act, unless the parties express a contrary intent in their agreement for the sale and purchase of fungible goods, title passes at the time of the agreement, providing the mass from which a specific amount of goods is to come has been ascertained. Only the mass need be ascertained and agreed upon.

> To Illustrate: *A* has a crib containing an unknown quantity of corn. *A* sells *B* 1000 bushels of corn, and they agree that the corn is to come from this crib. *B* has immediate title to 1000 bushels of corn in the crib. Assume it turns out that the crib contains 2500 bushels. *B* owns an undivided 2/5ths of the mass even though his corn has not been separated.
>
> Now, assume, that some of the corn is destroyed, but that 1000 bushels of it are salvaged. *B* would suffer the loss of 600 bushels (2/5 × 2500=1000) and *A*, 900 bushels.
>
> Finally, assume the seller was to sack the corn and the loss occurred prior to the sacking. *A* would take the entire loss as title would not pass until goods were in a deliverable state. (U.S.A. Sec. 19 Rule 2) until the corn was sacked.

B. BAILMENTS

Because some rules of determining intent require a knowledge of bailments, we will now consider this topic and then return to the balance of the law of sales.

I. In General

A bailment is a temporary transfer of possession of personal property from one person to another for a specific purpose. Whenever you check your coat, rent a boat, leave your car in a garage for repairs, borrow a book, or take your clothes to the cleaners, you have created a bailment. The person transferring the property is called the bailor and the one taking possession is known as the bailee.

a. Characteristics of a Bailment

There are four characteristics that create a bailment: (1) there must be both delivery and acceptance of personal property; (2) under an expressed or implied agreement that the transfer of possession is without intent to pass title; (3) that the transfer of possession is for some temporary purpose; and (4) that possession is to revert to the bailor or someone entitled to possession either upon the fulfillment of the purpose of the bailment, at the expiration of an agreed period of time, upon the happening of a specified event, or at the bailor's demand.

Normally, the exact goods bailed are to be returned to the bailor in their same or altered form, and if such is not the case, the transaction is not a bailment. An exception to this rule is made in the case of fungible goods where the law recognizes a bailment relationship even though the identical article delivered is not to be returned to the bailor in its original or altered form.

II. Sale Or Bailment?

A bailment transfers possession only (not title) to the bailee, title remaining in the bailor (assuming the bailor is the owner). Since risk of loss follows title, it is important to determine whether a given transaction is a sale or a bailment. Thus, if logs are delivered to be sawed into boards, or olives are delivered to be made into oil, or wheat into flour, if the product of the identical article delivered is to be returned to the original owner in a new form, we have a bailment and for this reason title was never vested in the processor. But if the processor is not bound to return the finished product processed from the identical item furnished, but may deliver any finished product of equal quality, we have a sales transaction, and title to the article delivered vests in the processor.

A consignment sale is where the buyer is given possession of goods and authority to sell them and to account for the proceeds as sales are made, but the seller retains title. Unsold goods are held subject to the order of the furnisher, and the consignee may return the goods which remain unsold. Thus, a consignment is another type of a bailment relationship. The owner may prefer to consign goods and authorize the retailer (bailee) to sell them on his behalf because of the retailer's poor credit or in order to control the retail price of the goods. The retailer may insist on this method in order to avoid the risk of ownership (adverse price changes, fire, etc.) and/or to keep his investment in inventory at the minimum.

If the agreement does not meet the requirements of a consignment in that the goods must be paid for whether sold or not, and payments are remitted on general account and not on basis of goods sold, the transaction is a sale and not a bailment, even though the contract was called a "consignment."

To summarize:

(1) Bailee cannot transfer good title—vendee can.
(2) Bailee's creditors cannot attach the goods—vendee's can.
(3) Risk of loss follows title and is on the bailor if we have a bailment, but is on the vendee if the transaction was a sale.

We have mentioned that delivery and acceptance are required in order to have a bailment. An exception is made for what is termed a constructive bailment. Suppose a storm tosses goods on to your property; well, you then hold such goods as bailee for the true owner. Or, if you find a textbook, you are a bailee even though there was no true delivery of the book to you by the bailor. In each case, you possess the property under such circumstances that the law imposes on you (the bailee) the obligation of delivering it to the true owner. The last two illustrations differ in that in the first you are an involuntary bailee and in the latter a voluntary bailee. This distinction is important as to determining your duties, which will be discussed at a later point.

III. Types of Bailments

There are three basic types of bailments which are important to keep in mind. The first type of bailment is a bailment for the sole benefit of the bailor. This would occur when a bailee is keeping property for a bailor without compensation or other benefit to himself. For example, the taking care of a neighbor's dog while your neighbor is on vacation—if you do it for free. The next type is a bailment for the sole benefit of the bailee. Example: You borrow your neighbor's lawnmower. The third and last type is a bailment for the mutual benefit of both bailor and bailee. This is the usual commercial type bailment. An example is the leaving of your car at a parking lot, the lot receiving 35¢ an hour in return. These three types of bailments become important in determining the duties of a bailor and a bailee.

IV. Duties of a Bailor

If bailment is for benefit of bailor or mutual benefit, the bailor is liable to bailee for any injury or loss to bailee caused by defects in the property which the bailor knew or should have known. If bailment is for benefit of bailee, the bailor is liable to bailee only if he failed to warn the bailee of defects which he, the bailor, had actual knowledge.

> Illustration: I'm driving a rented car and have an accident, the cause of which was a defective steering wheel. Bailor is liable. Now if I were driving a friend's car, the bailor is liable only if he knew of the defect and failed to warn me.

V. Duties of a Bailee

The duties of a bailee as to the degree of care required depend upon the type of bailment, as the duties of the bailor so vary, unless the contract of bailment fixes the duties in some other fashion.

(1) For Sole Benefit of Bailor. Under such bailment, the bailee must use only slight care, must be guilty of gross negligence before he will be liable for loss to the bailed property.

(2) For Sole Benefit of Bailee. Here the bailee must give the property great care and will be liable for any loss or damage to the property bailed if he is guilty of slight negligence. In case of fire, for example, the bailee must save the bailed goods in preference to his own if he is to escape liability for negligence.

(3) Mutual Benefit Bailment. Here the bailee must use ordinary care and will be liable for loss or damage to bailed goods only if guilty of ordinary negligence.

The bailee is not liable to bailor for loss of or damage to the bailed property unless he has failed to exercise the proper degree of care, unless he has exceeded his authority in some manner. This will be noted later. We should define "ordinary care." Ordinary care is the care a reasonably prudent person usually exercises over his own property under similar circumstances. Ordinary care varies according to the nature of the subject matter. What might be great care as to a baseball might be gross negligence as to a valuable diamond ring.

VI. Duties of Innkeepers and Common Carriers Acting As Bailees

Innkeepers and common carriers (those who serve the public generally), when acting as bailees of personal property, have a greater duty of care than others. They are responsible for goods while in their possession as though they were an insurer. They are liable for loss, even when such was not caused by their negligence, unless the loss was caused by an act of God, an act of the shipper, an act of a public enemy, or because of the inherent nature of the goods.

The reason for this strict liability is basically historical. In early England, when travel was by stagecoach and inns were in remote places, and law enforcement was inadequate, the common law developed this extraordinary liability in order to encourage these businesses to protect those to whom they were rendering a service and to discourage their taking advantage of their guests and freight shippers by faking hold-ups and robberies. Because certain losses would be difficult to fake, and would be the result of such notorious occasion that the cause would be known to all, certain exceptions to the rule that they are "insurers of goods" were recognized. These exceptions are:

(1) Acts of God: Rain, flood, winds, lightning, etc., are all Acts of God, but to excuse one from liability they must be unforeseeable, i.e., unprecedented floods, high winds, etc., or a tornado.

(2) Acts of Shipper: Loss from improper packing done by the bailor, or electing to ship perishables without icing in

anticipation of cool weather, but instead it turns hot and spoilage results.

(3) Acts of Public Enemy. Public enemy means an armed force acting against the government and not "Public Enemy No. 1," or mobs, or strike rioters.

(4) Inherent Nature of the Goods: If in No. 2 above, the goods had been shipped properly but the railroad negligently failed to maintain the refrigeration of the cars, the railroad would be liable. But if corn spoils in transit due to some defect inherent in it, the railroad would not be liable.

These duties of innkeepers and common carriers may be limited by contract. They cannot, however, contract not to be liable for their own negligence, but losses resulting from other causes may be limited or avoided. An example is the limiting of the amount of loss to an agreed value in the event goods are lost or damaged. This is merely a liquidated damage provision. Also risk of loss due to strike, riots, fire, etc., may be limited by contract, so long as the fire or what-have-you was not caused by the innkeeper's or common carrier's negligence.

VII. Bailee's Duty Not to Exceed His Authority

A bailee has the duty not to depart from the contract of bailment. He makes himself absolutely liable for the property if he uses it in an unauthorized manner. So, if a parking lot owner drives your car home to lunch without your permission and the car is damaged, the bailee is liable, even though the damage was not caused because of his negligence. Unauthorized use by a bailee is treated the same as a "conversion" and one remedy for conversion is to force the convertor to buy the property converted at its market value.

VIII. Liens

Many people do not pay their bills, and in order to aid collections various legal and commercial devices have been developed whereby personal property may be charged with the obligation, in the event the obligor fails to discharge his personal debts. These include chattel mortgages, mechanic's liens, artisan's liens, conditional sales contracts, bailee liens, etc.

The bailee's lien is dependent upon his retention of possession, and consists of his right to retain possession until he has been paid. Thus, if he voluntarily surrenders possession to the owner, he loses his lien. But the common law bailee's lien was given only to the extent the bailee expended money or services to improve or alter the condition of the bailed property. Thus, a garageman would have a lien for repairs, but not for storage. And if the owner had several cars stored, only one of which was repaired, and the garageman allowed the owner to take the repaired car, no bailee's lien would be had by the garageman on the remaining cars, since the bailee's lien is a specific and not a general lien.

The lien holder cannot sell the property directly to enforce his lien, but instead must sue and get a judgment and then levy on the property held so it can be sold by judicial proceedings.

Public service businesses who must serve the public generally without discrimination, including chiselers, thieves, etc., are given a specific retaining lien on the subject-matter of the bailment as security for their compensation, regardless of whether they altered or improved the condition of the bailed property.

C. SALES (Continued)

We now resume the question of when title passes in absence of expressed intent. We have already concerned ourselves with unconditional contracts to sell and also contracts of sale for specific (or ascertained) goods and fungible goods. We now shall concern ourselves with conditional sales contracts and sales of unascertained goods.

I. Conditional Sales

a. Sale on Approval

Upon a sale on approval, the Uniform Sales Act provides as follows regarding the passing of title:

> "When goods are delivered to the buyer on approval or on trial or on satisfaction, or other similar terms, the property therein passes to the buyer:
>
> (a) When he signifies his approval or acceptance to the seller or does any other act adopting the transaction.
>
> (b) If he does not signify his approval or acceptance to the seller, but retains the goods without giving notice of rejection, then if a time has been fixed for the return of the goods, on the expiration of such time, and, if no time has been fixed, on the expiration of a reasonable time. What is a reasonable time is a question of fact." (U.S.A. 19 (3) (2)).

Here the buyer is given possession of goods in hopes they

will meet his requirements. Title does not pass until he expressly or impliedly indicates his acceptance. Until such time, the buyer is merely a bailee. Thus, if goods are damaged without fault, the seller takes the loss.

b. Sale or Return

The following is provided by the Uniform Sales Act regarding a contract on "sale or return":

> "When goods are delivered to the buyer on 'sale or return,' or on other terms indicating an intent to make a present sale, but to give the buyer an option to return the goods instead of paying the price, the property passes to the buyer on delivery, but he may revest the property in the seller by returning or tendering the goods within the time fixed in the contract, or, if no time has been fixed, within a reasonable time." (U.S.A. 19 (3) (L)).

Here we have a present sale with buyer having an option to return goods and revert title in seller. Until the option is received, title is in the buyer. Thus, if goods are destroyed before he returns them, the buyer takes the loss.

II. Unascertained Goods

Here the Uniform Sales Act provides:

> "Where there is a contract to sell unascertained or future goods by description, and goods of that description in a deliverable state are unconditionally appropriated to the contract, either by the seller with consent of the buyer, or by the buyer with the assent of the seller, the property in the goods thereupon passes to the buyer. Such assent may be expressed or implied, and may be given either before or after the appropriation is made." (U.S.A. 19 (4) (1)).

From this we should note that a contract relating to unascertained goods is a contract to sell and therefore title does not pass until the specific goods have been agreed upon. Passing of title is dependent upon a subsequent act of appropriation with assent of both parties. Usually the buyer impliedly gives his previous assent to the seller to make the appropriation when the goods are ordered. Thus, when the seller unequivocally indicates an intent that certain goods of kind and quality specified have been assigned to the performance of the contract to sell by (1) setting the goods aside and marking them for the buyer;

(2) pointing the goods out to the buyer; (3) or delivering the goods to a carrier for transmission to the buyer—any of these are sufficient to pass title to the buyer, but there are exceptions to #3 as follows:

> "If the contract to sell requires the seller to deliver the goods to the buyer at a particular place, or to pay the freight or cost of transportation to the buyer, or to a particular place, the property does not pass until the goods have been delivered to the buyer or reached the place agreed upon." (U.S.A. 19 (5)).

Thus, the terms of sale affect the determination as to when title passes. A sale from Lincoln—F.O.B. (1) Lincoln shipping point; (2) Chicago intermediate point; or (3) New York destination, title would pass respectively (1) when goods were loaded in Lincoln; (2) when car reached Chicago; or (3) when car reached New York.

But in a C.I.F. sale (C.I.F. meaning cost, insurance and freight), title passes at point of shipment. This is based on the fact the quoted price includes freight, and therefore the buyer is in effect paying the freight.

The basis for these rules as to when title passes is that the carrier is acting as agent for the party who pays the freight. So where the parties expressly provide for delivery F.O.B. destination, the presumption that delivery to the carrier or delivery to the buyer is rebutted until the goods reach the point the parties intended.

There are other types of shipments—C.O.D. and bills of lading. Sellers at times find it necessary to secure payment of the purchase price before they relinquish control of the goods to the buyer. This can be done by making use of a C.O.D. sale or by shipping goods on an order bill of lading with draft attached.

A C.O.D. shipment is a device by which the seller appoints the carrier his agent to collect the purchase price as a condition precedent to delivering the goods to the buyer. This does not change the presumption that title passes when the goods are delivered to the carrier nor does it imply a cash sale. It is merely a security device for the seller to retain possession until the price has been paid. The carrier is an agent of the buyer for transporting the goods and an agent of the seller to collect the purchase price.

A bill of lading is a contract between the shipper and the carrier for the transportation of the described goods. It is also a receipt for the goods delivered to the carrier. Straight bills are not negotiable and can therefore be transferred only by assignment. Thus, a carrier which has not received notice to the contrary from an assignee of the bill, can safely deliver to the person designated in the bill of lading and without securing the surrender of the bill. But an order bill is negotiable and may be transferred, the transferee being entitled to receipt of the goods even though no notice has been given to the carrier. The carrier should not deliver goods shipped under an order bill without securing the surrender of the bill.

This being the case, a seller may ship goods naming himself as the consignee on the order bill. The buyer cannot get the goods from the carrier without surrendering the bill of lading. This being so, the seller attaches a draft to the bill and sends both to a bank in the buyer's town. The bank notifies the buyer who comes in and pays the draft and is then given the bill of lading. The U.S.A. considers such merely a security device and holds that such a shipment is an act of appropriation as much as if the goods had been shipped on a straight bill. Thus, if the buyer pays the freight, risk of loss while in transit is still on the buyer, as the seller retained title only for security of payment of purchase money.

U.S.A. Sec. 20 (2) states this rule as follows:

> "Where goods are shipped, and by the bill of lading goods are deliverable to the seller or his agent, or to the order of the seller or his agent, and the seller thereby reserves the property in the goods. But, if except for the form of the bill of lading, the property would have passed to the buyer on shipment of the goods, the seller's property in the goods shall be deemed to be only for the purpose of securing performance by the buyer of his obligations under the contract."

Obviously, the operation of all these rules heretofore set out are subordinate to any expressed intent to the contrary. This would be a good point to review again the importance of determining when title passes.

D. WARRANTIES

A warranty is in the nature of an assurance from the seller

to the buyer in respect to the character, quality, and/or title of the goods. Warranties may be either expressed or implied by law. The seller assumes the responsibility that the goods are as represented. To this extent the seller guarantees the goods.

"Any affirmation of fact or any promise by the seller relating to the goods is an express warranty if the natural tendency of such affirmation or promise is to induce the buyer to purchase the goods, and if the buyer purchases the goods relying thereon. No affirmation of the value of the goods, nor any statement purporting to be a statement of the seller's opinion only, shall be construed as a warranty." This is the U.S.A. (Sec. 12) definition of an express warranty.

Note the elements required in order to have an express warranty. First, an affirmation of fact is required. The seller need not say "I warrant" or "I guarantee" in order to have a warranty. A bare statement of fact is sufficient. But it must be a statement of fact and not opinion. "Sales talk" and "puffing" are considered opinion and not fact. "Wear like iron" or "best buy in town" are illustrations of mere sales talk and the buyer must learn to discount such statements. Only statements a reasonable person would rely upon qualify as warranties. This is a $110 diamond—no warranty, mere opinion. This is a 3 K. diamond—a warranty, a fact.

Secondly, as already explained, the affirmation of fact must be made for the purpose of inducing the buyer to purchase the goods and finally the buyer must rely on the affirmation and not on his own judgment. On this latter point, the buyer may absolutely rely upon the facts as represented and must be under no duty to inspect the goods, investigate, or in any other manner ascertain the correctness of the facts. The buyer may inspect and yet show he relied, if he can convince the jury that his inspection was not of a nature that made him aware (and would not have made a reasonable person aware) of the defect he is now claiming to be a breach of warranty.

Implied Warranties are based upon the presumed intent of the parties, and cannot be assumed if it clearly appears from the contract that the buyer and seller intended that no implied warranties were to apply to the transaction. Thus, waiver of implied warranties by the buyer is possible, but only if done with knowledge and intent. In such instance it is, but if the seller puts in the contract a phrase "there are no warranties, either express or implied." There are a number of important warranties implied by law, as follows:

(a) Implied Warranty of Title. One who sells goods or makes a contract to sell goods, unless a contrary intent appears, impliedly warrants: (U.S.A. Sec. 13)

(1) in the case of a sale he has a right to sell the goods and in the case of a contract to sell he will have a right to sell the goods at the time when the property is to pass;
(2) that the buyer shall have and enjoy quiet possession of the goods as against any lawful claims existing at the time of the sale;
(3) that the goods shall be free at the time of the sale from any charge or encumbrance in favor of any third person, not declared or known to the buyer before or at the time when the contract of sale is made;
(4) that the buyer shall not be held liable to a sheriff, auctioneer, mortgagee, or other person professing to sell by virtue of authority in fact or law, goods in which a third person has a legal or equitable interest.

(b) Implied Warranty as to Quality. Ordinarily there is no implied warranty as to quality, the rule being "let the buyer beware." Exceptions are made when goods are sold by sample and/or description as disclosed by U.S.A. Section 14 and 16.

"Sec. 14. Where there is a contract to sell or a sale of goods by description, there is an implied warranty that the goods shall correspond with the description and if the contractor sale be by sample, as well as by description, it is not sufficient that the bulk of the goods correspond with the sample if the goods do not also correspond with the description."
"Sec. 16. In case of a contract to sell or a sale by sample:
"(a) There is an implied warranty that the bulk shall correspond with the sample in quality."

Do these implied warranties of quality apply even though the buyer inspected the goods? The answer is "yes" unless the examination would have disclosed the defect to a reasonable purchaser.

In sales by sample, the sample must be furnished by the seller. If the goods are present and the buyer merely inspects at random some of the goods, such is not a "sale by sample" unless the seller agrees that such testing may be so treated.

(c) Implied Warranty of Merchantability. This warranty applies only if the seller is a dealer, and it merely means that the seller warrants the goods sold to be fit for the general use to which goods of a like nature would ordinarily be used. This warranty also applies only if the buyer has no opportunity to inspect, or if his inspection did not disclose the defect and an inspection by a reasonable person would not have disclosed the defect. The reason the warranty is limited to sales made by dealers is that dealers are presumed to know the ordinary purposes the goods they handle are to serve, whereas there is no basis for this assumption when an individual makes a casual sale of the same item.

(d) Implied Warranty of Fitness for a Particular Purpose. For the same reason as just stated, this warranty applies only to dealers also. If you order a machine intending that it should do a particular job, but upon receipt of the machine it fails to do what you had intended, you have no legal right to return such item to the seller.

On the other hand, if you acquaint the seller with the purpose for which the machine is to be employed and rely on his skill and judgment, and the seller selects the particular machine for you, the law implies that the machine will reasonably fit your needs.

The elements needed are:

1. Buyer makes known his purpose to seller.
2. Buyer relies on seller making the selection.
3. Seller accepts the commission to make the selection and the buyer does not interfere in the choice made by the seller.

If I go in and order a product by its trade name, or trademark, no implied warranty of fitness attaches, as I have not relied on the seller's skill and judgment. But if the elements above are present, the mere fact the seller picks a trade-marked product does not prevent the warranty of fitness from being applicable.

Warranties run only to the immediate vendee. If the original vendee should resell the goods, the new purchaser would have no recourse as against the original vendor on any warranty the original vendor may have made, expressed or implied. This rule is frequently phrased, "there can be no implied or expressed warranties without privity of contract." There are certain recognized exceptions to this rule as where the thing causing the injury is inherently dangerous or where the thing is not inherently dangerous, but the manufacturer has been negligent in producing the item. But, so much for warranties.

E. DOCUMENTS OF TITLE

I. Negotiable Bills of Lading and Warehouse Receipts

Bills of lading and warehouse receipts originate when goods are placed in the hands of a railroad, or other carrier, or a warehouse. Since delivery of goods to a railroad is a transfer of possession without transfer of title, this transaction results in a bailment. The bill of lading issued by the railroad upon receipt of the goods is a receipt and evidences the railroad has the goods in its possession.

Bills of lading and warehouse receipts may be negotiable or non-negotiable. A non-negotiable bill of lading is known as a straight bill whereas a negotiable bill of lading is known as an order bill. If the railroad issues a straight bill, it need only deliver the goods to the person specified therein or his assignee, all contract law dealing with assignments being applicable to straight bills of lading. A straight bill acts as a receipt as well as a contract of shipment between the shipper and carrier, but it is not a document of title.

An order bill is a true document of title in addition to being a receipt and a contract between the railroad and shipper. It will always have on its face that the goods are to be delivered to the person specified "on order" or "or bearer." Title to goods shipped on a negotiable bill may be transferred by delivery (if bearer) of the bill, or by endorsement and delivery (if order bill) just like a check is transferred. It is possible that title to the goods may change hands many times while the goods are being transported across the country in possession of the railroad which issued the bill of lading. For this reason, the railroad will not surrender the goods shipped on an order bill to anyone except in exchange for the bill of lading, for if the railroad delivered the goods to someone not the owner of the bill, it would be required to make good to the true owner.

To negotiate a document of title one need but deliver a bearer instrument, but an order instrument must be endorsed and delivered. If endorsed in blank (consignee's signature only), an order document becomes bearer paper and can be negotiated by delivery. If instead, an order document is endorsed specially ("Deliver to Richard Roe" and signed by consignee), such remains order paper and would require Richard Roe's signature to be further negotiated. Greater detail will be given concerning endorsements under negotiable instruments at a later point.

II. Consequences of Negotiability

a. Negotiability and Title

The general rule of law is that a person cannot transfer better title than he possesses. Do these documents of title change this? For example, could a thief put stolen goods on a train, get a negotiable document of title, sell this to a bona-fide purchaser and the latter get good title? The answer here is "no." The document of title gives the consignor no greater rights in the goods represented than he actually possessed. But, the holder of a negotiable bill of lading is able to transfer better title than he possesses. To illustrate, if *A* sells goods to *B*, *B* gets no better title than *A* had. If it turns out that *A* had stolen the goods, the true owner could recover the goods from *B*. *B*'s recourse would be against *A* for breach of contract of implied warranty of title. On the other hand, a thief or a finder of a negotiable bill of lading payable to bearer, or an order instrument endorsed in blank, can pass good title to the goods the instrument represents if the purchaser is a bona-fide purchaser for value and without notice. Thus, the quality of the title to goods represented by a negotiable bill of lading can be improved as it is negotiated to what is called a holder in due course. The same is true of negotiable instruments, and is discussed in a later section.

The Uniform Bills of Lading Act, Sec. 31, explains this as follows:

> "A negotiable bill may be negotiated by any person in possession of the same, however such possession may have been acquired if, by the terms of the bill, the carrier undertakes to deliver the goods to the order of such person, or if at the time of negotiation, the bill is in such form that it may be negotiated by delivery."

The Uniform Warehouse Receipts Act and Uniform Sales Act say that a negotiable document of title may be negotiated by the owner or by any person to whom possession or custody has been entrusted by the owner. Thus, warehouse receipts are restricted as to their negotiability, and a finder or thief, since not entrusted with the instrument by the owner, cannot transfer good title even to a bona-fide purchaser for value.

b. Warranties in Negotiations

The transferor of a negotiable document of title warrants, unless a contrary intent appears, that:

> "1. The document is genuine;
> "2. He has a legal right to negotiate or transfer it;
> "3. That he has knowledge of no fact which would impair the validity or worth of the document, and
> "4. That he has a right to transfer the title to the goods and that the goods are merchantable or fit for a particular purpose, whenever such warranties would have been implied if the contract of the parties had been to transfer without a document of title the goods represented thereby." (U.S.A. Sec. 36.)

Similar warranties are made by the Uniform Bills of Lading Act, Sec. 35, and the Uniform Warehouse Receipts Act. You should note warranty #3 above is based on knowledge. If the transferor had no knowledge of the fact which impaired the validity (original bailor had stolen the goods) or worth (goods previously destroyed without fault of bailee) of the instrument, he would not breach this warranty. Also it should be noted that the transferor does not warrant the bailee will perform. Thus, if the railroad fails to deliver the goods, the holder of the instrument can sue only the bailee railroad unless non-performance was due to breach of warranty, e.g., the document was a forgery. It should be noted that the bailee railroad is required to hold possession of the goods for a transferee of a negotiable bill of lading under the terms of the document just as if the railroad and the transferee had contracted directly.

F. SPECIAL SALES TRANSACTIONS

I. Conditional Sales and Chattel Mortgages

Conditional sales are made extensively in the retail sale of appliances on credit. In a conditional sale, the buyer gets possession, but the seller retains title until the condition has been fully complied with by the buyer. The condition upon the happening of which the buyer gets title is the payment of the purchase price.

A chattel mortgage serves a similar purpose as a conditional sale, but the transactions differ. In a chattel mortgage, the sale is absolute; the buyer gets title immediately. Then the buyer gives back a chattel mortgage as security for the unpaid purchase price. A chattel mortgage is a conveyance of title, which conveyance is agreed to be null and void if the payments (interest and principal) are made as agreed.

In a conditional sale, the buyer gets possession, but not title, and the question becomes whether such conditional vendee can transfer good title to a bona-fide purchaser. The normal rule is one cannot transfer better title than he possesses, but how can a purchaser know what title one has in property? At common law, the risk was on the purchaser, but today most states have recording statutes which require a conditional vendor to record his conditional sales contract at the county recorder's office in the county where the vendee resides, and the failure to do so results in a bona-fide purchaser of such goods sold on a conditional sales contract getting absolute title. Chattel mortgages are also required to be recorded and if not, a purchaser gets title free from the chattel mortgagor's lien. Thus, whenever one purchases goods from an individual, the public records should be checked to see that the vendor has good title free from recorded liens. Today, a purchaser gets good title unless the conditional sale is recorded or unless he had actual notice of the conditional sale if not recorded.

This precaution need not be taken when one purchases from a dealer. In such cases, a purchaser gets good title even though the dealer is a conditional vendee or has given a chattel mortgage on his inventory. This is because the courts say such persons have been given an indicia of title and, by the very nature of their being in the business, are authorized to sell in the ordinary course of trade and, therefore, the dealer's conditional vendor or mortgagee has waived his security as against a subsequent purchaser.

The rights of parties to a conditional sale are unique, and will therefore be set forth.

a. Rights of a Conditional Vendee

A conditional vendee has the following rights and duties:

(1) Has all rights and duties of an owner including risk of loss. This is an exception to the rule that risk of loss always follows title in that the risk is on the vendee even though title is in the conditional vendor.

(2) May use and enjoy the property as long as he makes his payments.

(3) May sell or assign his beneficial ownership as long as he is not attempting to deprive the conditional vendor of his security.

(4) Cannot destroy the conditional vendor's security by destroying the goods or taking the goods out of the county without the seller's approval. Many states provide criminal punishment for a conditional vendee who does such acts with intent to render vendor's security ineffective.

(5) Is entitled to absolute title upon payment of the full contract price. Title vests automatically in the conditional vendee as a matter of law as soon as the price is paid or tendered and refused.

b. Rights of a Conditional Vendor

A conditional vendor has the following rights:

(1) In case of default, he may sue for each payment as it comes due, but if he sues for payment after the last payment is due, this is considered an election to treat the sale as absolute, and he thus surrenders his alternative remedy of repossession.

The acceptance of a note from the vendee at the time of the sale is not regarded as a payment which divests the conditional seller of his title. Usually this provision is stated in the note to be double-sure. If the seller should transfer the note, title vests in the new owner of the note on the basis that security follows the debt.

(2) Right to repossess upon the vendee's default is an alternative remedy. Here, the seller declares the full purchase price due and payable, and demands such payment or for the property to be surrendered to him. The vendor is entitled to use reasonable force (self-help) in repossessing, as long as such does not cause a "breach of the peace." If such is not possible, he must resort to the courts for an order allowing him to repossess.

c. Rights of the Parties after Repossession

The parties, after repossession, have the following rights:

(1) Conditional vendor may elect to retain or resell the

property. If he resells, he is entitled to keep all payments made by vendee plus amount realized on resale.

(2) If resale proceeds plus prior payments of vendee do not equal the contract price, the conditional vendee need not make up the deficit unless the contract so provides. In the event of a surplus, such may be retained by the vendor, unless the contract states such belongs to the vendee.

Since the contract is generally drawn by the vendor, the vendee generally makes up a deficit but is not entitled to any surplus. The Uniform Conditional Sales Act is more equitable in that it requires a public sale of repossessed goods with any surplus to be paid to the vendee and any deficit to be made up by the vendee.

G. MISCELLANEOUS PROTECTIVE PROVISIONS

In the law of sales, there are a number of rules that protect bona-fide purchasers or creditors. A few follow:

I. Bulk Sales Act

The Bulk Sales Act aims to prevent a dishonest merchant from selling his stock of merchandise in secret and absconding with the cash, thereby defrauding his creditors. The act declares void a sale of a merchant's stock in bulk unless proper notice has been given to the seller's creditors. Since the seller generally gets cash, it means the buyer is the loser if the provisions of the act are not followed. The act generally provides for notice to be given the seller's creditors 10 days prior to the consummation of the pending sale.

II. Possession Left with Seller

Section 25 of the U.S.A. provides:

"Where a person having sold goods continues in possession of the goods, or of negotiable documents of title to the goods, the delivery or transfer by that person, or by an agent acting for him, of the goods or the documents of title under any sale, pledge, or other disposition thereof, to any person receiving and paying value for the same in good faith and without notice of the previous sale, shall have the same effect as if the person making the delivery or transfer were expressly authorized by the owner of the goods to make the same."

The basis for this section is that when the buyer leaves goods purchased in the possession of the seller he has created a condition whereby the seller is able to sell the goods again to an innocent third person and thereby perpetrate a fraud. Thus, we have another exception to the rule that a person cannot transfer better title to goods than he possesses. The loss is placed on the first purchaser because he created the misleading conditions which trapped the second purchaser. Note carefully the elements needed to give the second purchaser good title.

(1) He must buy in good faith, without notice of the prior sale,
(2) Must pay value for the goods, ...
(3) Actually receive the goods.

These elements must all be present and concluded before the second purchaser obtains better title than the first purchaser. Thus, if the first purchaser gets possession after his seller with whom he left the goods had resold them to another, the second buyer cannot claim the goods. Likewise, if the second buyer buys in good faith, without notice and for value, but is then told of the prior sale before he takes possession, the first purchaser again has the better title, assuming he gets possession before a third sale is made to one who meets all the requirements.

III. Sale by One Having Voidable Title

Section 24 of the U.S.A. provides:

> "Where the seller of goods has a voidable title thereto, but his title has not been avoided at the time of the sale, the buyer acquires a good title to the goods, provided he buys them in good faith, for value, and without notice of the seller's defect of title."

If through fraud *A* induces *B* to sell goods to *A*, one of *B*'s remedies is to rescind. *A* has voidable title to the goods. Now if *A* sells the goods to a bona-fide purchaser for value, the bona-fide purchaser gets good title, and *B*'s remedy of recision is eliminated.

H. REMEDIES IN SALES

I. Remedies of Seller

a. Action for the Price. This may be done in three instances:

(1) Title has passed to the buyer. U.S.A. Sec. 63 (1) provides:

"When under a contract to sell or a sale, the property in the goods has passed to the buyer, and the buyer wrongfully neglects or refuses to pay for the goods according to the terms of the contract or the sale, the seller may maintain an action against him for the price of the goods."

(2) Where the price is payable on a certain day and the buyer wrongfully neglects or refuses to pay such price. U.S.A. Sec. 63 (2) provides:

"Where, under a contract to sell or a sale, the price is payable on a certain day, irrespective of delivery or of transfer of title, and the buyer wrongfully neglects or refuses to pay such price, the seller may maintain an action for the price, although property in the goods has not passed, and the goods have not been appropriated to the contract. But it shall be a defense to such an action that the seller at any time before the judgment in such action has manifested an inability to perform the contract or the sale on his part or an intention not to perform it."

(3) If goods cannot readily be resold. U.S.A. Sec. 63 (3) provides:

"Although the property in the goods has not passed, if they cannot readily be resold for a reasonable price, the seller may offer to deliver the goods to the buyer, and if the buyer refuses to receive them, may notify the buyer that the goods are thereafter held by the seller as bailee for the buyer. Thereafter, the seller may treat the goods as the buyers and may maintain the action for the price."

b. Action for Damages

(1) Sec. 64 (1) of the U.S.A. provides:

"Where the buyer wrongfully neglects or refuses to accept and pay for goods, the seller may maintain an action against him for damages for non-acceptance."

(2) Sec. 64 (4) provides:

> "If, while labor or expense of material amount are necessary on the part of the seller to enable him to fulfill his obligations under the contract to sell or the sale, the buyer repudiates the contract on the sale, or notifies the seller to proceed no further therewith, the buyer shall be liable to the seller for no greater damages than the seller would have suffered if he did nothing towards carrying out the contract on the sale after receiving notice of the buyer's repudiation or countermand. The profit the seller would have made if the contract or sale had been fully performed shall be considered in estimating such damages."

c. RECISION

U.S.A. Sec. 65 provides:

> "Where the goods have not been delivered to the buyer, and the buyer has repudiated the contract to sell or sale, or has manifested his inability to perform his obligations thereunder, or has committed a material breach thereof, the seller may totally rescind the contract or the sale by giving notice of his election so to do to the buyer."

U. S. A. Sec. 61 allows a seller to sue for damages even though he has elected to rescind, and therefore recision is a cumulative and not an alternative remedy. Notice need not be given by the seller of his election to rescind, but it is best to do so as notice of the intent to rescind is relevant in any issue involving the question whether the buyer had been in default an unreasonable time before the right of recision was asserted.

d. LIEN

In addition to the above-enumerated remedies, the unpaid seller has a lien against the goods in his possession and may retain possession until the purchase price is paid. Since this lien is dependent upon possession or the right to possession, the lien is lost if possession is extinguished. However, a qualified delivery to the buyer will not defeat the seller's lien. An illustration would be where, on a C.O.D. sale, the buyer paid by check and the check was dishonored by the drawee bank due to the buyer having insufficient funds on deposit. The reasoning for calling this a qualified delivery is that a check is not considered payment until it has been honored by the bank. Thus, the delivery by the seller was conditioned upon the check being honored. Of course, a bona-fide purchaser from the buyer may cut off the seller's lien.

An unpaid seller's lien is not applicable to sales on credit unless the credit has expired or the buyer is insolvent. It is applicable where goods have been sold without stipulation as to credit. The seller may exercise his lien even as to goods he is holding as agent for bailee for the buyer. (U.S.A. Sec. 54)

e. STOPPAGE IN TRANSIT

Stoppage in transit is really a mere extension of the unpaid seller's lien. The right to regain possession of the goods is an exception to the rule that the seller loses his lien when he delivers the goods to a carrier for the purpose of transmission to the buyer without reserving title to or the right to possession of the goods. (U.S.A. 56 (a)).

In order to exercise the right of stoppage in transit the following conditions must be met:

A. Buyer must be insolvent (Sec. 57). The seller must not have known of the buyer's insolvency until after the sale. The buyer may have been insolvent for weeks without the seller knowing it. Knowledge is the important issue here. "Insolvent" means the buyer cannot meet his obligations as they come due and not that he is bankrupt or has committed an act of bankruptcy.

B. The goods must be in transit and reclaimed by the seller while in transit. Only when the goods are in transit or the goods considered under the seller's control and thereby subject to "stoppage in transit." U.S.A. Sec. 58 gives the following rules concerning the determination as to whether goods are or are not in transit:

Goods are in transit:

1. (a) From the time they are delivered to a carrier by land or by water, or other bailee for the purpose of transmission to the buyer, until the buyer, or his agent in that behalf, takes delivery of them from such carrier or other bailee.
   (b) If the goods are rejected by the buyer, and the carrier or other bailee continues in possession of them, even if the seller has refused to receive them back.
2. Goods are no longer in transit:
   (a) If the buyer, or his agent in that behalf, obtains de-

livery of the goods before their arrival at the appointed destination.

(b) If, after the arrival of the goods at the appointed destination, the carrier or other bailee acknowledges to the buyer or his agent that he holds the goods on his behalf and continues in possession of them as bailee for the buyer or his agent; and it is immaterial that a further destination of the goods may have been indicated by the buyer. Thus, if goods arrive at destination and the carrier notifies the buyer of their arrival, unless the buyer rejects the goods, it is presumed that the railroad is now holding the goods for the buyer and such goods are considered "delivered" even though the carrier still has physical possession.

(c) If the carrier or other bailee wrongfully refuses to deliver the goods to the buyer or his agent in that behalf.

3. If part delivery of the goods has been made to the buyer, or his agent in that behalf, the remainder of the goods may be stopped in transit, unless such part delivery has been made under such circumstances as to show an agreement with the buyer to give up possession of the whole of the goods.

Sec. 59 of U.S.A. explains how the seller exercises stoppage in transit by either obtaining actual possession or giving carrier or other bailee, in whose possession the goods are, notice at such time and under such circumstances so as to prevent a delivery to the buyer.

When proper notice has been given to the carrier, he must redeliver the goods to, or according to the seller's directions. But if the goods are represented by a negotiable document of title, the carrier need not deliver the goods to the seller unless the document is first surrendered. This latter is further explained in Sec. 62 which provides that a bona-fide purchaser of a negotiable document of title either prior or subsequent to seller's notification to carrier of right of stoppage in transit, that such bona-fide purchaser's right shall be protected against the seller's claim to lien or right of stoppage in transit. Other than this, the seller's rights are not affected by any sale or other disposition of the goods made by the buyer, unless the seller has assented thereto.

f. Resale by the Seller

This is a remedy already discussed. Resale may be by private or public sale so long as the seller exercises reasonable care and judgment in making the resale. Such resale may be made without giving the original buyer any notice of the time or place of such resale, but where the right to resell is not based on the perishable nature of the goods or upon expressed provision of the contract or the sale, giving or failure to give notice is relevant in determining whether the buyer had been in default an unreasonable time before resale was made. If the goods are resold at a profit, such belongs to the seller, but if resold at a loss, the seller may recover such loss from the buyer who defaulted. (U.S.A. Sec. 6d)

II. Rights and Remedies of the Buyer

a. Examination

The buyer has the right to examine (inspect) any goods which he has not previously examined, and until the buyer has had a reasonable opportunity to inspect and see if the goods are in conformity with the contract, it will not be deemed that he has accepted them. The inspection must be accomplished with reasonable promptness and if the goods do not conform with the contract the buyer need but inform the seller he refuses to accept. Failure to notify the seller is construed as acceptance, but this still allows the buyer to sue for damages due to breach of contract even though the seller loses his right to refuse the goods. (U.S.A. Sec. 47) (U.S.A. Sec. 48) (U.S.A. Sec. 49)

The buyer waives his right to inspect if terms of sale are C.O.D., as such terms indicate that the buyer agrees to pay for the goods before delivery by the carrier, unless the right of inspection is specifically provided for.

If goods do not conform with the contract, the buyer need not return them to the seller as long as the buyer rightfully refused to accept them. He need only to inform the seller that he refuses to accept them. (Sec. 50)

b. Sue for Conversion

If the seller wrongfully withholds goods after title has passed to the buyer, the buyer may elect to sue to recover (repleven) the goods in specie; or rescind the contract and sue for damages (value of goods) he has suffered (normally a return of the purchase price paid). (Sec. 66)

c. Sue for Damages

When title has not passed to the buyer, and the seller wrongfully neglects or refuses to deliver the goods under a contract to sell, the buyer may sue for damages. Like all contracts, the buyer has the duty then to mitigate damages—he must buy the goods elsewhere if they are available, and if available at the same price, he has then suffered no damages except that for delay.

d. Specific Performance

Specific performance is the remedy if the goods are unique and a contract to deliver is broken.

e. Sue for Breach of Warranty

If the goods when delivered do not conform to the contract, or if the implied warranties are breached, the buyer has an election of the following alternative remedies:

(1) Rescind, by refusing to accept the goods, or if already received, return them or offer to return them and recover the price or any part thereof which has been paid. This remedy is not allowed if the buyer knew of the breach of warranty when he accepted the goods, or if he fails to notify the seller of his election and/or fails to return or offer to return the goods to the seller within a reasonable time and in substantially as good condition as they were at the time he acquired title, unless the deterioration was due to the breach in warranty.

(2) Refuse to accept the goods if title has not passed, and sue for damages for breach of warranty.

(3) Accept or keep the goods (affirm the sale) and maintain an action against the seller for damages for breach of warranty.

(4) Accept or keep the goods and set up against the seller the breach of warranty by way of recoupment in diminution or extinction of the purchase price when sued for by the seller.

So completes the law of sales and bailments. As should now be obvious to the student, the law is primarily "statutory." This chapter herein has only attempted to set forth the important statutory provisions and explain them when necessary. It must be here emphasized that one's knowledge of the law of sales can never be sufficient without a reading of the Uniform Sales Act (or the Sales Act in force in your State).

Chapter 3

AGENCY

A. INTRODUCTION

The law of agency is an important facet of the law to the businessman nowadays, as most businesses are now carried on by means of agents. Under the corporate form of business organization, each time a person properly acts for the corporation in dealing with other persons, the law of agency is applicable. Obviously a corporation, not being a natural person, can act only through its agents, but even individual proprietorship and partnerships may and do transact much of its business through agents.

I. Relationships: Employee-Agent-Independent Contractor

People serving or working for others do so in one or more of several capacities. These people may be employees, servants, agents, or independent contractors. Employees or servants merely work for the employer and have no power to bind the employer (principal) to a contract with a third person. An agent, on the other hand, is the right arm of his principal in business transactions with third persons. Thus, it is apparent that agency involves contractual duties with third persons, whereas an employer-employee relationship contemplates only two parties, the employer and the employee. Since an agent acts not for himself but for his principal, the contract with third parties, if properly entered into, is between the principal and the third person, and not that of the agent. It is quite possible that a single person may be an agent at one time, and at another time an employee. For example, a horsetrainer would be an employee while training the horses, and an agent in purchasing feed for the horses (assuming he had been authorized to make such purchases).

An agent is distinguished from an independent contractor by the amount of discretion possessed in carrying out an objective. If a person hires another to do a job, the person hired will be an agent or employee if the employer can dictate both the results and the means of accomplishing those results. On the other hand, if the employer cannot dictate the means of accomplishing the result, the person hired is an independent contractor. Thus, it is frequently said that an agent or employee is told what to do and how to do it, while an independent contractor is only told what to do. So we come to the real test—the amount of control an employer can exercise over the person hired determines whether that person is an agent (or employee) or an independent contractor.

II. Importance of Relationships

For several reasons it is important to know in what class a person belongs. For example:

A tort is a wrong, not arising out of a contract, for which the law provides a redress. It is usually a negligent or willful act. An example is an automobile accident caused by the negligence of some person. Now, a principal is liable to a third party for the torts of his employees or agents if the employee was then acting within the scope of his authority. However, a principal is not liable for the torts of an independent contractor—the independent contractor alone is liable for any such torts.

Secondly, a principal is bound and liable for all contracts made by his agent if the agent is acting within the scope of his authority. A principal is not bound or liable for any contracts made by an employee or independent contractor.

Finally, a principal is required by law to do certain acts (such as pay social security taxes) if he has agents or employees, whereas if he has only independent contractors, nothing may be required.

III. Formation of the Agency Relationship

Generally, the relationship of agency is formed by either a written or oral contract between the principal and the agent. This agreement may fall short of being a contract, since all that is actually needed to create the relationship is an appointment by the principal and an act thereunder by the agent. Thus, it is probably more accurate to state that the relationship arises by consent. Mutuality of consent by both parties is all that is required, and this consent may be either express or implied.

In the formation of the agency relationship, the agent may be either a special agent or a general agent for his principal. A general agent is one who has broad powers to act for his principal, and he may act in many ways with a continuity in his service. An example of a general agent would be the president of a corporation. A special agent acts under more limited powers and restrictions, and is generally engaged to perform a more specific task or tasks. An example would be a stockbroker who is hired to negotiate a sale of securities for his client (his principal). Another example of a special agent is a salesman for a corporation who may bind his principal to deliver goods that he sells, but who cannot bind his principal to purchase any materials.

In an expressed agency contract, the details concerning the agents powers, duties, directions, and other terms are stated in the agreement. Details that may be too numerous to express are made clear by the actions of the parties, customs of the trade, or from other pertinent circumstances. Often these details not expressly stated act so as to enlarge the agent's powers significantly, but we shall take this up at a later place herein.

B. CREATION OF THE AGENCY RELATIONSHIP

I. In General

We have already spoken some of the creations of the agency relationship. However, there are certain other important rules to keep in mind. For example, it has been previously stated that an agency relationship may be created either orally or in writing. This statement must be qualified by adding that if an agent is given authority to make contracts for the principal, and these contracts are required by the Statute of Frauds (see Contracts Section) to be in writing, then so, too, must be the instrument which created the agent's authority. This rule is known as the "Equal Dignities Rule." In other words, both the agent's authority and the contract which the agent enters into for his principal must be of equal dignity. When an agent's power to act is given in writing, this written authority is called a power of attorney, and the agent is known as an attorney in fact.

The legal qualifications of a principal are that he must be of sound mind and must have reached majority. A minor may act through an agent, but any contracts so made are those of the minor and are thus voidable. (See Capacity in Contracts Section.) This power of the unqualified principal to disaffirm extends to contracts made by the agent with third persons, the torts of the agent committed within the scope of his authority, as well as the contract creating the agency. In short, the limits of one's capacity to appoint agents is the same as one's capacity to make other contracts.

Even though a minor cannot do through a competent principal what he lacks the capacity to do directly, a minor can act as an agent for a competent principal. Where a minor acts as an agent, the contract he makes with a third party is the contract of the principal. The principal cannot rescind or disaffirm the contract despite the fact that a minor made it for him. Thus generally, any person may do through an agent anything he could do himself, except for a few minor things of so personal a nature that the law will not recognize their attempted delegation (voting, making a will).

The authority of an agent always comes from some act by the principal. A third person dealing with an agent has the burden of proving that the agency does, in fact, exist if he is to be successful in making a claim against the principal. (Of course, proof of the agency does not have to be made if the principal does not dispute its existence.) The following are ways of showing that the principal has given an agent authority to act for him:

1. Expressed Appointment
2. Appointment Implied from Conduct
3. Appointment by Ratification

These methods of appointment and proofs of agency will now be discussed in greater detail.

a. Express Appointment

The principal may expressly appoint an agent, either orally or in writing, to act for him. If an agent is to deal with many persons, the creation of the agency should be in writing so that the agent can readily prove the extent of his authority to third persons with whom he is to make transactions for his principal. The authority given in the writing (or orally) is known as expressed authority. Certain implied authority accompanies the expressed authority as it is generally impossible to cover all details of an agent's powers in any expressed grant. This implied authority will be discussed in detail in the next chapter.

b. Appointment Implied from Conduct

There are situations where the principal may not expressly

appoint an agent but, nevertheless, imply the creation of the agency by his conduct. When the relationship is implied by conduct, the agent is known as an ostensible agent, and it is said that the agent has implied or apparent authority or authority by estoppel.

> Illustration: *A* managed a store in his own name, the store being owned by *P*. *P* tells *T* he owns the store. *A* buys goods from *T* on credit. *P* is liable for such purchases to *T*. Now, if *P* did not, in fact, own the store or have any interest therein, he would nevertheless be liable to *T* to the same extent. The basis for this is to protect third persons. In our illustration the conduct of *P* led *T* to reasonably believe *A* was his agent. *T* was misled by these actions to the extent that he changed his legal position in justifiable reliance on this belief. For this reason, *P* is estopped to deny the agency relationship.

As stated by the Supreme Court of Michigan, "If a person, with full knowledge and without protest, allows another to appear to be an agent with authority to act in a given capacity, he will be estopped from denying such actual authority on the part of the agent insofar as third persons, acting in good faith and having exercised reasonable prudence, have dealt with the agent in reliance on the apparent authority." *Plankenton Packing Co. v. Berry,* 199 Mich. 212.

c. Appointment by Ratification

Usually the act of establishing the agency precedes the action by the agent, but it is possible for a person to act without authority and then acquire the authority to act by getting the principal's ratification of his prior act. In such a case, the purported agent must represent himself as an agent of his principal with authority to act, and the third party must believe the purported agent is acting for the principal at the time the contract is entered into.

At the time the contract is entered into, the principal is not bound as the purported agent had no authority. Once the principal learns of the agent's act and has acquired full knowledge of all the facts, he may elect to either ratify or denounce the agent's act. If the principal elects to ratify, the effect is the same as though the agent had prior authority, and the principal becomes bound to the agreement with the third party the same as he would have been had the agent been given previous authority. The ratification must meet the same requirements as for conferring authority in advance. If the purported agent's contract is in writing as required by the Statute of Frauds, the ratification must be in writing. The principal must have capacity to appoint an agent at the time of the ratification as well as at the time of the purported agent's act which is being ratified. (See Corporations Section on acts of a promoter being ratified by a subsequently organized corporation.)

To summarize, the requisite elements to grant authority by ratification are:

(1) The agent must allege he is acting for a principal. The principal need not be named or disclosed to the third person.
(2) The third party must reasonably believe there is a principal.
(3) The principal must exist and have capacity to contract at the time the agent acted as well as at the time of ratification.
(4) The principal need not ratify, it being strictly at his option.
(5) Once the principal ratifies with full knowledge of all the facts (and he must know all the facts or he may later disaffirm), the agent's authority relates back and is the equivalent to prior authority.
(6) The ratification must be made within a reasonable time and in the same manner required for conferring original authority; for example, compliance with the Statutes of Frauds if applicable.

Normally, the ratification will be expressed by words. But it may also be implied by conduct, such as when the principal accepts the benefits of the contract with full knowledge of the facts or when he retains the benefits received without full knowledge after learning all of the facts.

Another important rule to remember with regard to ratification is that if the principal elects to ratify, he must do so in full. In other words, he cannot accept any benefits that he might gain by ratification without accepting also any liabilities that might have accrued. Thus, if the agent committed a tort within the scope of his ratified authority, the principal is liable for this tort along with the agent as is true in other types of appointments of authority.

Illustration: *A* has the authority to deliver milk for the *P* Dairy Company, but has no authority to find new customers and contract with them for *P* Dairy to deliver milk. However, being ambitious to get ahead, *A* goes from house to house, in his spare time, contracting for new customers. *P* Dairy happily accepts ten new accounts *A* has contracted for them. However, *P* Dairy later finds out that *A* has tramped over the flower beds of fifteen persons whom he had called upon. *P* Dairy, along with *A*, is liable for this tort.

One final question arises. May the third party withdraw from the contract because of the lack of authority of the agent at the time the contract was made? The answer is "Yes," if the third party notifies either the agent or the principal before ratification by the principal. Any subsequent ratification by the principal after notice to himself or the agent would be ineffectual, and the third party would not be bound by the contract.

C. PRINCIPALS AND THIRD PERSONS

We have previously discussed the creation of an agent's authority. Equally important as the existence of an agent's authority is the extent of his authority. Third persons who deal with an agent assume the responsibility of determining the agent's authority, and this includes both the existence thereof and the extension to the act in question. This the third person would have to do to be successful in holding the principal liable for the acts of the agent. The proof of the agent's authority closely parallels the proof of the creation of the agency relationship, as will be self-evident in the following discussion.

I. Determination of an Agent's Authority

The extent of the agent's authority is derived from three sources. These are:

1. Expressed Authority
2. Implied Authority
3. Apparent Authority

Expressed authority is quite simple—the agent merely has

the authority to do those things which his principal expressedly stated, either orally or in writing, he could do. The remaining types of authority are not wholly that simple.

a. Implied Authority

Implied authority is that which is inherent in the scope of the expressed powers, even though not stated therein. It is inconceivable that even a comprehensive written appointment of an agent would cover every detail, and the gaps are therefore taken care of by implied authority. Implied authority may be further broken down into incidental authority, authority by custom and usage, authority by course of dealings, and authority by necessity.

Incidental authority includes those acts ordinarily done in the course of carrying out the main purpose of the agency. For example, a third person may reasonably assume that a sales agent is empowered to make the ordinary warranties concerning the goods he is authorized to sell, but this would not include the power to make extraordinary warranties.

Customary authority is that which is justified by custom and usage in the particular line of business or in the particular locality where the custom has become so widely known as to warrant a reasonably prudent third person to rely on the presumption. Thus, the incidental powers may be enlarged (or diminished) by custom and usage.

Authority through course of dealings by the particular principal may also enlarge or diminish the agent's authority. For example, a salesman not in possession of goods does not have implied power to collect money for any goods his customers might order. But if the salesman regularly collects money and remits it to his employer and the employer never objects, eventually it will be implied that he has authority through course of dealings to make these collections.

Authority by necessity is dependent upon an unusual or unexpected emergency under which a decision to act must be made by the agent because there is no time or opportunity for him to communicate with his principal for special instructions.

The courts have held certain acts generally to be implied, and other acts only rarely. Some acts or powers which are frequently implied to an agent are to give the usual warranties in making the sale of goods, to collect the purchase price of goods sold if the possession of the goods is entrusted to the agent, and to appoint sub-agents (as further discussed below). Powers which the courts rarely imply and which therefore must be established by the third party by the showing of an expressed grant are the powers to borrow money on the principal's credit, to sign a deed or formal contract requiring a seal, to give extraordinary warranties, or to receive payment for the sale of goods not in the agent's possession.

b. <u>APPARENT AUTHORITY</u>

The third major source of an agent's authority is apparent authority. The term apparent authority is used in at least two different fashions. If *P* appoints *A*, we have seen that certain implied powers accompany the expressed powers granted. Now, if *P* informs *A* that these implied powers are not to be assumed, then *A* does not possess them, that is as between *P* and *A*. But third persons who have not been informed of these limitations placed on *A* may presume *A* has the normal implied powers. Under such a situation, *A*'s authority is said to be apparent. This was summarized in *<u>Anderson v. State</u>,* 22 Ohio 305, as follows:

> "As between a principal and a third person dealing with the agent on the faith of his apparent authority, the law conclusively presumes the actual authority of the agent to be what it openly appears to be; while, as between the principal and agent, the extent of the actual authority may be shown."

The term apparent authority is also used to describe an agent's authority when the agency arises not through appointment but through a principal's holding out another as his agent so that it appears reasonable for a third person to assume that the agency exists. This situation is more correctly described as authority by estoppel. Regardless of what we denominate it, there still exists the necessity that a third person change his position in some manner in reliance on this apparent authority before this third person might hold the principal liable.

c. <u>SUB-AGENTS</u>

Although the above heading, sub-agents, does not precisely fit into the outline at this point, it is a subject illustrative of implied and apparent authority.

A sub-agent is one employed by an agent to assist in carrying out the business of the principal. An agent, unless specifically forbidden by his principal, can generally delegate his powers to another person under the following situations:

1. When delegation is specifically authorized by the principal . . .
2. When it is the custom and usage of that type of business in the locality for an agent to delegate his powers . . .
3. When the act to be done by the sub-agent is purely mechanical or ministerial . . .
4. When the act to be performed by the agent is such that the agent himself cannot lawfully perform, but can be by a sub-agent.

An example of number 4 would be where an agent was required to supply certified financial statements regarding a business when he is not a certified public accountant. He could therefore hire a C.P.A. to prepare the statements for him. Numbers 2 and 3 may be clarified with some illustrations. An agent employed to manage a 25,000-acre ranch could appoint sub-agents as the job is clearly too large for him to handle alone, but for a 1500-acre ranch, he would not necessarily have such implied authority. A real estate broker engaged to sell a home may delegate the job to a sub-agent, but an agent employed to buy rare portraits could not do so because of the high degree of personal knowledge involved. Thus, the creation of sub-agency depends on the nature of the job to be done and should not be implied indiscriminately. After all, the principal selects the agent because he has faith and confidence in the skill and judgment of the agent, and to arbitrarily deny the principal in his selection would certainly be an injustice. Obviously, the act of the sub-agent will not bind the principal unless the same act if done by the original agent would have bound the principal.

The relationship of the parties when an agent appoints a <u>sub-agent</u> depends on whether the agent did or did not have authority, expressed or implied, to hire a sub-agent. If the hiring was authorized, the sub-agent becomes the agent of the principal. There then is no agency relationship between the agent and the sub-agent. If the hiring was unauthorized, there is no relationship between the principal and the sub-agent. Rather, the agent becomes the sub-agent's principal, and the agent becomes liable for the contracts made by the sub-agent.

Problem:

> Assume an agent has the authority to hire a sub-agent, but in authorizing such the principal has placed secret

limitations on the agent's authority; specifically, not to pay the sub-agent more than $300 per month. The agent, however, in violation of this limitation hires a sub-agent at $350 per month. What are the rights and liabilities of the agent, the principal, and the sub-agent?

Answer:

The principal would be liable to the sub-agent for $350 per month. This is a case of apparent authority—or in other words, since the agent had the authority to hire a sub-agent, it is reasonable that the sub-agent may rely on the authority (apparent) of the agent to pay a reasonable salary. However, the principal may recover this $50 per month from the agent for, as will be discussed in more detail later, an agent is liable for any loss caused the principal by his exceeding his authority.

II. Knowledge of Agent—Knowledge of Principal

If a third person conveys certain relevant information to the agent, to what extent will this knowledge of the agent be imputed to the principal? In other words, if you tell something to an agent, is that as good as telling his principal? This is an important question in the law of agency, for a person's duties are frequently limited by his knowledge or notice. For example, no person can charge that he has been defrauded by misrepresentations as to facts when he already had knowledge of the true facts. Now, assuming *P* sends out *A* to buy some land from *T*, hoping there might be some oil thereon. *A* investigates the land and ascertains that there is absolutely no oil. However, *T* represents to *A* that there is oil, and for some unknown reason *A* buys for *P*. Can *P* then get out of the contract because of the misrepresentation? If *A*'s knowledge that there was absolutely no oil is imparted to *P*, he cannot. The general rule is that notice or knowledge of the agent is imputed to the principal if the agent obtained his knowledge within the scope of his authority, which was the situation above. Suppose, again, that an applicant for insurance tells the insurance agent that he had had a previous heart attack. The agent fails to tell the company. Again, the insurance company could not get out of the contract that it might issue, for notice to its agent is notice to itself. This general rule is based on the theory that it is the duty of an agent to keep his principal informed concerning the subject matter of the agency. To this general rule, however, we have the following exceptions where notice to the agent is not notice to the principal.

1. When the agent has an adverse interest which would lead him to conceal rather than disclose information to his principal. For example, when the insurance applicant makes the agent the beneficiary of the policy, thereby giving the agent an adverse interest to his principal which might influence the agent to neglect from disclosing his knowledge.
2. When the agent's knowledge was acquired prior to the creation of the agency—unless the third person shows the knowledge was present in the agent's mind at the time the agent acted for his principal. Thus, if the insurance agent had known about the applicant's heart condition prior to the time he went to work for the company, and had forgotten all about it, and the applicant failed to remind him, then the insurance company may rescind any policy it might issue. However, if the applicant could prove that the agent remembered about the applicant's heart condition at the time of the application, then the company could not rescind.
3. If the agent and the third person conspire to defraud the principal; for example, if the insurance applicant pays the agent $50 to keep quiet about the applicant's heart condition.

III. Liability of the Principal to Third Persons for Torts of His Agent

a. Scope of Employment

On the assumption that a principal has the right and ability to control his agent (and employee), that a principal reaps the benefits of his agent's acts, and that accidents are inevitable and therefore merely another cost of doing business, the law makes the principal responsible to third persons for injuries done to them by his agents. A basic limitation to this rule, which is a source for much court litigation, is that the principal is liable only for torts of his agents or employees committed by them while they are in the scope of their authority or employment. Thus, a third person injured by the negligence of an agent acting within the scope of his authority may recover from either the agent or the principal, or both. These explanations of why the principal is liable for his agent's torts are summed up by the legal profession in two Latin words—*"respondeat superior."*

Assume that the third person sues the principal and collects. Then may the principal sue his agent? Yes, but in practice this is seldom done, for the loss is usually covered by insurance. In practice, the end result is the discharge of the agent.

As has been mentioned, the real problem here is the question of whether the agent or employee was within the scope of his authority or employment at the time and in the act of committing the tort. Scopes of authority and employment raise questions as to whether the agent was acting during authorized times (e.g., during his shift), at his authorized place, and accomplishing an authorized job.

To summarize all the court rulings on these questions would take a library. Suffice it to say here that the courts have been quite liberal in finding that an agent was acting within the scope of his authority when committing the tort, and therefore allowing a third person to recover from the principal. A few illustrations will point this up:

1. An agent was in charge of a saloon, and part of his authority was to keep order. One intoxicated customer came in and refused to leave when asked to do so. The agent forcibly removed him, fracturing the customer's skull. Held: The agent acted unreasonably since he used too much force, but was within the scope of his authority. Thus, the principal was vicariously liable even for malicious injuries caused by the agent.
2. A customer argued with the manager of a chain store. The manager struck the customer. Held: The store manager was within the scope of his authority and thus the store was vicariously liable.
3. A salesman left in charge of a store erroneously thought a customer had stolen some goods and had her arrested. It turned out the customer had not "shop lifted" any merchandise. The customer sued for false arrest and imprisonment. Held: The store owner was liable for the act of the agent since the agent was within the scope of his employment. He was acting, although mistakenly, to protect his principal's property.
4. A collector for a company went out to collect a bill. The

customer said he had not paid the bill as he had never received a bill. The collector called the customer a liar. There was a fight, the customer was injured and sued the company. Held: The company was liable. The bill collector had authority to collect the bill and the injury was incidental to its collection. The injury occurred within the scope of the agent's authority.

What if the principal in the above illustration had told his bill collector never to use force? Would the principal then be liable? The answer is yes, for a principal cannot avoid being liable to third persons for the acts of his agents merely by instructing the agent "to be careful," "don't use force," "don't slander anyone," and so forth. The logic of this rule is more easily understood when you consider the possibility of a principal avoiding all liability of his truck drivers by merely admonishing them to "drive carefully." Although a truck driver would never be authorized to drive carelessly, the question is not how he was authorized to drive, but merely was he authorized to drive and was he pursuing his principal's business at the time of the accident?

b. DEVIATION

We have seen that a principal is liable to third persons for the torts of his agent during the course or in the scope of his agent's authority or employment. We now add to this the rule that the principal is also liable for torts of his agent while the agent is pursuing both his own and his principal's business at the same time. Now, what if the agent departs wholly or largely from his course of employment? The answer is that the principal will not be liable for torts occurring during such a departure or so-called deviation. It seems most reasonable that a principal cannot be expected to answer for the misdeeds of his agents which are unrelated to his work. Thus the question frequently arises, "Did the agent, at the time of the commission of the tort, substantially deviate from the course of his employment—was he on business or a frolic of his own?"

We shall look at a few examples of how some courts have answered the question in specific cases:

1. A truck driver picked up a hitch-hiker who was injured in a subsequent accident. Held: The principal is not liable, as the truck driver had no authority to pick up passengers.

Therefore the agent's act was not within the scope of his employment. This explains why many trucks have signs on them stating "no riders allowed."

2. A butler, without authority, drove his master's car to meet his master at the airport—the chauffeur could not be located. Due to the butler's negligence, a third party was injured. Assume no possibility of arguing "authority by necessity." The principal would not be liable because the butler was not within the course of work for which he was employed at the time of the accident.
3. The chauffeur is on his way to pick up his master at the airport and has a wreck while speeding. He had been told never to speed or drive carelessly. The principal, nevertheless, would be liable to a third person, as the chauffeur was within the scope of his employment and was acting with an eye to his master's benefit, even though he was disobeying instructions by speeding.
4. A truck driver on his return to the plant drove past the plant several blocks in order to pick up his laundry and dry cleaning. After passing the plant, the truck hit a pedestrian. Held: The principal would not be liable because there had been a substantial deviation from the course of the agent's employment.

In the above examples, ask yourself if the act was done within the course of employment and with an eye to the employer's benefit. The answer to both of these must be "yes" or the principal is not liable. If the answer to both is "yes," the principal is liable regardless of how stupid or negligent the employee might have been.

One final problem. Assume a truck driver on his way to the freight depot on business for his employer stops by his home, which is five or six blocks out of the way. Before he deviates and after he is back on the route, he is no doubt pursuing his employer's business, but the question is when did the deviation start and when did it end. Sometimes the beginning and the end of the deviation may be clearcut, but more often it is quite a problem. There is no all-inclusive rule to provide you with, but it might be kept in mind that when the fact situation provides a close question, the courts generally hold the employer liable. But even this statement is not always true.

c. Direct Orders

We have seen that an agent who has committed a tort may be liable to the third person, and also to his principal. What liability, though, does an agent have to a third person and his principal if he unknowingly commits a tort in carrying out his principal's orders? For example, *P* tells *A* to repossess *T*'s radio because of *T*'s failure to keep up in his payments, whereas in reality *T* has not been in default in these payments. *A* takes possession of the radio, and *T* sues *A* for conversion (wrongful taking of property). Is *A* liable to *T*? Yes, for everyone is liable for his torts. But, *A* may sue *P* to be reimbursed for this loss as he was merely following *P*'s directions. Obviously *T* could have sued *P* and collected if he had not elected to sue *A*.

IV. Liability of the Principal to Third Persons for Contracts of His Agent

a. In General

The liability of the principal to third persons for a contract made by his agent may depend on the degree of disclosure of the agency relationship during the contract negotiations. Three types of situations may arise in these negotiations:

1. Disclosed Principal: the agent revealing the agency relationship and naming his principal
2. Partially Disclosed Principal: the agent revealing the agency relationship but not revealing the identy of his principal
3. Undisclosed Principal: the agent not revealing that he is even an agent, and the third person therefore unaware of any agency relationship

b. Disclosed Principal

Disclosure of the agency relationship and the identity of the principal is the usual situation in contract negotiations by an agent. If the principal is disclosed and the agent acted within the scope of his authority, then the principal is the only person who can enforce the contract against the third party and vice versa. The agent has no liability or rights in the contract. This is true even if the agent signs his own name and capacity (i.e., Jones, agent), for the intent of all the parties was to bind only the principal and a third person.

c. Partially Disclosed Principal

In business dealings it is often advantageous not to reveal the identity of the real party in interest. For example, a third person may refuse to do business with a particular principal, or the price of goods might be raised if the principal were disclosed. Therefore, it sometimes occurs that an agent enters into a contract with a third person, disclosing that he is acting for another party but withholding the identity of that party.

If the principal is only partially disclosed, the liability and rights of the principal, agent, and third person remain exactly the same as if the principal was fully disclosed.

d. Undisclosed Principal

The general rule is that an undisclosed principal can enforce the contract of his agent even though neither the agency or the principal's identity has been revealed at the time of the contract. However, there are at least three exceptions to this general rule.

1. Where unique and personal services are involved
2. Where the third party has relied upon the agent's credit, and is not satisfied with the principal's financial status
3. Where the contract involves a negotiable instrument, and the controlling negotiable instrument law provides, "No one is liable on the instrument whose signature does not appear thereon . . ." (See Negotiable Instruments Section herein)

Number one above is analagous to the assignability of contracts. If the contract is one that may be assigned, then an undisclosed principal may enforce it. And the enforcement by the undisclosed principal is limited to the same extent of that of an assignee enforcing a contract, viz., the undisclosed principal's rights under the contract cannot be any greater than those that his agent might have had. Thus, if *T* contracted with *A* to purchase some goods at which time *A* owed *T* \$500, *P,* who was undisclosed, in enforcing the collection of the purchase price would be subject to \$500 set-off by *T*. Subject to this limitation, an undisclosed principal may enforce a contract, and this is true even though a third person may prove he would not have entered into the contract had he known of the agency relationship. However, should a third party ask the agent if there is an agency and the agent denies it, or if a third party should state to the agent that he does not wish to deal with any other person than the agent, the third party then would be under no obligaion to any principal.

The third party may enforce the contract against either the agent or the principal, but he must elect to hold one or the other. However, there can be no effective election unless the third person is informed of the undisclosed principal, the reasons for which are obvious, so if the third party obtains a judgment against the agent without knowledge of the principal, the principal would not be released as would be the case if the principal's identity was known to the third person. Thus, if a contract between an undisclosed principal and a third person is breached, the agent should inform the third person of the agency or otherwise the third person will surely proceed against the agent.

One final word. It is quite possible for an undisclosed principal to act through an agent and settle with the agent in good faith before the third person is informed of the existence of the undisclosed principal. In such a situation, the third person cannot enforce the contract against the undisclosed principal. To illustrate: *A* purchases goods from *T* for an undisclosed *P*. In making the sale, *T* relied solely on *A*'s credit. *A*, in turn, surrenders the goods to the undisclosed principal who pays *A* for the gods and reasonably believes *A* will pay *T*. Under such facts, *T* would be able to enforce his rights against *A* only. This does not denty *T* any rights, for he is getting all he bargained for. There is no sound reason for allowing *T* to sue *P*, and thus force *P* to bear an added burden. Of course, if *P*'s settlement with *A* is not in good faith and he is in collusion with *A* to defraud *T*, then *T* may still hold *P* liable, even though *P* has settled with *A* prior to *T*'s finding out the existence of the undisclosed principal.

D. RELATIONS OF AGENT AND PRINCIPAL

The rights of the agent or, conversely, the duties of the principal to the agent generally result from the contract creating the agency, but as to some particulars, these rights or duties are imposed by law. So, too, for the rights of the principal or, conversely, the duties of the agent to his principal. We shall look at some of these duties that are imposed by law whenever the agency contract may be silent as to such.

I. Duties of a Principal to an Agent

The principal owes the agent the duty of compensating him for his services upon the agent's completion of the assigned task, or in the event the agent is discharged without cause prior to performance or completion. In the event that the agency contract does not specify the amount of compensation, the law imposes the duty on the principal of paying the agent a reasonable amount for his services. The time of payment, or what condition precedent must be met prior to payment, is decided either by the terms of the contract or by what is reasonable.

The principal owes the agent the duty of reimbursing him for the reasonable expenses incurred in carrying out the agency assignment unless the agreement expressly states otherwise.

Finally, the principal owes the agent the duty of indemnifying him for any liability the agent may incur to a third person by following the instructions of the principal. Thus, if *P* directs *A* to sell a car which *P* does not own, and the real owner recovers his car from *T*, the buyer, *P* must indemnify *A* for any claim recovered by *T* against *A*.

II. Duties of an Agent to a Principal

An agent is a fiduciary and, therefore, must always act with an eye to his principal's best interests. The breach by an agent of any of the duties hereinafter set forth will cause the agent to be liable to his principal.

An agent has the duty of obedience in carrying out his principal's instructions and must remain within the scope of his authority. We have seen that if a principal places a secret limitation on an agent's authority, an agent will still have certain apparent authority as to third persons who do not know of the limitation. If the agent should violate this limitation and thereby bind his principal to a contract with a third person, the agent will be forced to indemnify his principal for any loss occasioned by his disobedience to his instructions. The agent may also be discharged for cause by such disobedience.

An agent has the duty of loyalty. It is the policy of the law to eliminate every possible motive or incentive for unfaithfulness, and it thus brings forth this second duty. It is well recognized that no man can serve two persons having adverse interests and serve both faithfully. Therefore, the courts held as follows:

1. An agent employed to sell certain goods cannot secretly sell any of these goods to himself. Similarly, an agent employed to purchase certain goods cannot buy from himself. If an agent does either of these, the principal may get out from under the contract even though the agent may have acted in the principal's best interests, and even though the contract was as favorable as could be obtained anywhere.
2. A single individual cannot secretly act as an agent for both the buyer and seller of property and thereby collect double commissions.
3. A full-time salesman cannot carry a side-line product, even though the side-line does not compete with his principal's business. If he should, any profits he realizes from the side-line would belong to his principal.
4. An agent may not disclose or use any trade secrets of his principal, even after termination of the agency, unless his principal consents.

The third duty of an agent to his principal is that of care and skill. This degree of care and skill that the agent is required to use is equal to that possessed by ordinary persons engaged in the same business as that of the agent.

The fourth duty of an agent is the duty to account for all money and property of the principal that may come into his possession. To do this, the agent should keep his principal's funds earmarked and separate, and keep proper records of receipts and expenditures. In regard to keeping funds separate, one court held an attorney liable to his client for money collected and deposited in the attorney's personal account when the bank for this account became insolvent. And this the court held even though the attorney's bank balance had always exceeded the amount due the client, and even though the court found that the attorney was not negligent in selecting the bank. Liability was based on the facts that the funds were co-mingled with the attorney's funds. The court reasoned that allowing the co-mingling of funds would be conducive to misappropriation and fraud, and wholly fail to afford protection to principals in general.

The fifth and final duty of the agent is to keep the principal informed of all material facts concerning the subject matter of the agency. This duty is required to offset the rule that notice to the agent when acting within the scope of his authority is notice to the principal.

E. TERMINATION OF AN AGENCY RELATIONSHIP

I. Notice

Whenever an agency relationship is terminated, third persons with whom the agent has dealt, or who merely know of the relationship, must be given notice of the termination. Without this notice, a third person might enter into a contract through the former agent which he could enforce against the former principal on the basis of apparent authority. To illustrate: *A*, a servant in the private home of *P*, had regularly purchased groceries from *T* on her employer's credit. After being discharged, *A* continued to buy on *P's* credit. Held: *P* was liable for failure to give proper notice to *T*. Of course, *P* can be indemnified by *A*—if *A* is not judgment proof, that is, broke.

There are two types of notice, actual notice and notice by publication. Actual notice of termination must be given to all those with whom the agent dealt, but notice by publication in a newspaper is sufficient for others. Actual notice may be given orally or in writing. If the agency is terminated by operation of law (e.g., death of the principal), no notice need be given.

II. Accomplishment of the Termination

Termination of the agency may be accomplished either by acts of the parties or by operation of law.

a. Operation of Law

Termination of operation of law includes death, insanity, or bankruptcy, of either the principal or the agent. In the case of the agent's banruptcy, termination by law is effected only if the agent's bankruptcy affects the subject-matter of the agency. For example, where the agent's credit would affect the interest of the principal. Supervening illegality due to a change in the law and destruction or sale of the subject-matter of the agency are other methods of termination by operation of law. Supervening illegality is illustrated by the agent who is hired to sell lottery chances, and a law comes into effect making lotteries illegal. Destruction or sale of the subject-matter is illustrated by the case of a home seller listing his home with four real estate firms. As soon as one of these agents finds a ready, willing, and able buyer, the agency as to the other three firms is terminated automatically by operation of law.

In the event any agent acts after the termination of the relationship by operation of law, the principal cannot be bound in any way. Neither can the agent, unless, as previously shown, the agent has failed to disclose any agency relationship wherein the agent is liable along with the principal.

b. ACTS OF THE PARTIES

Termination by acts of the parties may be provided for in the agency agreement. The relationship may also be ended by subsequent acts of the parties, such as by mutual consent, revocation by the principal, or renunciation by the agent.

In connection with termination by revocation or renunciation, the right to terminate must be distinguished from the power to terminate. A principal has the power to revoke an agency at any time, or an agent the power to renunciate the agency, but this does not mean the right to revoke or renunciate and either might be subject to being sued for damages if either has breached the agency contract. There is one exception to the principal's power to revoke. This is in the case of an agency coupled with an interest. Such an agency is irrevocable and even termination by law, such as death of the principal, will not operate as a revocation. An agency coupled with an interest arises when an agent has an interest in the subject-matter of the agency prior to the creation of the agency relationship. For example, if a creditor is given by a debtor a power of attorney to collect the debt out of the debtor's assets (thus creating an agency relationship), this would be an agency coupled with an interest, for the agent (the creditor) had an interest in the subject-matter of the agency (the debt) prior to the creation of the principal-agent relationship.

F. RELATIONS OF AGENT AND THIRD PERSONS

I. Liability of an Agent to Third Persons

Since the acts of an agent are the acts of the principal, if the agent was authorized and acted within the scope of his authority and at least partially disclosed his principal, the principal alone will be liable for the contracts entered into by his agent. To hold only the principal liable on the contract in such instances is merely carrying out the intent of the parties as expressed in the contract and disclosed by the fact that the signature of the agent discloses he is merely an agent acting for a disclosed principal.

As already indicated in previous sections, there are several situations under which the agent might be liable on the contract which he negotiates with third persons. These are:

1. If the agent contracts for an undisclosed principal, as already seen.
2. If the third person insists in contracting with the agent and not with the principal, and to this the agent agrees. The third person may do this because he may have greater confidence in the agent's credit or other ability to perform.
3. If the agent signs a negotiable instrument so that the agency is not disclosed thereon, even though the third person may know of the agency. The law sets forth this rule to protect those parties in the future into whose hands the negotiable instrument might come.
4. If the agent exceeds his authority or lacks authority because of the lack of capacity of his principal. In this regard, a person who acts as an agent impliedly warrants that he is an agent, that his principal is in existence and has capacity to enter into the contract, and that his principal has authorized him to make this contract. Thus, if the agent exceeds his authority, or has none, a third person may sue for breach of warranty. To avoid this liability from breach of warranty, an agent might make a full disclosure of all the facts and then let the third person determine the scope of his authority and the capacity of his principal. And public officials and corporate officers are held to have always made a full disclosure of the facts because their authority and their principal's capacity are public records, so they automatically come within this last limitation.
5. Finally, if the agent intentionally misrepresents his authority. This liability has previously been explained under the rule that a person is always liable for his own torts even though he was acting for a principal at the time he committed the wrong.

It should be noted that in numbers 4 and 5 above, the third person at the time he dealt with the agent never intended the agent to be bound. In spite of this, the third person may hold the agent liable by showing that he justifiably relied on the agent's authority, that is, he did not know and had no reason to suspect that the agent lacked authority.

II. Liability of Third Persons to Agent

Normally, the agent cannot enforce the contracts made by him for his principal. The agent has no rights on such contracts against the third person, for the contract is between the third person and the principal. There are, however, at least four exceptions to this general rule:

1. If an agent appears to be the real contracting party. For example, if he is acting for an undisclosed principal.
2. If a contract makes the agent a party thereto.
3. If it is customary in the trade for an agent to enforce the contract.
4. If the agent has a special interest or property in the subject matter, i.e., an agency coupled with an interest.

As to the agent's rights against third persons on torts committed against the agent, the only point worthy of comment here is that if a third person wrongfully influences a principal to terminate an agent's employment, the third person may be liable to the agent for any damages suffered by the agent. This rule of law is not peculiar to agency or employment contracts only, but applies to any contract wherein a third person maliciously and without cause induces one of the contracting parties to breach the contract.

Chapter 4

BUSINESS ORGANIZATION

I. INTRODUCTION

Whenever an individual (or a group of individuals) decides to enter into a business venture, a decision must be made as to the legal form of business organization in which the venture should be conducted. Each type of business organization has certain advantages and disadvantages when compared to some alternative choice. The problem of selecting the business organization which will suit an individual's purpose should be discussed with an attorney, a tax consultant, and a certified public accountant. Some of the factors which will influence the choice of legal form of business are the impact of income taxes, liability of the owners, transferability of ownership in the business, cost of formation, division and specialization of management, etc. Depending on whether the business is organized as an individual proprietorship, general partnership, limited partnership, corporation, joint stock company, or business trust will determine the impact of taxes and these other factors. No general rule or rules may be itemized in order to make the correct selection automatic, as the organization must be tailor-made to fit the particular individual faced with the problem.

Many misleading generalities may be made and have been made about the advantages and disadvantages of various business forms. For example, many writers have itemized and discussed the relative advantages of a partnership with a corporation. Unfortunately, they have unconsciously or through ignorance really compared a large business organized as a corporation with a small business operating as a partnership. They state that a corporation has limited liability which is an advantage when compared to the unlimited liability of a partnership. Technically this is true, but if a small partnership incorporated, the local banker is certain not to lend money to the corporation without insisting on the stockholders co-signing the note. Thus, the limited liability advantage of incorporation has been at least partially lost. I state partially lost for we must not overlook the fact that the corporation would still have a sizable advantage in that the stockholders are shielded from unlimited tort liability, but then good management would generally take care of this through an adequate insurance program.

Other advantages of a corporation which are frequently mentioned are the ease of transferring ownership, and the fact that such transfer has no effect on the life of the business. Also, that the death of the owner (stockholder) in no way affects the life of the business. Again, this is true of large corporations such as A.T.&T., but how about a small corporation where stock is closely held and for which there is no ready market. In such a corporation, the death of a key stockholder may vitally affect the business even though the corporation's legal existence is not affected. The same fallacy applies to the argument that corporations are staffed with specialists whereas in a partnership a few individuals must perform all managerial functions. To argue that a partnership if turned into a corporation will automatically be staffed with experts is utterly ridiculous.

Some disadvantages attributed to a corporation are the difficulty and high cost of organizing, that a corporation is limited by its purpose clause as to the business activities it may pursue, and the greater variety of taxes imposed upon the corporate form. These disadvantages are questionable, as a small corporation's charter may be obtained at a cost of from $400 to $500 or even less; the purpose clause may be broadly drawn; and the annual franchise tax for a small corporation capitalized at $100,000 is as little as $50 in some states.

The above is included at this point because of the confusion which exists in many people's mind concerning the choice of business organization. The confusion must be attributed to some extent to the broad conclusions drawn by many so-called experts, whereas, as previously mentioned, the choice of organization must be determined according to the particular circumstances of each case.

To illustrate the need of selection on an individual basis we might consider the impact of taxes, which today is frequently the determinative factor. The presence of double taxation in the case of a corporation does not mean the tax rates in the aggregate will necessarily be higher than if the same business were carried on as a partnership. Such aggregate tax would be higher if all corporate income, after taxes, was paid out in dividends, but this need not be done. If the stockholders do not need this income, they may plough it back into the business and thus build up the value of their stock which they might later sell and have this income taxed at the capital gain rate. Or, instead of selling their stock, they may declare varying amounts of dividends from year to year, to even off income at the individual level and thereby prevent the owners from being taxed at the higher rates under our progressive income tax. Finally, the corporation might be able, if small enough, to take advantage of the federal tax law applicable to small corporations which allows for avoidance of the double taxation.

Where funds are needed in the business, the corporate form permits accumulations of additional working capital. To illustrate, if the profits of a partnership ($100,000) are distributed to individuals in the 70% tax bracket, there would only be 30% ($30,000) left for reinvestment in the business. Under the corporate form the tax rate is 30% for the first $25,000 profit and 52% for any additional profit. Thus, in our illustration 53½% ($53,500) of the profit would remain, after taxes, for reinvestment.

Of course, there are or may be tax disadvantages to operating a business as a corporation. This discussion is included herein merely to emphasize the fact that there is no clear-cut answer to the question as to which form of organization is best in any or all cases. The selection should be made only after a critical review of the factors in each case. With this preface to forewarn the student, the following comparisons are made subject to the limitations set forth above.

II. CONSIDERATIONS IN SELECTING THE LEGAL FORM OF BUSINESS ORGANIZATION

1. Extent of individual liability. In a general partnership, each partner has unlimited liability. This means that the creditors of the business can reach the private assets of each partner in the event the assets of the partnership are insufficient. In a corporation, each stockholder has limited liability. His liability is limited to the extent of his investment.

2. Control of the business. In the absence of an agreement to the contrary, each partner in a general partnership has an equal right of management. In a limited partnership, one in which there are one or more general partners and one or more limited partners, a general partner has unlimited liability, where-

as a limited partner's liability is limited to the extent of his investment, providing he does not participate in the management of the business. In a corporation, the stockholders right is merely to vote for and elect a board of directors who, in turn, elect and appoint those who will manage the business.

3. Transferability of ownership. The proprietary interest of a stockholder in a large corporation whose stock is listed on the exchange is readily transferable. The transfer of stock ownership in a corporation does not interrupt or impair the existence of the corporation, whereas if a member of a general partnership transfers his interest in the business, the entire partnership is dissolved. Dissolution of a business should not be confused with termination; the former means the legal existence ceases, whereas the latter term includes winding up and liquidating the the business operation.

4. Division of profits and losses. The basis of distribution of profits and losses is usually based on the amount of each participant's investment, but adjustments may be made when a partner or stockholder devotes more time than others to the business by salary differentials.

5. Financing the capital. If outside financing is necessary either initially or due to expansion, a corporation is generally considered the best type of organization since it allows the raising of money through the sale of stocks to the general public. The public is willing to make such investments because of the corporation's limited liability. In a partnership, a new partner may be admitted but such may not be desirable because each general partner has the power to bind the partnership on business transactions. A person who desires to invest in a partnership but who does not want to participate in management may willingly become a limited partner and thus secure the same limited liability advantage he would obtain by buying stock in a corporation.

6. Cost and ease of formation of the organization. The cost of obtaining a corporate charter for a business with a capitalization of $100,000 would be around $500, whereas a partnership agreement would not exceed $100. Thus, the percentage cost is not important unless the capital of the business is small ($3,000 to $5,000) because the cost of organizing would be about the same. The corporate charter must be secured from the State, whereas no consent is needed to form a partnership.

7. Government regulation. The corporation is subject to

more governmental regulation than a partnership, but this is not necessarily a deterrent factor to forming a small corporation, as large corporations are subject to greater regulation than small corporations.

8. Continuity of existence. Corporations continue to exist until dissolved by election of the stockholders or until the state revokes its charter. The death of a stockholder or the transfer by a member of his interest in the organization does not affect the life of the corporation. A partnership, on the other hand, has a limited existence. The death of a general partner or the transfer of his interest dissolves the partnership.

9. Income taxes. For income tax purposes, a partnership is treated as a conduit. No income tax is imposed at the partnership level, but each partner is taxed on his distributive share of the partnership income as such income is earned. A partnership must file a partnership return, but such is for information purposes only. Under the 1954 Revenue Code, a partnership may elect to be taxed as a corporation.

A corporation, on the other hand, is a separate taxable entity and must pay income taxes on its income. In addition, the individual stockholders must pay income taxes on the dividends received from the corporation. This "double taxation" has been minimized to a degree by the exclusion from tax of the first $50 in dividends received. Also, if the corporation is a small, closely held one, there is no double taxation. Two partners could thus form a corporation and not pay any greater income taxes.

III. OTHER BUSINESS FORMS

While our discussion of the law of business organization will be limited to partnerships and corporations, it might be well to describe and explain other forms of business organizations to a limited extent.

a. JOINT STOCK COMPANY

A joint stock company is similar to a partnership in that it is an unincorporated association, each member of which has unlimited liability. Ownership is evidenced by shares of stock and these may be transferred without causing a dissolution of the business. The death of a shareholder does not affect the company's existence. Management of a joint stock company may be delegated, as in a corporation. Some states tax a joint stock company like a partnership, whereas others treat it as a corporation for tax purposes.

b. Business Trust

The business trust form of organization originated in Massachusetts, and is also known as a Massachusetts Trust. In this type of organization, the assets are placed under the control of one or more persons, who act as trustees and manage the business for the owners. The owners may not take part in this management of the business and have limited liability. Ownership is evidenced by transferable certificates. The trustees have legal title to the assets, are charged with the responsibility of management, and have unlimited liability unless each contract they enter into negates this unlimited liability. A business trust is taxed in the same manner as a corporation.

c. Joint Venture

A joint venture is an association of two or more persons to carry out a specific transaction or series of transactions. It is usually of a temporary nature, whereas a partnership is of a more permanent nature. Many types of partnerships are possible in joint ventures. Some are:

1. Ostensible—known and held out to the public as being a partner in the firm.
2. Active—partners who do the work of the firm.
3. Silent—known to be a partner in the firm, but not active in the operation of the business.
4. Dormant—has a financial interest in the business but such is not known to outsiders as he takes no part in the business (other than sharing in profits) and his name is not associated with the partnership.
5. Secret—one who is active in the management of the firm, but not known or held out to be a partner.
6. Nominal—a former partner whose name is used in the partnership name although he no longer owns a share of the capital nor is he entitled to a share in the profits.
7. Limited—this will be discussed at a later point.

IV. CREATION OF A PARTNERSHIP

There are few formal requirements in organizing a partnership. A written agreement is not necessary unless required by the Statute of Frauds (partnership to last more than a year). Even though not required, a written agreement setting forth the terms of the partnership is desirable as a means of preventing disputes. The agreement should include the name of the partnership, the purpose for which the business is organized, the limitations on the powers of the individual partners, and provisions as to how capital is to be contributed, how profits and losses are to be shared, and how the assets are to be divided upon dissolution of the partnership. In the absence of a written agreement to the contrary, the law will impose the terms of the agreement, e.g., if the agreement does not mention how profits and losses are to be divided, the Uniform Partnership Act provides they shall be shared equally.

The Uniform Partnership Act has been adopted by 31 States. It defines a partnership as being "an association of two or more persons to carry on a business as co-owners for profit." (U.P.A. Sec. 6).

A partnership can commence only by voluntary contract—"an association." No one may be forced to become a partner. The "persons" to become partners must have capacity to contract. Capacity has been explained in the section on Contracts except as to the ability of a corporation becoming a partner. This is generally denied unless the charter expressly authorizes the corporation to be a partner.

"Carrying on a business" means continuous, and not a mere isolated, transaction. An isolated transaction would probably be a joint venture. "For profit" means the association must have the pursuit of profits and not pleasure as their main objective. "Co-owners" does not preclude one person's contributing capital and the other the skill of management. The court in *Ash v. Guie,* 97 Pa., 493, a case decided before the adoption of the U.P.A., said a partnership is a "combination of two or more persons of capital or labor, or skill for the purpose of business for their common benefit." This is still an applicable definition today.

Since individual profits are subject to withdrawal at any time, they do not represent partnership capital which is a permanent investment, returnable to the partners only at the time the partnership is dissolved or all partners agree to vary their capital investments. Of course, the partnership agreement may provide that a portion of the profits are to be retained as capital, and thus not subject to being withdrawn.

If one partner contributes the capital and the other the labor and skill, the latter has no claim to the original capital but may acquire a claim to a portion of the capital if the partners agree to the retention in the business of a portion of their profits. This may be desired in order to expand a growing business. If no agreement is made to leave the profits in the business to increase the capital, the profits do not constitute capital and may, therefore, be withdrawn by both partners at any time.

Should a loss occur (instead of a profit), the partner who contributed labor and skill would be required to share in these losses in the same manner he was to share in the profits, and if no mention of this is made in the agreement, profits and losses are shared equally. Of course, the agreement may provide that a partner is not to share in the losses and, as between the partners, such would be valid.

Finally, no interest is allowed to partners on their capital contributions nor are wages allowed to partners unless such are specified in the partnership agreement. If wages are agreed upon, they are not treated as expenses to be deducted in determining net profits, but as a means of determining the distribution of the profit or loss. On the other hand, a loan by a partner to the firm (not an increase in his capital) would be entitled to interest and would be treated, as between the partners, the same as though obtained from an outside source such as a bank.

Illustration: *A* and *B* form a partnership; *A* to be paid 6% on his capital contribution of $25,000 and *B* to be paid wages of $6,000 per year. At the end of the year assume the profits of the business (prior to the above interest and wages to partners) are as follows:

		I.		II.		III.
Profit or (Loss)		$10,000		$5,000		($5,000)
Interest to *A*	$1,500		$1,500		$1,500	
Wages to *B*	6,000		6,000		6,000	
Total		$7,500		$7,500		$7,500
Balance		$2,500		($2,500)		($12,500)
Balance distributed equally:						
½ to *A*		$1,250		($1,250)		($ 6,250)
½ to *B*		$1,250		($1,250)		($ 6,250)

In illustration I. *A* got $2,750 and *B* got $7,250 of the $10,000 profit.

In illustration II. *A* got \$ 250 and *B* got \$4,750 of the \$5,000 profit.

In illustration III. *A* took \$4,750 and *B* took \$250 of the \$5,000 loss.

B's loss in Illustration III makes him owe the partnership \$250, he having a deficit in his capital account of \$250, and *A* has a credit balance in his capital account of \$5,250—net capital of the business being \$5,000.

Assume the partnership is terminated at this time, *B* must contribute \$250 to the firm to cover his share of the loss.

V. EXISTENCE OF A PARTNERSHIP

Rules for determining the existence of a partnership are set out in Section 7 of the U.P.A. The ultimate test as to the existance of a partnership is of course the intent to carry on a business as co-owners for profit. But when the agreement of the parties does not sufficiently express their intent to do such, the rules laid out in Section 7 of the U.P. are applied.

Section 7 of the U.P.A. provides that joint ownership of property and/or the sharing of gross returns does not of itself establish a partnership, but the sharing of profits is prima facie evidence that one is a partner. The section goes on to explain that this inference is negated if the share of profits is received as payment of a debt, wages to an employee, rent to a landlord, an annuity to a widow or representative of a deceased partner, interest on a loan, or in consideration for the sale of goodwill of a business. As the sharing of profits constitutes prima facie evidence of a partnership, the burden of proof that one is not a partner or that the business is not a partnership lies with the person sharing in the profits.

Even though not mentioned in the U.P.A., showing that an individual shares in the losses of the business is stronger evidence that he is a partner than is the showing he shares in the profits. In either case, the contention that the individual is a partner may be rebutted if he is in fact not a partner.

Section 7 of the U.P.A. also sets forth the rule that persons who are not partners as to each other cannot be partners as to third persons. An exception is made, however, to this rule by what is called "partnership by estoppel." This is covered by Sec. 16 of the U.P.A.

Section 16 of the U.P.A. provides for the creation of partnership by estoppel when a person by words or conduct holds himself out, or permits himself to be held out, as a member of an existing partnership, and the third party alleging the partnership by estoppel has justifiably relied on such holding out and changed his position thereby, such as by extending credit to the partnership. The person so holding himself out is liable in the same manner as if he were actually a partner, and the partnership is also liable if it participated in the misrepresentation. Thus, as to third persons, one may be held to be a partner to another even though no actual relationship exists by means of "partnership by estoppel."

VI. PARTNERSHIP PROPERTY

Section 8 of the U.P.A. provides:

> "(1) All property originally brought into the partnership stock or subsequently acquired by purchase or otherwise, on account of the partnership, is partnership property.
>
> "(2) Unless the contrary intent appears, property acquired with partnership funds is partnership property.
>
> "(3) Any estate in real property may be acquired in the partnership name. Title so acquired can be conveyed only in the partnership name.
>
> "(4) A conveyance to a partnership in the partnership name, though without words of inheritance, passes the entire estate of the grantor unless a contrary intent appears."

Sections 24 through 28 of the U.P.A. define and explain the property rights of a partner. Under common law, a partnership was not a legal entity and thus partnership property was held in the names of one or more of the partners, but under the U.P.A. (Section 8 (3)) a partnership may own property under its fictitious name or under the names of the individual partners. The partnership property is held by the partners as tenants in partnership. The characteristics of such a tenancy are set out in Section 25 of the U.P.A. as follows:

(1) Equal rights of possession for partnership purposes but no right to possess such property for any other purpose without the consent of his partners.

(2) This right is not assignable except in connection with the assignment of the rights of all other partners in the same property.

(3) The specific partnership property may not be attached

to satisfy a personal claim against a partner; it is subject to attachment only on a claim against the partnership.

(4) On the death of a partner, his rights in the partnership property vests in the surviving partners who must account to the widow or heirs of the deceased partner for the value of the property received.

(5) A partner's right in specific partnership property is not subject to dower, courtesy, or allowance to widows, heirs, or next of heirs.

Thus, a partner does not own any specific partnership property personally, and any sale not within the scope of the partnership business by one partner without full authority will not pass title.

Besides his interest in the specific property as set out above, a partner has an "interest" in the partnership, i.e., the rights to his share of the profits and surplus, and this is personal property even though all the assets of the partnership are realty. Even though an individual partner's creditor cannot levy on the specific assets of the partnership to satisfy a judgment, such personal creditors may levy on the "partner's interest."

Upon the application of a judgment creditor, a court may order a sale of the debtor partner's interest in the partnership. If the partnership interest is then sold to a person or persons outside the partnership, the partnership is dissolved. Section 27 provides for a partner to pledge his "interest," and such will not of itself dissolve the partnership. The pledgee of such interest does not become a partner but is merely entitled to receive, in accordance with his contract, the profits and surplus to which the assigning partner would otherwise be entitled. Of course, if the partner selling his interest withdraws from the firm and the remaining partners and the purchaser all agree, a new partnership may be formed which would include the purchaser as a partner.

From the above discussion, it should not be presumed that all property used by the partnership is partnership property, and this may be the situation even though title is in one or several partners. Whether property is or is not partnership property depends largely on the intentions of the parties as expressed in the deed and/or partnership agreement. Where there is no expressed intent, many factors may be relied upon to determine the question of ownership. Some of these are the purpose and manner in which the property is used, how the transaction of acquisition is carried on the books, and any other conduct of the parties which implies an intent. A question which has been frequently litigated in the past is whether the partnership name is partnership property. The courts uniformly hold that the firm name is a part of the good will and is a partnership asset. Some states require the filing of a certificate with the county recorder setting forth the names of the partners when the business is conducted under an assumed or fictitious firm name. Failure to comply with the statute precludes the partnership from enforcing their contracts.

The third and final property right of a partner is his right to share in the management of the business. Partners are all agents of one another while conducting transactions within the scope of the partnership business irrespective of how much capital each has contributed. In the event there is a dispute as to ordinary business within "the scope of the partnership business" in absence of any expressed provision to the contrary, the majority is to prevail; but to implement a fundamental change in the objectives of the association requires a unanimous assent. In either case the partnership agreement may specifically provide how such disputes are to be settled and, if so, such agreement will prevail.

VII. LIABILITIES OF PARTNERS AND THE PARTNERSHIP

The principal disadvantage of a partnership is that each partner is liable for the contracts and torts committed by other partners acting within the scope of the partnership business. A partner is also liable for the criminal acts of other partners if he expressly or impliedly authorizes them by accepting the benefits therefrom with full knowledge of the facts. This liability of partners is merely the law of agency which is applicable to partnerships, as partners are all agents of one another.

Section 13 of the U.P.A. provides: "Where, by any wrongful act or omission of any partner acting in the ordinary course of the business of the partnership, or with the authority of his copartner, loss or injury is caused to any person, not being a partner of the partnership, or any penalty is incurred, the partnership is liable therefore to the same extent as the partner so acting or omitting to act."

Section 14 of the U.P.A. provides: The partnership is bound to make good the loss:

"(a) Where one partner acting within the scope of his apparent authority receives money or property of a third person and misapplies it

"(b) Where the partnership in the course of its business receives money or property of a third person and the money or property so received is misapplied by any partner while it is in the custody of the partnership."

Section 15 of the U.P.A. provides: "All partners are liable:

"(a) Jointly and severally for everything chargeable to the partnership under Sections 13 and 14

"(b) Jointly for all other debts and obligations of the partnership, but any partner may enter into a separate obligation to perform a partnership contract."

Thus, all partners are liable jointly and severally for the torts committed by other partners acting within the scope of the partnership business. This means the injured third party may sue the partnership and name all the partners as defendants or he may sue each separately. "Several liability" means that the injured party has as many causes of action as there are partners. Where the partnership obligation is a debt or contract (Section 15 (b) above), the partners are only jointly liable. This means that the injured third person has only one cause of action. Thus, he should sue all the partners and the partnership together as he cannot later bring a suit against a partner whom he failed to name in his original action. The reason for suing all, or as many as you can get jurisdiction over, is to give the greatest assurance of collecting any judgment awarded to the plaintiff. An individual partner cannot be held liable if he is not named in the complaint or if he is not served with a summons.

Suppose a partner accidently injured his wife while conducting partnership business and that the wife sued the partnership for damages. Applying Section 13 of the U.P.A., a partner is liable for the torts of other partners to the same extent as the partner committing the tort. At common law, a wife cannot sue her husband (or a husband his wife) for damages resulting from a tort. Thus, the partnership could not be held liable since the husband, the partner committing the tort, could not be held liable. Now, if the husband had been a stockholder in a corporation and had injured his wife while conducting business for the corporation, the wife could have recovered from the corporation. A corporation is considered by law as a person separate and distinct from the stockholders.

The liability of a new partner being admitted into an existing partnership for obligations arising before his admission is covered by Section 17 of the U.P.A. The act provides such incoming partner is liable for these past obligations the same as though he had been a partner when such obligations were incurred except that this liability shall be satisfied only out of partnership property. Thus, is a partner is admitted into an existing partnership upon a contribution of $10,000 and creditors later bring suit against the partnership for obligations incurred before the new partner was admitted, the creditors may attack all partnership property, including the $10,000 invested by the new partner, and the separate personal property of those who were partners at the time the obligations were incurred. They may not get at the separate personal property of the new partner.

The liability of a retiring partner for partnership obligations contracted while he was a partner continue unless the partnership creditor and the persons continuing the business expressly or impliedly agree to release him of this obligation. If all the partners and the creditors consent to his release, a retiring partner is released of his obligation through the "novation."

In many aspects a partnership is treated as a single entity under the Uniform Partnership Act and, to a degree, this is true as to the enforcement of claims by partnership creditors and creditors of the individual partners. Section 40 (H) of the U.P.A. provides that when partnership property and the individual properties of the partners are in possession of a court for distribution, partnership creditors shall have priority on partnership property and separate creditors on individual property. This is merely applying the doctrine of "marshaling of assets" whereby a creditor having a first lien on two different properties of the debtor and another creditor has a junior lien on one of these; the creditor having the two liens is required to resort first to the property on which he has an exclusive lien, thus saving the lien of the other creditor to the extent possible.

This doctrine applied to partnerships requires partnership creditors to exhaust their remedy as to partnership property before going against an individual partner's property. In the case of a personal creditor of a partner, even though he cannot attach specific partnership property, he can under the U.P.A.

Section 28 get a receiver appointed to collect the debtor partner's share of the partnership profits and may, when circumstances of the case require, force the debtor partner's interest to be sold in order to collect the judgment. In case the debtor partner's interest is sold to an outsider, the partnership is dissolved. In any event, the personal creditor of a partner will not be allowed to enforce his claim against partnership property to the prejudice of partnership creditors. Thus, partnership creditors have first claim on partnership property and a second claim on the personal assets of the individual partners, whereas personal creditors have a first lien on personal assets of individual partners only. If all partners are insolvent and there are no firm assets, partnership creditors and individual creditors all share equally in the amounts of the individual partners. The same holds true if a partner fraudulently converts partnership property to his own use.

As to partnership debts, the property of the partnership as well as the personal assets of the partners may be attached if necessary to enforce their collection. Should the partnership creditors be required to collect from the personal property of the partners, they need not do so pro rata as to each individual partner's liability, but may collect the entire amount from any one or several of the partners and let the partners settle the question of contribution among themselves. If necessary, the partner paying more than his pro rata share may sue in equity for an accounting, and thus require the others to contribute their pro rata share. Thus, it is said as to outsiders each partner is liable for all partnership debts, but as between themselves, each is liable only for his share.

VIII. RIGHTS AND DUTIES OF PARTNERS TO ONE ANOTHER

The relationship of partners is of the same fiduciary character as agent and principal, which has been previously discussed. Being a relationship of trust and confidence, the law demands they act in good faith and integrity towards one another. Section 21 of the U.P.A. brings out this duty by requiring every partner to account to the partnership for any benefit or profit derived by him, without the consent of the other partners, from any transaction connected with the formation, conduct, or liquidation of the partnership or from any use by him of its property. Thus, a partner cannot carry on a competitive business without the consent of his associates; he cannot renew a partnership lease for his own benefit or advantage; he must use ordinary care and skill in performing his partnership duties; and so forth.

Of course, the above duties as well as those set out below may be varied by the original partnership agreement or by subsequent agreements among them; but assuming the agreement does not cover the point in issue, then the U.P.A. (Sections 18 to 23 and 9 (3)) provides the rules which govern the rights and duties of the partners in relation to the partnership. The following are rules which are subject to change by agreement between the partners:

(1) Each partner shall be repaid his contributions, whether by capital or advances, to the partnership property and share equally in profits and surplus remaining after all liabilities, including those to partners, are satisfied; and must contribute towards the losses, whether of capital or otherwise, sustained by the partnership according to his share in profits.

(2) The partnership must indemnify every partner in respect to payments made and personal liabilities reasonably incurred by him in the ordinary and proper conduct of the business, or for the preservation of the business or its property.

(3) A partner, who in the aid of the partnership makes any payment or advance beyond the amount of capital which he agreed to contribute, shall be paid interest from the date of the payment or advance. This wording precludes allowing interest on advances made when such is not needed by the partnership as well as on individual profits not withdrawn from the firm.

(4) A partner shall receive interest on the capital contributed by him only from the date when repayment should be made.

(5) All partners have equal rights on the management and conduct of the partnership business regardless of their proportionate share in the business.

(6) Any difference as to ordinary matters connected with the partnership business may be decided by a majority of the partners; but no act in contravention of any agreement between the partners may be done rightfully without consent of all the partners. Thus, in a retail sales appliance partnership, the majority could decide to change the firm's product line from *A* Company to *B* Company products unless the partnership agreement required approval of all partners to make such a switch.

But to change the nature of the business from retailing to wholesaling would require unanimous consent.

(7) No person can become a member of a partnership without the consent of all partners.

(8) Unless authorized by the other partners or unless they have abandoned the business, one or more but less than all the partners have no authority to:

(a) Assign the partnership property in trust for creditors.
(b) Dispose of the goodwill of the business.
(c) Do any act which would make it impossible to carry on the ordinary business of a partnership.
(d) Confess a judgment.
(e) Submit a partnership claim or liability to arbitration.

(9) No partner is entitled to remuneration for acting in the partnership business, except that a surviving partner is entitled to reasonable compensation for his services in winding up the partnership affairs.

The partnership books shall be kept, subject to any agreement between the partners, at the principal place of business of the partnership, and every partner shall at all times have access to and may inspect and copy any of them. This does not mean that the partner is entitled to formal financial statements or that he may use the information secured for an improper purpose. A partner, however, does have the right to a formal account (financial statements) as to partnership affairs if he is wrongfully excluded from the partnership business or its property by his copartners, if the partnership agreement gives the right, if a partner has breached his fiduciary relation by making a secret profit, or whenever other circumstances render an accounting just and reasonable, such as when an execution of judgment has been made against an individual partner's interest.

Whenever a partner is forced to take court action in order to secure a formal accounting, such action must be brought in a court of equity. A partner may not sue in a court of law a partnership of which he is a member because it is impossible to determine one partner's indebtedness to another until all partnership transactions are settled and a balance between partners determined.

IX. RELATIONS OF PARTNERS TO THIRD PERSONS DEALING WITH THE PARTNERSHIP

Every partner is an agent of the partnership for the purpose of its business, and the act of every partner, including the execution in the partnership name of any instrument, for apparently carrying on in the usual way the business of the partnership of which he is a member binds the partnership, unless the partner so acting has in fact no authority to act for the partnership in the particular matter and the person with whom he is dealing has knowledge of the fact he has no such authority.

Thus, a partner has actual authority as granted by the partnership agreement and, in addition, implied authority as derived from the nature of the partnership business when the partnership is silent. This implied power includes doing all things necessary to conduct the ordinary business of the firm, and its extent will obviously vary as between trading and non-trading partnerships. Even though the partnership agreement withholds from a partner certain implied authority, the partner will still have apparent authority to bind the partnership as to third persons with whom he deals—persons who have no knowledge of his lack of authority.

In a trading partnership, each partner has implied authority to purchase personal property and resell those items which are included in the ordinary course of such business. This power includes the execution of the necessary documents to effectuate the transaction. But to sell the business's fixed assets, the partner conducting the transaction must have been given authority to do so or the partnership will not be bound. In the case of realty, the title of which is in the name of the partnership, a sale by a partner who has not been authorized by the other partners, may be avoided unless the grantee from the partner has, in turn, conveyed the property to a bona-fide purchaser. Of course, if the partnership is engaged in the real estate business, a partner may sell such realty the same as in the case of any partner selling goods in the ordinary course of the partnership business.

If the realty (fixed asset) title is in the name of one or more but not all the partners, and the record does not disclose the right of the partnership, the partners in whose name the title stands may convey good title for value to a bona-fide purchaser who has no knowledge of the partnership interest in the property.

One must not forget that the law of agency determines a partner's power to bind the partnership. Obviously, a partner in a trading partnership (buying and selling goods) has greater implied powers than a partner in a non-trading partnership (professions: e.g., doctors, attorneys, etc.) when it comes to borrowing money, pledging assets as security, etc. In either case, torts committed by a partner in the ordinary course of partnership business will make all partners vicariously liable thereon.

An act which is not apparently for carrying on business of the partnership in the usual way does not bind the partnership unless expressly authorized by the other partners. If a partner wrongfully claims power beyond the partnership agreement which is not apparently for carrying on partnership business, and if other partners with knowledge of these facts remain silent, the partnership will be held on the basis of estoppel.

Assume a partnership agreement limits the power of a partner. Will such be effective as to third persons who have no notice of the limitation? As between partners, such would be effective and any partner who violated the agreement would be liable to the other partners for any damages resulting, but as to third persons who have no notice of the limitation, the partnership would be liable. For example: A partnership agreement provides that the senior partner must approve all contracts. A junior partner makes a contract with a third person (who has no knowledge of the partnership agreement) without obtaining the necessary approval. The partnership will be liable for the contract. The liability of a partnership to a third person is not affected by partnership agreements of which the third person is not aware. As between the partners, the partner who acted beyond the agreed range of his authority, would be liable to the other partners for any resulting damages.

In holding a partnership liable, it is often necessary to prove that the partnership had knowledge or notice. Well, the U.P.A. provides that notice to any partner of any matter relating to partnership affairs, and the knowledge of the partner acting in the particular matter, acquired while a partner or then present to his mind, and the knowledge of any other partner who reasonably could and should have communicated it to the acting partner, operates as notice to or knowledge of the partnership, except in the case of a fraud on the partnership committed by or with the consent of that partner. Thus, notice to a partner is notice to the partnership, and a partner has the same duty to keep the other partners informed as an agent has to keep his principal informed, and any loss resulting from a break of this duty by a partner to the partnership must be born by the partner who failed to fulfill this duty. (U.P.A. Sec. 12)

An admission or representation made by any partner concerning partnership affairs within the scope of his authority is evidence against the partnership. (U.P.A. Sec. 11)

X. DISSOLUTION AND WINDING UP A PARTNERSHIP

The dissolution of a partnership is defined in Sec. 29 of the U.P.A. as the change in the relation of the partners caused by any partner ceasing to be associated in the carrying on of the partnership business. "Winding up" the partnership, on the other hand, is the method of settling partnership affairs after dissolution. Thus, the partnership is not terminated upon dissolution, but continues in existence until the winding up of the partnership affairs is completed, at which time the partnership is said to terminate. (U.P.A. 30)

Partnerships may be dissolved by acts of the partners or by operation of law. The acts of the partners causing dissolution may or may not be in violation of the partnership agreement.

A. Dissolution by Acts of the Partners

Dissolution is caused without violation of the agreement between the partners (a) upon the expiration of the term or upon completion of the particular undertaking specified in the agreement; (b) by express will of a partner to dissolve the partnership where no period or particular undertaking is specified; (c) by express will of all partners to dissolve the partnership; and (d) by expulsion of a partner in accordance with the original agreement between the partners, e.g., the agreement may provide that a member may be expelled by a majority vote of the partners. It should be obvious there is no right for expulsion of a member unless such is specifically provided for in the partnership agreement.

Suppose that *A* and *B* form a partnership for a period of five years. Under the common law, the partnership would be automatically dissolved at the end of the five-year period. Under the U.P.A. Sec. 23, which modifies the common law rule, the partners may, upon expiration of the five-year period, continue to do business, as a partnership at will. A partnership at will may be dissolved rightfully by any partner at any time. The rights and duties of the partners remain the same as they were at the expiration of the term so far as is consistent with a partnership at will.

A partnership may be dissolved if a partner violates the partnership agreement by refusing to continue in the partnership business. The partner refusing to continue is breaching the contract, and his partners may recover damages from him if the breach is unjustified. Thus, a partner (like an agent or a principal) has the power to terminate the partnership even though he may not have the right to do so. The basis of the law is that the courts will not order specific performance of a personal act. The U.P.A. Sec. 38 (2) (a) (ii) (iii) provides for the partners who have not wrongfully caused the dissolution to elect to continue the partnership for the agreed term and for that purpose may possess all the partnership property including the withdrawing partner's interest, provided they post bond to secure the payment of the withdrawing partner's interest at the end of the agreed term of the partnership, or they may pay to the partner who wrongfully caused the dissolution the value of his interest at the time of dissolution less damages for breaching the agreement. In either case, the goodwill of the business is not considered in ascertaining the value of the interest of the partner who wrongfully caused the dissolution. In addition, the partners continuing the business must post bond to indemnify the withdrawing partner against all present or future partnership liabilities.

B. Dissolution by Operation of Law

Dissolution of the partnership by operation of law may be caused by supervening illegality, death of a partner, or bankruptcy of a partner or the partnership.

Anything which makes it illegal or impossible to continue the partnership for the period agreed causes dissolution. Supervening illegality and its effect on contracts as previously explained (see Contracts) is applicable to partnership. An example would be if Nevada should pass a law prohibiting gambling, then partnerships operating gambling businesses in that state would be dissolved.

Death of a partner automatically dissolves the partnership. The partnership is not terminated, however, until the surviving partners wind up the partnership affairs. A new partnership relation may be formed between the heirs of the deceased partner and the surviving partners.

A partnership is dissolved upon the bankruptcy of either the partnership or a partner. Mere insolvency does not necessarily effect a dissolution. The distinction between insolvency and bankruptcy is that bankruptcy is provided for by federal statutes which establish definite procedures for taking over and distributing the assets of a debtor, whereas insolvency is that status of anyone whose liabilities exceed his assets. A company may be insolvent one day and solvent a month later.

Sec. 32 of the U.PA. provides for dissolution by a decree of the court. A court of equity may, upon application, order the dissolution of a partnership when (a) a partner is adjudged insane or is otherwise incapable of performing his duties; (b) a partner is guilty of an act which is prejudicial to the partnership business or which constitutes a breach of the partnership agreement; (c) the business can be further conducted only at a loss; and (d) any other circumstances which render dissolution an equitable remedy. Examples under (d) would include refusal to allow a partner to share in the management of the firm's affairs or to participate in the profits.

The occurrence of any cause for dissolution under Sec. 32 will not, of itself, cause the partnership to be dissolved as this section requires a positive act—application to the court. Thus, insanity or incapacity alone does not dissolve the partnership. The court will decide whether a partner's incapacity is grave enough to order a dissolution.

Notice of dissolution is a means of protection. If the partnership of *X, Y,* and *Z* is dissolved and *Y* and *Z* continue the business as a new partnership, they must give notice of dissolution of the original partnership in order to protect themselves against unauthorized acts and contracts of *X*. *X,* the retiring partner, to protect himself against future liability as a member of the partnership, must give notice of dissolution, unless the other partners give notice. Actual notice of dissolution must be given to persons who have extended credit to the partnership. General notice of dissolution by publication in a newspaper is sufficient as to all other persons. No notice need be given if dissolution was caused by supervening illegality or bankruptcy, as third persons are presumed to have notice of such public matters.

Dissolution terminates all authority of the partners to act for the partnership except to wind up the partnership affairs. However, a partner may bind the partnership as to third persons even after dissolution if proper notice has not been given as required. Even the death of a partner terminating the partnership by operation of law does not excuse the giving of notice as in case of bankruptcy or supervening illegality. Thus, a deceased partner's estate is bound by contracts made after dissolution caused by the death of a partner unless notice has been given. The notice should therefore be given by the deceased partner's legal representative.

A partner is liable for his share of any liability created by any partner acting for the partnership after the partnership is caused to be dissolved by act, bankruptcy, or death of a partner just as though no dissolution had occurred, unless the partner acting for the partnership had knowledge of the dissolution. Under the common law, a partner who made a contract after the death of a co-partner was the only one liable if a loss resulted. The U.P.A. is more equitable in that the acting partner should not be liable for something of which he had no knowledge. Thus, it appears the only dissolution by operation of law which is binding on the partners and adversely affects their right to contribution from co-partners for liability created after dissolution is dissolution by supervening illegality.

Sec. 37 of the U.P.A. provides that, subject to any agreement, the partners who have not wrongfully dissolved the partnership have the right to wind up the partnership affairs. This includes receiving payment of accounts receivables and giving discharge therefore, selling the firm's assets and paying the liabilities. The partner or partners winding up the partnership cannot create new obligations not incidental to winding up the partnership. Should a partner improperly create a new obligation, he alone assumes the liability for any loss resulting. As to liabilities existing at the time of dissolution, each partner's liability continues to the same extent as though no dissolution had occurred.

Sec. 40 provides the rules for settling the accounts between partners and the order of distribution of the partnership assets. Payments by the partnership are to be made in the following order: (1) to creditors other than partners; (2) to partners for money loaned in excess of the capital investment; (3) to partners in respect to capital investments; and (4) any balance is considered profit and is distributed as such according to the terms of the partnership agreement.

If the assets of the partnership are insufficient to meet the claims of creditors other than partners, the partners must contribute towards the losses according to their shares in the profits. If any, but not all, the partners are insolvent, the other partners must contribute their share of liabilities in the relative proportions in which they (the solvent) partners share in the profits.

To illustrate: *A, B,* and *C* share profits equally and have capital account balances of $7,000, $4,000 and $3,000. The assets of the partnership are sold for $25,000.

Illustration:

		1		2		3		4
The liabilities to outsiders total		$10,001		$11,999		$20,000		$23,000
Assets are paid:								
To outside creditors		$10,001		$11,999		$20,000		$23,000
To partners Capital *A*		7,000		7,000		7,000		7,000
To partners Capital *B*		4,000		4,000		4,000		4,000
To partners Capital *C*		3,000		3,000		3,000		3,000
Balance (Profit) to partners	*A*	333	loss	(333)	loss	(3,000)	loss	(4,000)
	B	333	"	(333)	"	(3,000)	"	(4,000)
	C	333	"	(333)	"	(3,000)	"	(4,000)
TOTAL		$25,000		$25,000		$25,000		$25,000

In illustrations 2, 3, and 4, the rule is to distribute the loss befor you pay out the capital. Thus,

A would receive $6,667, 4,000 and 2,000 respectively.
B would receive $3,667, 1,000 and 0 respectively.
C would receive $2,667, 0 and 0 respectively.

In illustration #4, A should have received $3,000 ($7,000-4,000) and may require *C* to contribute $1,000 (Capital $3,000 —share of loss $4,000). If *C* is insolvent, his loss is shared by *A* and *B* and thus *A* may require *B* to contribute $500.

XI. LIMITED PARTNERSHIPS

A limited partnership is one in which certain members' liability for the firm obligations is limited to their capital investment. Limited partnerships were not known under the common law. They are permitted by statute in 31 states, and the statute must be strictly (or at least substantially) complied with, or all the members will be liable as general partners.

A limited partnership is formed upon the filing of an appropriate certificate with the county clerk of the county in which the principal place of business of the partnership is situated. The certificate should include the following: name and location of the partnership, character of business, names and place of residence of each partner with indication as to whether they are general or limited partners, the amount of cash, and a description of and the agreed value of other property contributed by each limited partner, etc. (see local Statutes). Each partner must sign the certificate in the presence of a notary public. Many states require the publication of the certificate in a newspaper of general circulation in addition to its being filed. Certain businesses, such as banking and insurance, generally are denied to use this legal form of organization. At least one member must be a general partner with unlimited liability.

If the filing of the certificate is substantially defective, a limited partnership is not formed. A partner who does not know of the defect and who, in good faith, believes he is a limited partner, does not become liable as a general partner provided he promptly renounces his interest in the profits of the partnership upon discovering the mistake. Failure to so denounce will make such a person liable as a general partner.

The contribution of a limited partner may be cash or other property but not services. In fact, a limited partner becomes liable as a general partner if he takes part in the management (control) of the business. Also the surname of a limited partner may not appear in the firm name unless it is also the surname of a general partner; or else, if prior to the time when the limited partner became such, the business had been carried on under a name in which his surname appeared. A limited partner, whose name appears in the partnership name contrary to these exceptions, will be liable as a general partner as to creditors who do not have actual knowledge that he is not a general partner at the time they extend credit to the partnership.

A limited partner has the same rights as a general partner to insist and copy the partnership books, have a formal accounting, and to have his capital returned upon dissolution. A limited partnership is not dissolved by death of a limited partner or by his selling his interest in the partnership. Any act which would dissolve a general partnership, if committed by a general partner in a limited partnership, will dissolve the limited partnership.

Upon dissolution, the assets of a limited partnership will be distributed in the following order: (1) to outside creditors; (2) to limited partners as to capital and profit; (3) to general partners other than for capital and profit; and (4) general partners as to capital and profits.

Chapter 5

CORPORATIONS

I. IN GENERAL

A. Legal Entity

The corporate form of business organization was not known under the common law; it is a creature of state statutory law permitting its formation and existence if the statutes are complied with. A corporation is defined as a separate legal entity created by law. It is a group of persons empowered to act as a single artificial person, separate and distinct from the stockholders. It can sue and be sued in its own name, hold legal title to property, and, in general, is capable of doing the same business acts as any natural person. Since a corporation is a legal entity separate and distinct from its stockholders, the life of the corporation is not affected by the death of its stockholders, and its debts and obligations are not that of the persons (stockholders) who created the entity. This limited liability of stockholders (which means a stockholder is not personally liable for the debts of the corporation) applies even though one person owns all of the stock, and the sole purpose of incorporating was to protect the owners against personal liability. There are exceptional cases where the legal entity will be disregarded. If a person sells his business (including goodwill) and agrees not to re-enter the same business and forms a corporation for the sole purpose of competing with his vendee, the courts will "pierce the corporate veil"—not recognize such fraudulent scheme and would enjoin the corporation from competing.

B. Charter

When a state grants a corporate charter, such is considered a contractual relationship between the corporation and the State issuing its charter. This contract, like all others, is protected by the Constitution of the United States. Art. 1, Sec. 10 of the U.S. Const. provides: "No State shall pass any law impairing the obligations of contracts." Thus, once a state issues a charter, it cannot amend, alter, or repeal such charter unless such rights are reserved to the State when the charter is granted. Since this ruling was laid down by the historic Dartmouth College case in 1819, most States generally reserve these rights and/or grant a charter only for a fixed period of time, e.g., 50 years.

A corporation is said to be an artificial person. To what extent is a corporation protected by the 14th Amendment to the Constitution of the United States which provides: "No State shall deprive any person of life, liberty or property without due process of law," and Art. 4, Sec. 2 which provides: "Citizens of each State shall be entitled to all the privileges and immunities of the citizens of the several States." Corporations are deemed persons within the due process clause of the 14th Amendment, but not as to the privilege and immunity clause of Art. 4, Sec. 2. As to the latter, a corporation is a person only in the State of its incorporation and those other States which choose to admit it by allowing it to become domesticated. Thus, a corporation is a citizen of the State which granted its charter and in such State the corporation is known as a domestic corporation. In all other States than the one which granted its charter, the corporation is known as a foreign corporation.

C. Liability to Suit and "Doing Business"

When a State grants a charter, one of the conditions of granting it is that the corporation must maintain an agent within the State at all times upon whom service may be made in the event the corporation is named a defendant in a law suit. But, if a corporation breaches a contract in another State, the injured party may find it difficult, if not impossible, to serve the corporation with a summons in order to give his State court jurisdiction over the corporation. For this reason, most States have statutes which provide that before a corporation may "do business" within its borders, they must domesticate themselves, and if they fail to do so the Courts of the State will not aid the corporation in enforcing any of their legal rights. In addition, if a corporation does business within the State without domesticating itself (such includes naming an agent for service of process) the corporation will be deemed by statute to have appointed the Secretary of State (or some other State officer) as its agent for the purpose of service of summons.

These statutes are held constitutional since, as noted previously, a corporation is not a person under Art. 4, Sec. 2 of the Constitution and therefore is not entitled to the privileges and immunities of citizens of the several states as are natural persons. This makes the question as to what constitutes "doing business" of great importance when a corporation is suing or being sued in a State other than the one which granted its charter or one in which it has domesticated itself.

"Doing business" means more than carrying out an isolated transaction. The making of a sale or the solicitation of orders does not alone generally constitute "doing business." A corporation is "doing business" within the State when it transacts a substantial part of its entire business therein, and when such local activities have the quality of continuity (as distinguished from a single transaction) as might be evidenced by the investment of capital, maintenance of an office for the transaction of its business, establishment of bank accounts and stock of goods for sale within the State—all attest the corporate intent to avail itself of the privilege to carry on business.

D. Kinds of Corporations

There are two broad categories of corporations—public and private. Public corporations are owned by the general public. An incorporated city is an example. Private corporations usually are organized for the benefit of their individual members. A private corporation may be either a profit or a non-profit corporation. A retail store or a manufacturing corporation are examples of profit corporations. Religious, educational, or charitable organizations are examples of non-profit corporations.

II. CREATION AND EXISTENCE OF A CORPORATION

The right to obtain a corporate charter is granted by Statute which prescribes the procedures to be followed. Generally before a corporation is formed, articles of incorporation, signed by at least three persons (incorporators), must be submitted to the Secretary of State. If these articles conform to the law, the Secretary of State files them in his office. The Secretary of State then issues the charter which, upon receipt, must be filed with the county recorder of the county where the principal office of the corporation is located. Upon such filing, the corporate existence begins. At this time, the stockholders meet and prepare by-laws and elect the corporation's directors and officers. The articles of incorporation generally are required to include:

1. The name of the proposed corporation which must not be such that it may mislead the public nor may it be the same

name of any other corporation in the State.

2. The purpose and powers of the corporation. These should be made sufficiently broad so that the corporation may, if necessary, engage in any type of business in any part of the world.

3. A description of the capital structure which should include the maximum amount of stock authorized and its classification, e.g., common or preferred.

4. Names of the subscribers to the capital stock including the amount subscribed by each as well as the amount paid thereon.

5. The names of the incorporators.

6. The length of time for which the charter is issued.

7. Any other provisions, if legal, may be included. For example, the articles may provide that the corporation is to be a "closed corporation." Thus, a stockholder who wants to sell his stock must offer it to other stockholders before he may offer it to a non-stockholder.

Corporations, after attempted organization, may either be *de jure* or *de facto.* A de jure corporation is one in which the incorporators have complied with all mandatory requirements of the State's incorporation laws. Its existence as a corporation is by virtue of law and its existence cannot be successfully challenged even by the State of incorporation. A de facto corporation results when the incorporators have made minor technical errors in securing the charter which the law overlooks. Only the State granting the charter can challenge its existence because it exists as a corporation in fact and not by right. Thus, if a de facto corporation sues an individual, the individual cannot set forth the defense that a plaintiff is not a corporation.

For a de facto corporation to exist there must be (1) a general law under which it may be organized; (2) a bona-fide attempt in good faith to organize a corporation; and (3) an actual exercise of some corporate powers and functions. A business organization which is not a de jure corporation will not be considered a de facto corporation if it has not attempted in good faith to organize. Thus, where the articles were not filed with the register of deeds in the county, it was held that this defect was so great as to not constitute a bona-fide attempt to organize, and thus not even a de facto corporation existed. Thus, the organizers were held liable as partners. Some courts hold the person acting for the "corporation" personally liable because of breach of implied warranty of a competent principal.

Even when the defect is so great that a de facto corporation does not exist, the organization, under proper circumstances, may be held to be a corporation by estoppel. Here the "incorporators" want to deny the existence of a corporation when a third party sues the "corporation." Here the organizers represent the business to be a corporation when, in fact, no attempt to incorporate has been made, and the third party extended credit in reliance upon the false representation (changed his position). Under such facts, the courts would hold that the incorporators are estopped to deny the company to be a corporation as to such particular third person.

III. CORPORATE POWERS

The charter, which term includes the articles of incorporation and the general laws under which the corporation was created, limits and controls the powers of the corporation. These limitations are binding on the corporation because its existence is made possible only because of the permission granted by the State. In addition, the corporation's powers may be limited by its by-laws as well as by resolutions made by the board of directors. In the event of conflict—for example, articles give permission whereas statutes generally deny powers—the order of precedence is (1) statutes; (2) articles; (3) by-laws; and (4) resolutions.

A. Types of Powers

The powers of a corporation are generally classified as being inherent, expressed, and implied. Inherent powers are incidental to the creation of the corporation and include the right to have a corporate name, to sue and to be sued in such name, to make by-laws, to own and convey property and to have a corporate seal.

Expressed powers are those conferred by the charter and statutes.

Implied powers include those which are essential to the successful prosecution of the corporate purpose. They include all powers reasonably necessary or incidental to the performance of the expressed powers. Thus, an ordinary trading corporation would have implied power to buy, sell and mortgage its stock in trade, and to issue negotiable paper in aid of such transactions.

We have seen that a corporation's powers may be limited by its articles of incorporation and the laws under which its charter was obtained. Since the corporation may enter only into contracts which are necessary to accomplish the purpose for which it was created, the normal tendency is to make the corporate powers as broad as the statutes will permit in order to prevent its contracts from being challenged as being *ultra vires* (see next sub-section). The corporate powers have previously been classified as being inherent, expressed, and implied. The implied powers are the ones which usually cause difficulty since they are the ones frequently challenged as being ultra vires.

Some past cases have held that the power to manufacture firearms does not include the right to manufacture railroad locks; the power to manufacture automobiles does not include the production of explosives or cotton cloth; the power to buy and sell dairy products does not include buying and selling oysters; to manufacture railroad cars and hold real estate necessary for the conduct of its business does not include the laying out of a company-owned town for its employees. On the other hand, it was held the right to manufacture automobiles included the smelting of ore used in such manufacture, and the right to dig for minerals included the right to drill for oil.

It is possible for those powers held not to be implied to be expressly granted to the corporation by its charter or by the statutes under which it was created. If this is so, there is no problem. What we are concerned with is when the charter does not grant the power, will the power be implied?

Let us take some potential corporate powers and see if they would be implied:

1. To make contracts of guarantee. A corporation's power to be an accommodation party for a non-corporate purpose will not be implied, but if such is necessary to complete business of the corporation properly undertaken, the power will be implied.

2. To borrow money and to give mortgages and/or pledge property as security. These acts will be implied when they are necessary to carry out authorized business transactions. The power includes the making of necessary negotiable instruments and contracts.

3. To acquire and hold its own stock. A corporation may acquire its own stock by purchase or in settlement of a debt as long as such does not work an injustice on creditors or stockholders. Statutes frequently regulate such purchases by limiting the acquisition to the extent the corporation has surplus available for dividends. This protects creditors in that the original

capital will be maintained (barring subsequent losses). To protect other stockholders, the courts generally hold that the purchase must be at a fair price in order that non-selling shareholders' interests will not be diluted.

4. To purchase stock in other corporations. Some courts hold this may be done only if expressly authorized, whereas other courts imply such power if the purchase will further legal corporate objectives. Thus, the reason for the acquisition cannot be to restrain trade or to create a monopoly.

5. To purchase and hold title to real and personal property. This will be implied to the extent such is necessary for carrying out the corporate purpose.

6. To enter into partnership agreements. This will not be implied since such would result in other partners acting for the corporation whereas the board of directors elected by the stockholders is the sole body authorized to control and manage the corporation functions. If such were delegated to others by the corporation becoming a partner, the result may be to subject stockholders to risks not contemplated by them when they acquired their interest in the corporation.

B. Ultra Vires Acts

The term "ultra vires" means beyond the powers granted. If in the exercise of the powers granted to it by its charter a corporation exceeds its authority, the act in question may be challenged. As previously mentioned, the corporate powers include implied as well as express powers, and the question of ultra vires generally arises concerning what powers will be implied. The presumption is that in the exercise of the corporate powers the board of directors has acted in good faith and in conformity with the authority granted. Thus, the party pleading "ultra vires" has the burden of proof. The doctrine is applicable only to contracts. It has no application to torts or illegal acts. Fraud by a corporate officer within the scope of his employment, or the negligent driving of a truck by an employee, are obviously ultra vires. Nevertheless, the corporation would be vicariously liable for such acts. An illegal act is one which is wrong regardless of who did it, whereas an ultra vires act is wrong merely because the corporation exceeded its authority.

The state which issued the charter may raise the question of an act being ultra vires, and enjoin the performance of such act, and may even declare a forfeiture of the corporation's charter. Stockholders may also enjoin the performance of an executory ultra vires contract and even may have an executed contract set aside if they act promptly. Creditors cannot generally complain, but when the performance of the contract would or may result in fraudulent diversion of the corporate assets and thereby render the corporation insolvent, it has been held that they can enjoin the performance or have it set aside. In the event the contract is executed, the board of directors and corporate officers may be held personally liable for any loss caused the corporation.

Outside parties, although they may be in some way affected (e.g., competition) by the ultra vires act, cannot enjoin its performance.

As between the corporation and the third party who has entered into the ultra vires contract, the courts will not generally aid either party to rescind a fully executed contract or to enforce a fully executory contract. Third parties have no one to blame since the charter, once filed, becomes a matter of public record, and thus any restrictions as to the corporation purpose is presumed to be known by all persons dealing with the corporation. For this reason, third parties should ascertain the limits of the corporation charter before entering into contracts with the corporation. This argument obviously breaks down in a situation where the board of directors authorizes the purchase of land not for authorized but for speculative purposes, and the third party selling such land to the corporation does not know the secret intent, logically supposing the corporation desires the land for legitimate purposes. In such a case, the third person, therefore, may enforce the contract and the stockholders may hold the directors personally liable for any loss resulting from the unauthorized act.

When the contract is partially executed and partially executory, the courts are not in agreement as to the enforceability of ultra vires contract. A minority of state courts refuse relief on the contract, but allow recovery of what has been parted with in reliance on the contract so as to prevent unjust enrichment by one party at the expense of the party who has substantially performed. If the benefit cannot be returned, these courts allow recovery in quasi-contract for the reasonable value of the benefit conferred. This minority relief differs only slightly from the relief granted by a majority of the courts which is to recognize the contract when it is merely ultra vires and not illegal. The basis of enforcement by the majority rule is estoppel, i.e., both parties are estopped to deny the validity of the contract when part performance demands the courts to recognize it if justice is to prevail. Thus, under either theory, the results would be identical in a case where a corporation secured a loan in excess of the limits set forth in its charter. The majority would enforce the contract and demand the loan be repaid, the minority would require repayment of the loan (return of benefits received) to prevent unjust enrichment.

IV. PROMOTERS

The person who performs the preliminary work necessary to bring the corporation into existence is known as a promoter. This person not only secures the corporation's charter, but also prepares the prospectus as well as other necessary work to enable the procuring of subscribers to the corporation's capital stock. The services performed by the promoter and the expenses which he incurs in organizing the corporation are presumed to be gratuitous. Thus, he is not entitled to payment for his services and/or reimbursement for his expenditures unless there is a statute or a provision in the charter making the corporation liable therefor. Some states' courts hold that the corporation is liable for the reasonable expenses incurred in bringing it into existence. The difference in views results from two different approaches. Some courts feel it would be unjust to hold one liable for expenses they had no part in creating, whereas others feel the corporation should reimburse one for the expenses which inure to its benefit and which were never intended as a gift. All courts allow the promoter to recover reasonable expenses if the corporation, once formed, promises to do so. The promoter would sue in quasi-contract (reasonable value of benefit received by the corporation) and hence no consideration is needed to enforce the promise.

> Example: At first stockholders meeting, a resolution was passed approving the work of this promoter and promising compensation. When the corporation failed to pay, the promoter sued. Held: For plaintiff. Once approved by stockholders, the promoter is entitled to the reasonable value of his services rendered.

Thus, the two views may be summarized as follows:

1. Corporation is not bound to pay promoter unless a statute or charter imposes liability or if no statute, the corporation subsequently promises to pay.
2. Corporation must pay regardless of statute, charter and/or subsequent promise to pay. They accepted the benefits of necessary services which they knew were never intended to be a gift.

It is a general practice for the promoter, in setting up the corporation, to enter into contracts with third persons prior to the securing of the corporate charter. If a third person insists on dealing only with the promoter personally and not with the corporation to be, obviously the promoter is personally liable. Even if the promoter makes the contract for the "corporation," he may be held personally liable on breach of implied warranty of a competent principal. In either of these cases the promoter's liability would end if, after the corporation is formed, the third party agrees to look to the corporation alone, and the corporation and promoter have agreed to this. This would be the same as any other novation.

If the promoter is careful and draws the contracts in a manner which shows the third party did not intend to hold him liable but instead relied on the credit of the future corporation, no personal liability would attach to the promoter. In none of these three cases will the corporation be bound to the contract unless upon its formation it adopts, ratifies, accepts the continuing offer, or there takes place a novation, either actual or by implication. These are four theories used to bind the promoter's contract to the corporation.

Technically, the corporation cannot ratify because, at the time the promoter acted as a purported agent of the corporation, there was no existing principal. For this reason, the courts say the corporation adopted the contract, or the corporation accepted a continuing offer. Or, a corporation may become liable because of a novation, i.e., the corporation, promoter, and third person all agree that the contract is to be between the corporation and the third person. This is generally done expressly, but it may be by implication. The promoter's assent is generally always implied. The corporation's assent may be express or implied. If the corporation accepts the benefit of the contract with full knowledge of the facts, its assent to be bound by the contract will be implied. This would not apply when the corporation has no choice in electing to accept the benefits or to reject them. Such would be the case as to the promoter's contract with the attorney who secured the corporation charter. For the corporation to be liable in such a case, the corporation must expressly consent to the novation. To release the promoter's personal liability on the contract, the third party must consent to the novation, either expressly or impliedly. In other words, you cannot preclude the third party's rights against the promoter merely by having the corporation adopt the contract. If there merely is an adoption by the corporation, the corporation is bound and the promoter is a surety.

The promoter owes the duty of a fiduciary to the corporation and will be held liable if he attempts to gain personal advantage from his position of trust and confidence. He, like all agents, cannot make secret profits in dealing with the corporation or its stockholders. Thus, if a promoter buys an option with a view to selling it to a corporation to be organized, he must make a full disclosure of its cost, etc., when he sells or exchanges it for stock of the corporation. Failure to make a full disclosure results in the corporation being able to recover any secret profit realized by him on the deal. Thus, to protect himself, the promoter should (1) make a full disclosure to an independent board of directors or to all the stockholders; or (2) after the corporation is organized get the stockholders to ratify his contract with the corporation; or (3) buy all the stock himself. In the latter case, the promoter is the sole stockholder and thus assent by the corporation is presumed. Even here the courts will hold such invalid if the promoter's over-all purpose is merely a scheme to validate the transaction, and the scheme contemplated a resale of the stock to the public and is done without making a full disclosure of the facts.

V. CORPORATE LIABILITIES

The liabilities of the corporation may arise from the torts and crimes of its agents acting within the scope of their authority as well as from contracts properly entered into by its agents.

From the study of agency law, we have learned that the person committing a tort or a crime is always liable and that the principal is also frequently held responsible. A corporation is liable for the torts committed by its agents while acting within the scope of its authority just like any other principal. We have already seen that the corporation cannot defend on the basis that the tort was ultra vires, for such may be used only in actions on contracts.

A corporation is liable for crimes when the wrong committed provides for a punishment capable of being applied to a corporation. A corporation cannot be arrested and imprisoned, but its property may be taken and/or its charter forfeited, either as compensation for a private wrong or as punishment for a public wrong. A corporation may be guilty of conspiring to restrain trade and/or to gain a monopoly in violation of the Antitrust Acts, for violating income tax and pure food and drug laws, and even may be cited for contempt of court if it refuses to obey a court order. While a corporation cannot commit crimes involving intent (murder for example), it may be held liable criminally and/or civilly for non-feasance (failure to act when it had a duty, e.g., render an income tax return) as well as misfeasance (act negligently in violation of a law).

VI. CORPORATION STOCKS

A share of stock is a contract between the issuing corporation and the owner of the stock. The stock certificate, like any written contract, is merely evidence of the contract—evidence of the owner's interest in the corporation and the rights he acquires because of his ownership. The stock certificate is not property but is merely a written acknowledgment by the corporation that the person named therein is a stockholder. It is not essential that certificates be issued to stockholders. A person who properly invests in a corporation becomes a stockholder even though no certificate is issued. His name on the corporation books is sufficient evidence of his ownership.

A stockholder does not have any direct claim on the specific assets owned by the corporation. A stockholder's rights are to share in earnings when properly declared by the board of directors, to share in the distribution of assets in the event of dissolution, and to indirectly participate in the management of the corporation through his right to vote his shares at the stockholders' meetings. These will be discussed in detail later.

A. Stock Subscriptions

Pre-incorporation subscription agreements are generally treated as offers by the subscribers which the corporation may accept once its charter has been granted. Being a mere offer, the subscriber may withdraw his agreement any time before the corporate charter is issued and the offer accepted. Once the corporation is formed, the offer of the subscriber may be impliedly accepted by calling for payment and once this is done, the subscriber becomes a stockholder even though the stock is not fully paid for. Of course, the subscription contract may expressly provide that a subscriber is entitled to vote and receive dividends only on the shares fully paid for.

Post-incorporation subscriptions may be either a contract to purchase stock or a present subscription to stock. If a contract to purchase stock is broken, the corporation can only sue for damages, since the subscriber is not a stockholder until the contract is performed and the stock certificate issued. In a present subscription to stock, the subscriber becomes a stockholder as soon as the agreement is entered into and is, therefore, liable to the corporation for the full amount agreed upon in the contract. This distinction is equally applicable should the creditors have to enforce the corporation's rights due to its insolvency. A receiver in bankruptcy would have no greater rights than the defunct corporation.

B. Par

Par value stock is stock which has an arbitrary monetary figure placed upon the share of stock, whereas no-par stock does not have a stated value. If par value stock is issued at a discount, creditors of the corporation may hold such stockholders liable for such differences between par value and the amount paid, if the corporation should become unable to meet its obligations. Creditors are not prevented from doing this even though the corporation could not have enforced the collection due to their agreement and the issuing of the stock marked "paid in full." When the corporation issues stock at a discount but marks "paid in full," if the original purchaser should sell his shares to a bona-fide purchaser who had no knowledge of the original sale at a discount, even creditors would not to able to sue for the unpaid balance. If the purchaser had notice of the original sale at a discount, then his liability to creditors would be the same as though he were an original subscriber. If creditors knew that the stock was sold at a discount, some courts will not allow them to require stockholders to pay in the balance on such stock. The basis here is that the creditors have not been misled and therefore no fraud occurred. (Fraud theory is explained below.)

In contrast, no-par stock is deemed fully paid regardless of its sale price, and the holders of such shares are never held liable to the corporation or its creditors. It may be issued for money or property of any amount or value that the directors find reasonable. Some states require the stockholders to fix the sale price of no-par stock. Other states require a minimum value placed on no-par stock by the corporate charter or by its by-laws. This "stated value" is then treated like par value stock.

Watered stock is the term used to describe stock issued as fully paid for money at a discount or for property the value of which is not equal to the par value of the stock given in exchange for the property. We have seen that if the stock is issued by the corporation as "fully paid," the corporation cannot recover the difference from the stockholders, but creditors who do not know the facts of the stock's issuance may collect such discount from the original subscribers and/or from subsequent holders who acquired the stock knowing it had not been fully paid for. When the stock is issued for money there is no question as to the extent the stock is "watered," but when issued for property a valuation of such property must be made in order to determine the extent the stock is "watered."

In placing a value on the property given in exchange for stock, the courts generally follow one of two rules to determine the adequacy of payment. The true value rule requires the property to be equal to the face value of the stock issued. The alternative rule is one of good faith and is followed by most courts. Under this rule, the courts realize honest men may reach different conclusions as to value. If it is shown that the determination as to the value of the property was made by the board of directors in good faith and without fraud, such will be conclusively presumed to be correct, and the courts will not allow such to be questioned.

Assuming that watered stock has been issued and the issuing corporation has become insolvent, the suit by creditors to make the subscribers of the watered stock pay in the balance may be maintained under the trust fund theory or the fraud theory.

Under the trust fund theory, the capital stock is treated as representing a trust fund for the benefits of creditors, and the rights of the creditors have been violated when the stock was sold for less than its par value. The law implies a promise by original subscribers to pay the difference to the corporation if such is needed to satisfy claims by creditors.

Under the fraud theory, a purchaser of stock marked "fully paid," when in reality he did not pay par, has misrepresented a fact which, if justifiably relied on by creditors, constitutes fraud. The creditor suffers damages if the corporate assets are insufficient to pay his claim in full. Thus, the creditor may recover from stockholders the unpaid balance. This theory precludes recovery by a creditor who knew that the stock was issued at a discount since he cannot show reliance, whereas under the trust fund theory such creditor might well have recovered.

These problems of watered stock and stockholders contingent liability apply only to new corporations for the sale of its original shares. Once the corporation is active and its stock has an established market value, the corporation may sell its unissued stock at any price without the possibility of this contingent liability attaching thereto. Also, treasury stock (stock issued as fully paid and then reacquired by the issuing corporation through purchase or as a gift) may be sold at any price without the purchaser assuming this contingent liability. If these exceptions were not made, a corporation in desperate need of additional risk capital would find it very difficult, if not impossible, to acquire it by sale of its capital stock.

C. Common and Preferred Stock

Corporations issue primarily two kinds of stock, common stocks and preferred stock. In the absence of expressed provisions to the contrary, stock issued by the corporation has the right to vote but does not enjoy any preference over any other class of stock as to dividends or assets in the event of dissolution. When such preference is given to a class of stock, such stock is generally known as preferred stock.

The term "preferred stock" does not have a general meaning. We have previously mentioned that a stock certificate is a mere contract. The purchaser should therefore read the statutes, charter, by-laws, and provisions on the stock certificate to see what his rights are—to learn what preference the preferred stock has over the common stock. Some preferences which might be granted are: preference as to dividends over common stock, such dividends being either cumulative or non-cumulative and/or participating or non-participating; preference as to assets in event of dissolution over other stockholders, but never prior to creditors; the right to convert the preferred stock into common stock or bonds (of course, the right to convert a stock to a bond would be subject to the rights of creditors to the same extent as though the corporation were purchasing such stock); whether the preferred stock may be redeemable at a fixed date; this, too, subject to the rights of creditors. As mentioned before, the preferred stock has the right to vote unless such is expressly denied to the stock contract.

To call a stock "preferred," without any other express provisions concerning the dividend preference, results in the stock being cumulative preferred but not participating preferred. Cumulative means that the dividends, if not paid, cumulate and any dividends in arrears must be paid before a dividend may be paid to the common stockholder. Participating means that the preferred will share in dividends equally with the common stockholders. In such instance, the preferred receive their preferential dividend, then common receive an equal per share divident, and any additional dividend declarataion will be shared equally by the common and preferred stockholders on a per share basis.

VII. STOCKHOLDER CONTROL AND RIGHTS

The person having legal title to the stock ordinarily has the right to attend and vote his stock at the stockholders' meetings. This right may be denied to a class of stockholders (e.g., preferred stockholders) by the corporation's charter unless the statutes under which the charter was granted provide that all stockholders must be given the right to vote. In the event that the stockholder is dead, bankrupt, or incompetent, the right to vote his shares is vested in the person designated by law to take over control and management of said person's property. This is an exception to the general rule that the registered shareholder on the corporate records is the one entitled to vote the stock.

The books and records of the corporation determine who are its stockholders and thus, who have the right to vote. There is no privity of contract between the mere holder of the certificate and the corporation, and he is not a real member of that organization until his name is upon the books. For this reason, it is held that the pledgor of stock has all the rights of a stockholder, including the right to vote, as he is still the legal owner as well as the owner of record on the corporate books. Of course, the pledgor may transfer legal title to the pledgee who, in turn, records his title with the corporation. In such an event the pledgee, being the owner of record, would be entitled to vote.

A. Voting Trusts

There have been instances where stockholders have created a voting trust in order to assure continuity of voting policy as specified on the agreement and thereby keep present management intact, or accomplish some other policy purpose. This is accomplished by transferring title of the stock to a trustee, in order that he may become the owner of record on the corporation's books and be entitled to vote the stock. The trustee, in exchange for the stock, issues trust certificates evidencing the stock surrendered to him. These agreements, if made in good faith and for the betterment of the corporation and apparent advantage of all stockholders, are valid and not contrary to public policy, so long as no fraud or other wrong is committed upon other stockholders and the period of continuance is not unreasonably long. Thus, a trust cannot be set up for a period beyond the life of the participators or upon condition of an office to be granted.

B. Voting Pool

Another device frequently used by a group of stockholders, in order to effectively control the corporation, is the voting pool agreement. Here, a group of stockholders agrees to vote their stock as a unit in accordance with their majority vote. Such agreements are enforceable if they are not contrary to public policy. Since each stockholder casts his own vote at the regular stockholders' meeting, the presiding officer must accept the vote as cast, and cannot compel a stockholder to cast his vote in accordance with the agreement. Thus, other members of the pool would have to sue for specific performance.

C. Transfer of Stock

Under the common law, the ownership of stock was transferred by making an assignment—just like an ordinary contract was assigned. Like other contracts, the assignability could be restricted by making the necessary provisions in the stock certificate and the charter or by-laws of the corporation. In this regard, the courts frown on all restraints on alienation of property rights, and will uphold such restraints on the transferability of stock only if reasonable, for a valid purpose, and are made known to the stockholder at the time he acquires his stock. Thus, the restriction should be in the charter or, better yet, on the certificate itself. A restriction in the by-laws alone will not suffice, as by-laws are not binding until one becomes a stockholder and do not bind third persons unless they have had notice of them at the time they acted.

Thus, if a person buys stock with notice that it can be transferred only if certain corporate officials or all stockholders consent, such restriction would be void as being contrary to public policy in that it unreasonably restrains the free alienation of property. The same would be true if the purchaser of stock agreed never to transfer ownership of his stock. On the other hand, a provision requiring a stockholder to sell his stock to an outsider only after offering it first to the corporation or other stockholders would be valid and enforceable. Such restraint may be needed to keep rivals from acquiring control of the corporation or to keep the corporation supplied with stock to issue to its employees as a method of promoting loyalty and good management.

Today many states have in force the Uniform Stock Transfer Act which makes the stock certificate a quasi-negotiable instrument. Thus, if a certificate is endorsed in blank and then lost or stolen, a bona-fide purchaser from the finder or thief would get good title, but if the certificate is lost or stolen, the bona-fide purchaser from a finder or thief who forged the owner's endorsement would not get good title. Under the common law, a certificate was non-negotiable, and an assignee never gets better rights than his transferor had.

Under either method of transfer (common law or the Uniform Stock Transfer Act), the transfer is not complete as to the corporation until the corporation has been informed. This is done by surrendering the old certificate to the corporation who will cancel it and issue a new certificate to the purchaser and enter the purchaser on the corporate records as being the owner entitled to dividends, voting rights, etc. Until the transfer has been made on the corporate records, the corporation is protected if it pays dividends to the owner of record on their books.

If the corporation issues a duplicate certificate to a stockholder who transfers it and his original to a bona-fide purchaser for value, the corporation will be liable to such bona-fide purchaser as though both were valid. Also, if a thief forges an endorsement and presents the certificate to the corporation who issues him a new certificate, the thief can transfer good title to a bona-fide purchaser. The corporation, by issuing the certificate, warrants its validity. In addition, the stockholder whose name was forged has a claim against the corporation because he cannot be deprived of his title by a forged endorsement. The corporation would have a cause of action against the thief. Thus, the corporation's liability is similar to a bank which honors a forged check. This similarity will be apparent after a study of negotiable instruments.

D. Stockholder Information

The corporation has the duty to keep records and to supply stockholders with annual financial statements. In addition, the stockholder under common law has a qualified right to inspect and copy the records. If the corporation refused, he could sue for a court order to allow this by showing he was a stockholder, had demanded inspection for a proper purpose (e.g., who are other stockholders; e.g., to determine whether he should sell his stock and at what price), and at a reasonable time and that the request was refused. Today, many statutes make this an absolute right and to prevent it, the corporation must show the stockholder's motives are improper (e.g., idle curiosity, wants information to give to a competitor).

E. Pre-emptive Right

If the corporation increases its capital stock as authorized by the stockholders and approved by the State by amendment of the corporation charter, the existing stockholders generally have a preference to purchase such stock in proportion to the number of shares presently held by them. The right is needed to maintain a stockholder's proportionate voting power and financial interest in the surplus. The right does not apply to treasury stock, unsold portions of original authorized capital stock, or stock issued in exchange for property (not sold for money). But even in these latter cases, a stockholder may get equitable relief by showing such is being done by the directors to gain some unfair advantage.

Where stock is non-participating and has no voting right, a pre-emptive right would not apply. It will always apply to common stock, and in one case a court held it would apply to 7% participating preferred stock when the additional authorized stock was common stock because the increase in common shares might reduce the participating preferred stockholder's share in the profits.

F. Right to Dividends

In wasting asset corporations (mining, oil and gas, etc.) profits available for dividends may be determined without deducting any depletion expenses unless such is required by contract (a bond indenture, for example, might include such requirement). Other than for this exception, statutes generally provide that dividends must be paid only out of surplus or current year's profits. This restriction on dividend payments is necessary (since stockholders have limited liability) to protect creditors and preferred stockholders who would be the ones most likely to suffer loss if dividends were permitted to be paid out of capital, and thus impair the corporation's capital. The provisions made in state statutes concerning a corporation's right to declare a dividend are so varied it is felt to explore all possibilities would be more confusing than useful.

Merely because a corporation could legally declare a dividend does not mean the stockholders have an absolute right to have it declared and paid. The determination of when and how much should be paid out as dividends is discretionary with the board of directors, and who must by formal resolution declare dividends before stockholders have any vested rights to have the earnings of the corporation paid to them. This is true as to preferred stock dividends as well as common. Of course the directors cannot arbitrarily and fraudulently abuse this discretion. If they withhold the payment of dividends other than as required for the corporation's success (e.g., build-up of working capital, logical expansion of plant, etc.), the stockholders may sue in equity for a court order to require the directors to pay out dividends. To this extent the stockholders are merely asking for specific performance of their stock contract in that they acquired the stock for a source of income. On the other hand, dividends cannot lawfully be declared and paid to even preferred stockholders when the corporation has no surplus available for distribution. When such was attempted in order to prevent the preferred stockholders from succeeding to the right to vote (preferred stock contract gave them voting right if dividends were missed any three consecutive years), the court nullified the dividend on the basis that it was unlawfully declared.

Even though dividend declarations are generally discretionary with the board of directors, such discretion cannot be arbitrary and/or fraudulent. This is emphasized by court rulings which hold that when non-cumulative preferred stock is issued, the board of directors must issue dividends annually if the corporation could lawfully declare them. Other courts allow the directors to absolutely decide the question and in the event the dividend is not declared, the preferred stock just isn't entitled to a dividend for that year.

Once a dividend has been lawfully declared, the stockholders' rights are vested and the board of directors cannot revoke the dividend without the unanimous consent of the stockholders. Unless otherwise provided, the dividend vests upon its being declared. For this reason, the directors generally state a date of record (vesting) and date of payment. This protects the corporation if they pay the dividend to the stockholder of record even though such stockholder may have sold his stock prior to the time of payment.

If the directors of a solvent corporation pay a dividend out of capital, such unlawful dividend may be recovered by the creditors from the stockholders who had notice of its being illegal and from the directors personally—but not from stockholders who had no such notice. If a director dissents to the dividend, his liability is negated. On the other hand, if the corporation was insolvent or if the dividend rendered the corporation insolvent, such would be considered as fraud on creditors and they could recover the dividends from the directors personally and/or the stockholders who received such unlawful dividend, regardless of whether they had notice of its illegality or not.

G. Suit by Stockholder

A stockholder may sue the corporation if he suffers damages resulting from the fraud of the corporation's agents acting within the scope of their authority (e.g., fraudulent misrepresentation of stock, in inducing its purchase), or if the directors arbitrarily and without just cause refuse to declare dividends, but a stockholder cannot sue third persons who cause injuries to the corporation. The corporation, being a legal entity, should bring such suits in its own name. Where the directors make a secret profit which rightfully belongs to the corporation, the directors obviously are not going to have the corporation sue themselves for such profits, and in such cases and similar cases where the corporation fails to enforce or defend its rights, a stockholder may sue or defend on behalf of the corporation.

In bringing such a suit, the stockholder must plead that he

has demanded the board of directors to bring the suit and that they have refused, or that such demand would have been useless as the majority of the directors are in collusion to defraud the corporation. Since the corporation has refused to be a plaintiff, it is joined as a defendant since it is a necessary party to the action. If the stockholder wins, the judgment is in favor of the corporation, but a part of the judgment may be awarded the stockholder to reimburse him for the expense of the lawsuit. Obviously, the shareholder indirectly benefits from the judgment in favor of the corporation to the extent of his pro rata ownership in the corporation.

VIII. MEETINGS OF STOCKHOLDERS

Basically, the stockholders control the corporation through their power to elect the board of directors at their annual meeting. The statutes generally require that the charter prescribe the date, time, and place of such regular meetings and the by-laws generally prescribe the methods of calling any additional (special) meetings. By-laws generally provide for the selection of officers and their duties, how the by-laws may be amended, notice required to hold a special meeting of stockholders, time and place of meeting of directors, etc. These by-laws are binding on all stockholders, but since they are not matters of public record like the charter they do not bind third persons unless they had notice of them. By-laws to be valid must be reasonably consistent with the charter and statutes and consistent with the purpose for which the corporation was formed.

No notice need be given stockholders of the regular annual meeting as to time, place, or what business will be transacted since such is set out in the charter and all stockholders are presumed to have notice of all charter provisions (generally corporations give notice even though not required). But special meetings must be called according to the by-laws which must include notice of time, place, and business to be transacted. Only the business indicated in the notice may be acted upon. Failure to give proper notice of a meeting nullifies any action taken at such meeting unless all stockholders attend and participate and thus impliedly waive the notice requirement.

Thus, the majority of stockholders control and direct the corporation over the long run by electing directors who will carry out their desires. Even though the majority control the lawful exercise of the powers conferred by the corporate charter, to effect a fundamental change in business requires unanimous consent of the stockholders unless the charter or by-laws specify less. Many charters provide for a two-thirds majority only. Stockholders have no right to do the normal management functions directly as this is conferred upon the directors and officers exclusively.

In all meetings a legal quorum is required as provided by the charter or by-laws. If no provisions are made to the contrary, those present constitute a quorum, and a majority vote by the quorum will be sufficient to carry an item of ordinary business, but to effectuate a fundamental change in business or purpose requires unanimous consent or such consent as required by the charter or by-laws. This latter requirement is based on the fact that the charter is a contract between the corporation and the stockholders which cannot be changed without the consent of the contracting parties. An exception is made when a corporation cannot produce a reasonable profit. In such case, a majority can force liquidation of the corporation.

At common law each stockholder had one vote per share but directors were voted as a group—by slate. Thus, a person or group with 51% of the stock would elect all the directors and the minority stockholders would have no representation. Today, by statute, most stockholders are given the right to cumulative voting under which such method the stockholder has the number of votes he has shares multiplied by the number of directors to be elected, and is allowed to place all the votes on one candidate or divide it as he desires. This concentration of voting power gives greater assurance that minority stockholders will be represented on the board of directors.

A proxy is a power of attorney used by a stockholder to authorize another to vote for him as his agent. Usually no consideration is given for the proxy and thus it is revokable any time before it is exercised unless it is "coupled with an interest." If a second proxy is given, the first proxy is held to be revoked by implication. Directors are not allowed to vote by proxy because they are fiduciaries, and are elected because of their personal knowledge and skill in business matters. At common law even stockholders could not vote by proxy.

IX. DIRECTORS AND OFFICERS

The initial directors may be named in the charter. With this exception, the stockholders elect the directors, the principal agents of the corporation in carrying on its ordinary business. They cannot effectuate a fundamental change in the corporate powers purpose, as such is reserved to the stockholders as outlined above. Also, notice required for regular and special stockholders meetings apply to regular and special board of directors' meetings. Barring statutes, charter or by-law provisions to the contrary, a director need not be a stockholder to qualify being a director and a director is not entitled to any compensation. Compensation is ordinarily provided for in the charter. If a director performs unusual services not generally performed by a director, he may recover in quasi-contract for the reasonable value of such service. Better practice is to fix compensation of officers and directors in the by-laws in order to avoid disputes.

Directors must act as a unit, and not as individuals. Unless they act as a unit at a board meeting properly called, their actions will not be binding on the corporation. A majority of directors create a quorum, and a majority of the quorum will carry a proposition. Directors are fiduciaries and must act in good faith toward the stockholders' interest which they represent. They must, at all times, exercise reasonable care, skill, and diligence in fulfilling their duties. It is no excuse for a director not to possess such skills because by accepting his job he warrants he has such qualifications required to properly discharge his duties. Honest errors in judgment are an exception to this rule, and any loss resulting from such will not render a director liable to stockholders.

Directors, as mentioned, and officers are fiduciaries as to the corporation and the stockholders, and their rights, duties and liabilities are governed by the principles of agency. Consequently, directors and officers may not make secret profits. They may not enter into any contract, directly or indirectly, between themselves and the corporation without acting in good faith by disclosing all pertinent facts to a quorum of disinterested directors. A director contracting with the corporation cannot be counted to determine whether they have a quorum, may not vote on the issue, and some courts say he may not even attend the meeting where such business is discussed. Courts have applied the above rules to a director who participated in voting on a resolution fixing his salary.

Generally speaking, directors and officers have no duty to the stockholders as individuals. If they perform their duties to the corporation, the interest of the individual stockholders is automatically taken care of. But when a director or officer deals as an individual with a stockholder in the purchase of the latter's stock in the corporation, the question arises as to whether the director or officer must disclose the superior knowledge he possesses resulting from the position in the corporation which he occupies. The majority of courts do not require such a disclosure. The minority view is that the director or officer is a quasi-trustee to the stockholders. They need not disclose information as to market or book value, etc., which is available to all stockholders, but they must disclose facts they possess which are not accessible to stockholders and which, if known, generally would affect the selling price.

X. CORPORATE DISSOLUTION

At the expiration of the time specified in the charter that the corporation is to exist, the corporation is automatically dissolved unless the stockholders vote to renew the charter and such request is honored by the State.

Even before the charter expires, the stockholders may consent to dissolve the corporation. This right is given to a bare majority in the event that the corporation is insolvent and/or can only operate at a loss. Other than for this exception, unless the statutes or charter provide for a lesser number having this right, such dissolution requires unanimous consent of all stockholders. Corporations engaged in "public interest" business can dissolve only with the permission of the State.

The state's attorney general may bring a court action to cancel the charter of a corporation which has violated its charter (ultra vires acts), committed illegal acts (restraint of trade), or merely failed to function and/or pay its franchise taxes for the statutory period. Such action may be brought only by the State which, in effect, is merely asking for recision (forfeiture of charter), a remedy frequently granted for breach of contract.

If *A* and *B* corporation unite and become *C* corporation, *A* and *B* corporations being dissolved, such is known as a consolidation. The new corporation (*C*) takes over the assets of the old (*A* and *B*) corporations subject to their (*A* and *B*) liabilities. On the other hand, if *A* took over *B*'s assets and liabilities and *B* dissolved—*A* continuing in existence—such is known as a merger.

The rights and duties of parties during and after dissolution are: stockholders have limited liability except as to unpaid subscriptions and/or discounts on acquisition of stock as previously described; and the corporate assets are used first to pay creditors and corporate debts, in full. The preferred stockholders have next claim on the corporate assets and this includes cumulated unpaid dividends as well as the par value of their stock. Any remaining assets are then paid to the holders of common stock on a pro rata basis.

Chapter 6

NEGOTIABLE INSTRUMENTS

I. INTRODUCTION

A. History

Bills of Exchange were developed as convenient commercial devices by Italian traders in the thirteenth century. Knowledge of their instruments and their use spread northward to France and thence to England. The rules governing the use of these instruments were at first inadequate and confusing, but after a time they crystallized. They were first codified in France and later, in 1882, England codified the law of negotiable instruments by passing the Bills of Exchange Act.

These European laws were transplanted to the United States by the early colonists. Because of the sovereignty of the various states, a different set of rules was developed in each state. As commerce among the states increased it became apparent that greater uniformity in the law governing negotiable instruments was something worth attaining. In 1895 delegates were appointed to the National Conference of Commissioners on Uniform State Laws to revise and codify the law of negotiable instruments. The conference selected the best of the various state rules and completed its draft in 1896. This draft, the Uniform Negotiable Instrument Law, was eventually adopted in almost identical form by all of the states. Thus, the Uniform Negotiable Instruments Law is really a series of laws and not one law.

The Negotiable Instruments Law applies only to negotiable instruments, but it is used to determine, in the first instance, whether or not an instrument is negotiable. Thus, the law is applied to non-negotiable instruments only as a test to show they are not negotiable. If found to be non-negotiable, ordinary contract law applies and they are transferable only by assignment.

B. Negotiations vs. Assignment

The rights one has under an ordinary contract are transferred by assignment, whereas the rights possessed by the owner of a negotiable instrument are transferred by negotiation. This distinction is important because we have seen that an assignee can acquire no better rights than his assignor had—but a transferee of a negotiable instrument may obtain greater rights than his transferor possessed providing the transferee qualifies as a holder in due course. A holder in due course (See N.I.L. Sec. 52) takes the instrument free from certain defenses (personal defenses, e.g., fraud in the inducement, failure of consideration, etc.) which the obligor could have successfully asserted against the original payee. This allowing of a negotiable instrument to improve in quality as it is negotiated is the fundamental principle of negotiable instruments. It is desired that these instruments shall approximate money and thereby pass freely from hand to hand.

To illustrate the distinction between negotiable and non-negotiable instruments, suppose *A* has two contracts with *B*. One of the contracts is for the sale of lumber to *B* for which *B* agrees to pay $1000; the other is a negotiable promissory note in the principal amount of $1000 given by *B* to *A*. *A* offers *C* both of the contracts for $950 each, and *C* accepts and pays *A* for the two contracts. The date of the contract payments arrives, and *C* calls on *B* for the payment of the two obligations. *B* refuses to pay, claiming both were procured by fraud on the part of *A*. *C* sues *B* on the two contracts and *B* is able to prove his defense of fraud in the inducement. In the case of the lumber contract, the defense of fraud will be good because an assignee of a non-negotiable contract takes the contract subject to all defenses that would be good as against the assignor. In the case of the promissory note, *C* will prevail because a holder in due course of a negotiable promissory note takes it free from personal defenses.

Only promissory notes, drafts, and checks will be included in our consideration of negotiable instruments. Other types of instruments ("quasi-negotiable" instruments) such as warehouse receipts, bills of lading, and stock certificates, which possess certain features of negotiability, have been previously discussed.

C. Definitions

N.I.L. Sec. 184 defines a negotiable promissory note as being an unconditional promise in writing made by one person (maker) to another (payee) signed by the maker engaging to pay on demand, or at a fixed or determinable time, a sum certain in money to order or to bearer.

N.I.L. Sec. 185 defines a check as being a bill of exchange drawn on a bank payable on demand, and Sec. 126 defines a bill of exchange as being an unconditional order in writing addressed by one person (drawer), to another (drawee), signed by the person giving it (drawer), requiring the person to whom it is addressed (drawee) to pay on demand or at a fixed or determinable future time a sum certain in money to order or to bearer. The person to whom the drawee is to pay the money is known as the payee.

From these definitions one can readily see that a promissory note is a two-party instrument (maker and payee), whereas a bill of exchange (draft, trade acceptance, check, etc.) is a three-party instrument (drawer, drawee, and payee).

Many students gain the impression in studying negotiable instruments that if the instrument is non-negotiable that it is not enforceable. This is not true. Contracts, including non-negotiable instruments, are enforceable under the Law of Contracts. The rights one has in contract may be transferred by assignment. Since rights one has in a negotiable instrument are transferred by a "negotiation" and since the laws dealing with assignments and negotiation are vastly different, it is important to know whether an instrument is or is not negotiable in order to determine which law governs—but not to determine whether we have a valid contract.

II. ILLUSTRATIONS OF NEGOTIABLE INSTRUMENTS

A. Promissory Note

$100.00 Lincoln, Nebraska
September 1, 1961

For value received, I promise to pay to the order of Richard Roe, on January 1, 1962, the sum of $100.00, together with interest thereon from date hereof until paid, at the rate of 5% per annum.

/s/ John Doe

1. John Doe is called the maker of the note.
2. Richard Roe is called the payee of the note.

3. Only the underlined portions are absolutely essential for a negotiable note.

B. Bill of Exchange (Draft)

$100.00 Lincoln, Nebraska
September 1, 1961

Pay to the order of Richard Roe on January 1, 1962, the sum of $100.00, together with interest thereon from date hereof at the rate of 5% per annum.

/s/ John Doe

Wm. Smith
Omaha, Nebraska

1. John Doe is called the drawer of this bill.
2. Richard Roe is called the payee of this bill.
3. Wm. Smith is called the drawee of this bill.
4. Only the underlined portions are absolutely essential for a negotiable bill.
5. If the drawee had been a bank, the instrument would be called a check (N.I.L. Sec. 185).
6. If the drawee and drawer had both been banks, the instrument would be called a bank draft.
7. If the drawee and drawer had been the same bank, the instrument would be called a cashier's check.

III. NATURE AND REQUISITES OF NEGOTIABLE INSTRUMENTS

A. Requisites of Negotiability

The Negotiable Instrument Law contains the tests which must be applied to determine the negotiability or non-negotiability of any instrument. Since these tests are entirely formal, it is possible for one who is familiar with the law to tell at a glance whether or not an instrument is negotiable. The requirements for an instrument to be negotiable as set out in Sec. 1 of the N.I.L. are:

1. Writing Required

It must be in writing. There is no such thing as an oral negotiable instrument. A negotiable instrument must be something that can be passed from one person to another. It may be written in ink, pencil, crayon, or carved in wood or stone. The writing must be in a permanent form. Checks written on the side of a hog or carved on a watermelon have been honored on TV programs, but such practice would obviously not be normally accepted.

2. SIGNED BY MAKER OR DRAWER

It must be signed by the maker or drawer. This requirement is the same as for all written contracts. One may sign an assumed name if done in good faith, or one may sign through an agent (N.I.L. Sec. 18 and 19). It is not good practice to use a rubber stamp for a signature, but a rubber stamp is a valid signature if such was the intent of the user. The signature of the party creating a negotiable instrument need not appear at the end thereof. If his name is written by him in any part of the instrument with the intent to sign or for the purpose of authenticating the instrument, it is sufficient to bind him.

3. MUST CONTAIN AN UNCONDITIONAL PROMISE OR ORDER

It must contain an unconditional promise or order to pay a sum certain in money. There must be an unconditional promise in the case of a promissory note and an unconditional order in the case of a bill of exchange. "Unconditional" means that the promise or order must be absolute, subject to no qualifications or contingencies. The promise or order must not contain any "ifs." It must carry the general personal credit of the maker or drawer. Thus, a simple "I owe Jane Jones $5.00" or "Please pay John Jones $5.00" are not negotiable instruments since there is lacking the unconditional promise or order to pay, a necessary requisite of a negotiable instrument. Thus, a note "payable out of rent proceeds" is not a negotiable instrument because such note does not carry the general credit of the maker and is conditional upon there being adequate rent proceeds to liquidate the note. The same may be said when the following appeared in a note: "This note is given in payment of merchandise and is to be liquidated by payments received on account of sale of such merchandise."

To further illustrate the requirement that a negotiable instrument contain an unconditional promise or order, suppose *A* makes a promissory note payable to *B* upon the arrival of the *Queen Elizabeth* in New York harbor. This is not an unconditional promise because the *Queen Elizabeth* may not complete her next voyage or may never be routed to New York again. Even if the *Queen Elizabeth* docks in New York the day after this note is given to *B*, the note still does not meet the test for negotiability. The test of negotiability is applied and the instrument's negotiability is judged as of the time it was made. This is explained by Sec. 4 of the N.I.L. which states . . . "an instrument payable upon a contingency is not negotiable, and the happening of the event does not cure the defect."

But suppose *A* makes a promissory note payable to *B* upon the death of Fidel Castro. The promise is unconditional because everyone is certain to die although the date of one's death is indefinite.

4. There Must Be a Sum Certain in Money

The instrument must contain an unconditional promise or order to pay a sum certain in money. The sum must be either certain or ascertainable from the face of the instrument. Some uncertainties are permitted as provided by Sec. 2 of the N.I.L. For example, the sum payable is certain although it is to be paid with interest. Without this provision one could argue that since it cannot be known when a demand instrument will be paid, the amount of interest cannot be definitely known and therefore the sum is not certain.

Other allowable uncertainties provided for by N.I.L. Sec. 2 are provisions for payment by installments which may also include a provision that upon default in payment of any installment or of interest the whole shall become due and provisions for costs of collection or attorney's fees in event suit must be brought to collect the instrument.

The instrument must be payable in money, but it need not be United States currency. Obviously, a promise to pay a good horse would not be a sum certain in money, but if an option is given the holder to take payment in money or some other commodity, negotiability is not destroyed because then the instrument does contain an unconditional promise or order to pay a sum certain in money. If the option is given to the maker to pay money or a commodity, negotiability is destroyed, because then the instrument does not contain an unconditional promise or order to pay a sum certain in money.

5. Must Be Payable on Demand or at a Fixed or Determinable Future Time

The instrument must be payable on demand or at a fixed or determinable future time. An instrument is payable at a determinable future time when it is payable at a fixed period after the occurrence of a special event, which is certain to happen, though the time of happening be uncertain. But remember, an instrument payable on a contingency is not negotiable and the happening of the event does not cure the defect.

An instrument is payable on demand where it is expressed to be payable on demand, or at sight, or on presentment, or in which no time for payment is expressed.

The following meet the requirements: "Pay to John Jones on demand"; "Pay to John Jones on Dec. 1, 1968"; "Payable on or before 60 days after date"; "Payable 10 days after death of John Jones." On the other hand, "Payment 10 days after the docking of the *Queen Mary* in New York harbor," or "Payable upon John Jones' 50th birthday," are non-negotiable since the instrument is not payable at a fixed or determinable future time, but on a contingency—not a special event which is bound to happen—and the fact the contingency occurs will not cure the defect as negotiability is determined at the time an instrument is issued.

It is interesting to observe that the following clause makes an instrument non-negotiable: "Jones (payee) has full power to declare the note due at any time he may deem this note insecure, even before maturity of the same." When the holder is given unlimited authority to accelerate the maturity of the note, the time of payment is uncertain and therefore non-negotiable. Yet a note "Payable on Demand" is specifically provided to be negotiable even though such is obviously due at the whim and caprice of the holder. However, there is a real distinction.

In a later section, we will see that for one to qualify as a holder in due course he must become a holder of the instrument before it is overdue. Paper payable on demand is deemed overdue when negotiated an unreasonable length of time after its issue, whereas paper payable at a fixed or determinable future date is not overdue until after the fixed date specified on the instrument. To permit combining the two above due dates in an instrument by a clause such as "due January 10, 1965, but the holder may declare the note due at any time, even before maturity" would pose many problems as to whether a holder became such before the paper was overdue. However, an acceleration clause causing the entire note to become due upon default of a payment of any installment of principal or interest does not render the note non-negotiable. This is logical in that the holder cannot accelerate the due date at his whim or caprice as the acceleration is within the control of the maker of the instrument—so long as he keeps up his payments it would not be overdue.

6. Must Be Payable "To Order" or "To Bearer"

The instrument must be payable to order or to bearer. The words "to order of" or "to bearer" are standardized words of negotiability. Sec. 10 of N.I.L. provides that the instrument need not follow the language of the N.I.L., but any terms are sufficient which clearly indicate an intention to conform to the requirements. Instruments payable to "John Doe or assigns" have been held negotiable in some instances and non-negotiable in other cases. For the sake of certainty, the standard words of negotiability should always be used.

Sec. 8 of N.I.L. provides the instrument is "order paper" where it is drawn payable to the order of a specified person or to him or his order. It may be drawn payable to the order of a payee who is not the maker, drawer, or drawee, to a drawer or maker, to a drawee, to two or more payees jointly (*A* and *B*), to one or some of several payees (*A* or *B*), or to the holder of an office for the time being (Sec'y. & Treas. of ABC Co.). Where the instrument is payable to order, the payee must be named or otherwise indicated with reasonable certainty because to negotiate such instrument requires endorsement and delivery. Bearer paper, however, is negotiated by delivery alone.

Sec. 9 of N.I.L. provides the instrument is "bearer paper" when it is expressed to be so payable (pay to bearer), when it is payable to a person named therein or bearer (pay to *A* or bearer), when it is payable to the order of a fictitious or non-existent person and such fact was known to the person making it so payable (pay to "Mickey Mouse"), when the payee named does not purport to be the name of any person ("pay to order of cash"), when the only or last endorsement is an endorsement in blank. The reason an instrument payable to the order of a non-existent person or fictitious person are considered bearer instruments is that these instruments could never be endorsed, and it is thus assumed the maker or drawer must have intended them to be negotiated by delivery alone.

If no payee is named in the instrument, some courts hold such to be bearer paper and the blank may be filled in by the holder (N.I.L. 14). On the same point, other courts hold such instrument to be non-negotiable as long as a payee is not filled in. All courts agree that if a line is drawn through the space where the payee's name is usually inserted, the instrument is void for lack of a designated payee. Should the holder, as permitted by N.I.L. 14, fill in the name of the payee and then transfer the instrument to a holder in due course, such holder in due course could enforce the collection of the instrument. (Further explanation of N.I.L. 14 later under "Personal Defenses.")

7. DRAWEE MUST BE NAMED WITH REASONABLE CERTAINTY

In a bill of exchange, the drawee must be named or otherwise indicated therein with reasonable certainty. The purpose of this requirement is to make it possible for the holder to know the person to whom presentment for payment is to be made. The mere possession of a paper drawn in the form of an order, there being no drawee indicated, will not entitle the possessor to any rights under the instrument.

8. INSTRUMENT CANNOT REQUIRE DOING AN ACT IN ADDITION TO PAYMENT OF MONEY

Sec. 5 of N.I.L. provides that an instrument which contains an order or promise to do any act in addition to the payment of money is not negotiable, but the negotiable character of an instrument otherwise negotiable is not affected by a provision which:

> "1. Authorizes the sale of collateral securities in case the instrument be not paid at maturity; or
>
> "2. Authorizes a confession of judgment if the instrument be not paid at maturity; or
>
> "3. Waives the benefit of any law intended for the advantage or protection of the obligor; or
>
> "4. Gives the holder an election to require something to be done in lieu of payment of money."

This section provides that to be negotiable the instrument cannot require the obligor to do any act in addition to the payment of money. Quite often instruments contain acceleration clauses which provide for an earlier due date in event certain contingencies occur. If the maker is required to do an act other than to pay money in order to prevent acceleration, the instrument is held to be non-negotiable unless the wording is properly phrased in the negative. To illustrate: If the maker promises to furnish additional security if the collateral securing the note depreciates in value; otherwise the note shall mature at once—such would be non-negotiable. On the other hand, if the note states that if the debtor allows the collateral to fall below a certain value, then the note shall mature at once, such would be negotiable. The second clause does not contain a promise to do an act in addition to the payment of money. This is merely an acceleration clause causing an earlier maturity on the happening of a contingency outside the control of the holder and there is no direct promise to do an act in addition to the payment of money.

The provisions of N.I.L. 5 above and N.I.L. 4 which require the instrument to be payable at a determinable future time frequently overlap. Thus, if a maker promises to provide additional security if the collateral securing the note depreciates (N.I.L. 5) and if he fails to provide such as holder deems necessary, the note becomes due and payable immediately (N.I.L. 4)—the note would not be negotiable in that the maker promises to do an act in addition to the payment of money and also the time of payment is at the whim and caprice of the holder, is absolutely uncertain, and therefore is not payable at a determinable future time.

If the maker promises to pay taxes or to insure the building on which a mortgage was given in security of the note, these and any other collateral promises made by the maker in the note will render the note non-negotiable.

B. Omissions Which Do Not Affect Negotiability

Sec. 6 of the N.I.L. enumerates the following omissions as having no bearing on the validity or negotiable character of an otherwise negotiable instrument: the fact that it is not dated, does not specify any value was given for it, does not specify the place it was drawn or where it is payable, whether it bears a seal or not, or whether it designates a particular kind of money in which payment is to be made.

C. Rules for Interpreting Ambiguous Language in Instruments

Sec. 17 of the N.I.L. provides that where the language of the instrument is ambiguous or there are omissions therein, the following rules of construction apply:

"1. Where the sum payable is expressed in words and also in figures and there is a discrepancy between the two, the sum denoted by the words is the sum payable; but if the words are ambiguous or uncertain, reference may be made to the figures to fix the amount.

"2. Where the instrument provides for the payment of interest, without specifying the date from which interest is to run, the interest runs from the date of the instrument, and if the instrument is undated, from the issue thereof.

"3. Where the instrument is not dated, it will be considered to be dated as of time it was issued.

"4. Where there is a conflict between the written and printed provisions of the instrument, the written provisions prevail.

"5. Where the instrument is so ambiguous that there is doubt whether it is a bill or a note, the holder may treat it as either at his election.

"6. Where a signature is so placed upon the instrument that it is not clear in what capacity the person making the same intended to sign, he is deemed an endorser.

"7. Where the instrument containing the words 'I promise to pay,' is signed by two or more persons, they are deemed to be jointly and severally liable thereon."

IV. HOLDER IN DUE COURSE

A. Holder Defined

" 'Holder' means the payee or indorsee of a bill or a note, who is in possession of it, or the bearer thereof." (N.I.L. 191)

"A holder in due course is a holder who has taken the instrument under the following conditions:

"1. That it is complete and regular on its face;
"2. That he became the holder of it before it was overdue, and without notice that it had been previously dishonored, if such was the fact;
"3. That he took it in good faith and for value;
"4. That at the time it was negotiated to him he had no notice of any infirmity in the instrument or defect in the title of the person negotiating it." (N.I.L. 52)

It is only when a negotiable instrument is owned by a holder in due course that the distinctive features of a negotiable instrument come into operation. This is best explained by the following illustrations:

1. *A* executes a non-negotiable promissory note and delivers it to *B*. Whether or not *B* "negotiates" the note further, *A* can successfully assert any defenses he may have against collection on the note. The title to a non-negotiable note is transferred by assignment and you will recall the rule

that an assignee gets no better rights than the assignor had; and/or the assignee is subject to all defenses the obligor had against the assignor. (N.I.L. 58) "In the hands of any holder other than the holder in due course, a negotiable instrument is subject to the same defenses as if it were non-negotiable."

2. *A* executes a negotiable promissory note and delivers it to *B*. If *B* does not further negotiate the note, it is similar in every respect to an ordinary contract and *A* can raise any defense he may have against collection on the note against *B*, the original payee. But if *B* negotiates the note to *H*, who qualifies as a holder in due course, *H* takes the note free from personal defenses that *A* might have successfully asserted against *B* or a subsequent holder who did not qualify as a holder in due course. Obviously, a negotiable note is more attractive to a prospective holder than is a non-negotiable note.

Some students arrive at two erroneous conclusions. First they conclude that a negotiable instrument is a guarantee of its validity and second that a non-negotiable note is not enforceable. Obviously, a forged negotiable instrument is not valid in the hands of any holder and a non-negotiable instrument is enforceable to the same extent as any ordinary contract. The advantages of being a holder in due course are (1) the absolute presumption of delivery and consideration which arise in your favor, and (2) the cutting off of personal defenses the party primarily liable could have asserted against one not qualifying as a holder in due course. This provision of the law which permits a negotiable instrument to gain in stature as it is transferred to a holder in due course is the basis which makes them readily transferable and acceptable almost to the extent of money itself.

B. What Constitutes a Holder in Due Course?

A holder in due course is a holder who takes the instrument under the following conditions:

1. That it is complete and regular on its face. Thus, there cannot be any "material blanks" nor patent erasures or alterations on the instrument. Any such irregularities upon the face of the instrument would prevent one from qualifying as a holder in due course. An instrument written in two or more different handwritings, and undated instruments are considered complete and regular.

2. That he become the holder before it is overdue and without notice that it had been previously dishonored, if such was the fact.

The only serious problem that arises in connection with this requirement is in the case of paper payable on demand. N.I.L. Sec. 53 provides that when demand paper is negotiated an unreasonable length of time after its issue, the holder is not deemed a holder in due course. The standard of what is an "unreasonable" time will vary considerably, depending on the facts of the particular case, usage in the trade or business in respect to such instruments, and the nature of the instrument. (N.I.L. 193)

Checks and bank drafts normally become overdue much sooner than demand promissory notes and trade acceptances. Presumptively, checks are to be presented by the close of business on the day following their date of issue where the drawee, drawer, and payee are all located in the same town, whereas six months and longer has been ruled a reasonable time period in which to become the holder of demand notes and drafts. The courts prolonged the "reasonable" time period to include 24 days when the drawer of a check did nothing to regain possession of it even though the payee was readily accessible.

The logic behind this requirement of taking an instrument before it is overdue to qualify as a holder in due course is that people generally pay their debts as they become due, unless they have a reason for not doing so. Thus, a purchaser of overdue paper should make inquiry of the party primarily liable, as the fact that it has not been paid constitutes notice that the party liable thereon might have a good defense. This overlaps the third requirement which is:

3. That he took it in good faith and for value. "Good faith" means without actual knowledge of any thing that may be wrong with the instrument or with the circumstances of its execution. Whereas suspicion alone is not enough to destroy good faith, obviously suspicious circumstances must be investigated. Under such circumstances one who "closes his eyes" for fear an investigation might disclose a defense would not qualify as a good faith purchaser.

"Value is any consideration sufficient to support a simple contract. An antecedent or pre-existing debt is deemed such whether the instrument is payable on demand or at a future time." (N.I.L. 25) A mere promise to give value is not sufficient to make one a holder in due course, the value must actually be given.

4. Holder must acquire instrument without notice of defenses. The fourth requirement to qualify as a holder in due course is "that at the time it was negotiated to him he had no notice of any infirmity in the instrument or defect in the title of the person negotiating it."

"The title of a person who negotiates an instrument is defective within the meaning of this act when he obtained the instrument, or any signature thereto, by fraud, duress, or force or fear, or other unlawful means, or for an illegal consideration, or when he negotiates it in breach of faith, or under such circumstances as amount to a fraud." (N.I.L. 55)

"To constitute notice of an infirmity in the instrument or defect in the title of the person negotiating the same, the person to whom it is negotiated must have had actual knowledge of the infirmity or defect, or knowledge of such facts that his action in taking the instrument amounted to bad faith." (N.I.L. 56)

The subsections of N.I.L. 52 overlap in that a person who acquires an instrument which has blanks or patent erasures, or acquires it when past due, or with notice of other infirmities in the instrument or defects in the title of person from whom the instrument was purchased, obviously fails to also meet the "taken in good faith" requirement. But this requirement covers additional circumstances. For example, it has been held to purchase an instrument from a stranger or from a known thief or under other suspicious circumstances constitutes knowledge of such facts that the purchaser ought to make inquiry and his failure to investigate might constitute bad faith.

C. Payee As a Holder in Due Course

A payee does not generally qualify as a holder in due course unless he is not an immediate party to the transaction.

Illustration: *D* makes a note payable to *P* and leaves the amount blank. *D* gives the note to *A* authorizing *A* to fill in the amount but for not more than $200 and deliver same to *P* as payment for merchandise *A* is to pick up. *A*, instead, fills in the amount of $400 and misappropriates the excess merchandise purchase. Does *P* qualify as a holder in due course? Assuming *P* meets the requirements for a holder in due course (N.I.L. 52) the answer is held by many courts to be "yes."

"Immediate parties" does not mean "immediate on the instrument" (maker-Payee) but, instead, means parties immediate to the conditions and limitations placed on the delivery in the sense of knowing or being charged with notice of them. Ordinarily, the maker deals directly with the payee and it is this fact that gives the payee the knowledge of defects which prevents him from qualifying as a holder in due course. Obviously, this is not true in the above illustration and therefore, logically, *P* should qualify as a holder in due course.

V. DEFENSES

A. Introduction

Defenses which may be raised by parties charged on negotiable instruments are classified as personal defenses and real defenses. Personal defenses are those which arise between the parties in their mutual business relations, whereas real defenses are those which challenge the validity of the instrument. Real defenses, if proved, are good against all holders, whereas personal defenses are not good as to those who qualify as a holder in due course. As previously mentioned, one of the advantages of a holder qualifying as a holder in due course is the "cutting off" of personal defenses which might otherwise have been asserted by the party being sued.

B. Personal Defenses

Remembering that these are defenses which are not good against a holder in due course, there follows a group of such defenses.

1. No consideration, or failure of consideration (N.I.L. 28). A negotiable instrument has the same requirements regarding consideration as has any other contract. However, one aspect differs in that the fact that a negotiable instrument exists creates a presumption that it was delivered for valuable consideration, whereas with contracts no such presumption exists and a party seeking to enforce a contract must come forward and prove that consideration was given.

There are two aspects of consideration—consideration in the creation and consideration in the transfer. Failure of consideration in the creation is a personal defense, while failure of consideration in the transfer prevents the holder from being a holder in due course (which would mean any personal defenses would be good against him, including failure of consideration in the creation).

2. Non-Delivery of a Completed Instrument (N.I.L. 16). A negotiable instrument, to become legally operative as to the immediate parties or as to the holders not in due course, must be delivered with the intent that it become a valid claim against the party putting it into circulation.

N.I.L. 16 . . . "Every contract on a negotiable instrument is incomplete and revokable until delivery of the instrument for the purpose of giving effect thereto. As between immediate parties, and as regards a remote party other than a holder in due course, the delivery, in order to be effectual, must be made either by or under the authority of the party making, drawing, accepting, or endorsing, as the case may be; and in such case the delivery may be shown to have been conditional, or for a special purpose only, and not for the purpose of transferring the property in the instrument. But where the instrument is in the hands of a holder in due course, a valid delivery thereof by all parties prior to him so as to make them liable to him is conclusively presumed. And where the instrument is no longer in possession of a party whose signature appears thereon, a valid and intentional delivery by him is presumed until the contrary is proved."

Thus, the non-delivery of a completed instrument is a personal defense, not good as to a holder in due course. As to a holder in due course, valid delivery is conclusively presumed, just like consideration is conclusively presumed when the instrument is in the hands of such a holder in due course.

This section (16) also provides that a conditional delivery is not a delivery for the purpose of giving effect thereto until the condition has been met and this condition not being met is a good defense between the immediate parties and remote parties who do not qualify as holders in due course.

3. Blanks Improperly Filled In (N.I.L. 14). When a negotiable instrument is incomplete, or when there appears only a signature on a blank piece of paper but which has been delivered for the purpose of converting it into a negotiable instrument, then in either of those events the person in possession has prima facie authority to complete the instrument. If he does this within the actual authority granted, then even the immediate payee may enforce it against the maker. Should the party authorized to complete the instrument exceed his authority (e.g., make the instrument for more than authorized) then this would constitute a personal defense but not good against a

holder in due course.

4. Fraud in the Inducement. An example of fraud in the inducement is where a person is induced to sign a negotiable instrument through fraud, whereas he would not have signed if the true facts were known. It is fraud which has the effect of inducing or furnishing the motion of the execution of an instrument. It is by far the most common type of fraud. Example: *A* signs a note on payment of a watch represented as having a solid gold case, whereas the case is merely gold plated.

5. Illegality. Examples of illegality are when a note is given for the purchase of intoxicating liquor, or when a note is given in payment of a gambling debt, and when, in both instances, statutes make such transactions illegal. Since the instrument arises out of an illegal transaction, it would be contrary to public policy to permit the original payee to enforce it, but to a holder in due course, the defense of illegality would not prevail.

6. Payment before Maturity without Taking up the Instrument. Only payment in due course discharges the instrument, and N.I.L. 88 defines payment in due course as "when it is made at or after maturity—to the holder thereof in good faith and without notice that his title is defective." Since payment to the holder before maturity without taking up the instrument would permit him to transfer the instrument to a holder in due course, it is the maker's fault (by not taking up the instrument) that such holder in due course purchased the instrument. As between the maker and the holder in due course, the maker (primary party) should stand the loss.

7. Miscellaneous Defenses. Undue influence, personal duress, set-off, counterclaim, and breach of warranty are all defenses to contracts (see Contracts) and negotiable instruments not in the hands of a holder in due course.

C. Real Defenses

Real defenses are defenses good against all holders, including holders in due course. Some of them are:

1. Non-Delivery of an Incompleted Instrument (N.I.L. 15). When an instrument has neither been completed nor delivered, it will not be valid even in the hands of a holder in due course. Thus, an incomplete instrument which is stolen (or lost) and the thief (or finder) should complete it and negotiate it to a holder in due course, the holder cannot enforce the instrument

against any person whose signature was placed thereon before the thief (or finder) completed it. (Take note that subsequent indorsers would be liable as will be shown when N.I.L. 65 and 66 are discussed.)

2. Material Alteration. "Where a negotiable instrument is materially altered without the assent of all parties liable thereon, it is avoided, except as against a party who has himself made, authorized, or assented to the alteration, and subsequent indorsers.

"But when an instrument has been materially altered and is in the hands of a holder in due course, not a party to the alteration, he may enforce payment thereof according to its original tenor." (emphasis added) N.I.L. 124.

Thus, as to a holder in due course, material alteration is a real defense to the extent of the alteration. Example: *A* issues a check to *B* for $100. *B* raises it to $150 and negotiates it to *C*, a holder in due course. *C* can enforce the instrument as to *A* for $100 and must look to *B* for $50 under *B*'s warranties. (See N.I.L. 65 and 66)

3. Fraud in the Execution. Fraud in the execution, resulting in a real defense, occurs when a party executes an instrument without knowing or intending to sign a negotiable instrument. For example, an illiterate unwittingly signing a negotiable note based on representations that it is a receipt would have a real defense.

4. Incapacity. Incapacity is a defense only as to the person having the legal disability, other parties' liability on the instrument not being affected. Example: *A*, a minor, makes a note payable to *B* who indorses to *C*. Upon presentment on its due date, *A* pleads defense of incapacity. *C* can collect from *B* (N.I.L. 65 or 66) on breach of warranty, but not from *A*.

5. Forgery. "When a signature is forged or made without the authority of the person whose signature it purports to be, it is wholly inoperative, and no right to retain the instrument, or to give discharge therefor, or to enforce payment thereof against any party thereto, can be acquired through or under such signature, unless the party, against whom it is sought to enforce such right, is precluded from setting up the forgery or want of authority." (N.I.L. 23)

Examples: (a) *A* forges *B*'s signature to a note payable to *A* and negotiates it to *C* and *C* negotiates to *D*, a holder in due course. *D* cannot enforce payment against *B*, but may collect from *C* on his indorser's liability (Warranty of genuineness of the instrument).

(b) *A* steals a note payable to *B* on order and forges *B*'s indorsement and negotiates to *C*. *C* negotiates to *D*. *D* cannot collect from the maker as one gets no title through a forged indorsement. *D* can collect from *C* on his indorser's liability (warranty of title). In both examples, *C*, the person who dealt with *A*, the forger, will bear the loss, assuming he cannot collect from *A*.

(c) *A* was asked by *B*, the payee of a note, to be present at the closing sale of property by *B* to *C*, the maker of the note which was indorsed by *A*. Actually *A* had not indorsed the note, his signature being forged. *A* inspected the papers, including the note with his indorsement and said "Everything is all right." When *C* failed to pay the note at maturity, *B* sued *A* on his liability as an indorser (*C* having made due presentment and given proper notice to *A*). *A* was precluded from setting up the forgery as a defense. The same result would be reached if *C* had signed *A*'s name to the note, representing to be *A*'s agent and all done in *A*'s presence, and *A* did not deny this allegation even though *C* was not *A*'s agent. In such a case, *A* would be estopped to deny the agency.

6. Illegality. Illegality may be a real defense when such illegality voids an act. For example: *D* executed a negotiable instrument which was discounted at a usurious rate of interest so that the usury did not appear on the face of the instrument. A statute declares instruments charging a usurious rate of interest void. Even a holder in due course would not be able to collect such instrument over *D*'s objection.

7. Duress and Undue Influence. Duress and undue influence of such an extreme nature that the person is constrained to that which is against his will is generally considered a real defense.

8. Statute of Limitations and Mutual Mistake. The running of the statute of limitations and mutual mistake (see Contracts) are real defenses, good even as against a holder in due course.

9. Real defenses may be reduced to personal defenses when the wrong is made possible by negligent conduct on the part of the party primarily liable. Illustrations:

(a) Material alteration. When the maker, by careless execution of the instrument leaves room for alteration to be made by insertion without defacing the instrument, or exciting the suspicion of a careful man, and the instrument, by reason of the opportunity thus afforded, is subsequently altered, the maker will be liable upon it, as altered, to a holder in due course.

(b) Fraud in the execution. To sign an instrument without reading it (you are literate), even when you are misled to believe it to be, say, a receipt, is such negligence on your part that it will constitute only a personal defense.

(c) Non-delivery of an incomplete instrument. When the primary party is negligent in making an instrument accessible to a thief, the courts may reduce the real defense of non-delivery of an incomplete instrument to the status of a personal defense. To sign a check in blank is always deemed negligent conduct and the drawee bank will be protected unless a timely stop-payment is ordered by the drawer.

VI. NEGOTIATION

As stated previously, negotiable instruments are designed to pass freely from hand to hand, and the main purpose of the rules governing them is to facilitate such passage. The act of passing a negotiable instrument from one person to another is called a negotiation, but every transfer into the hands of another is not necessarily a negotiation. N.I.L. Sec. 30 provides "An instrument is negotiated when it is transferred from one person to another in such a manner as to constitute the transferee the holder thereof. If payable to bearer, it is negotiated by delivery; if payable to order it is negotiated by the indorsement of the holder completed by delivery." Thus, a delivery of order paper without indorsement is not a negotiation and, instead, is treated as an assignment with regard to the rights of the transferee. However, if the transferee gave value for the instrument, he has the right to require the transferor to indorse under N.I.L. 49.

VII. LIABILITIES OF THE PARTIES

Every negotiable instrument has the purpose of evidencing a contract between the parties to the instrument, in the form either of an unconditional promise (in the case of a note) or of an unconditional order (in the case of a bill of exchange). The maker of a promissory note and the acceptor of a bill of exchange are primarily liable—that is, their liability is absolute. The liability of all other parties on a negotiable instrument is secondary or contingent. If the parties primarily liable do not perform their obligation, then the liability of the secondary parties arises. Every negotiation of an instrument has two results: (1) it effects a transfer of title to the instrument and the right to enforce its payment, and (2) it sets up certain implied warranties in favor of the indorsee (the party to whom an instrument is negotiated by indorsement). If the indorsee, after having taken proper steps, is unable to collect from the maker, he can enforce payment against his indorser. The delivery of bearer paper imposes certain liabilities upon the person effecting the delivery. By the act of delivering the instrument he makes certain warranties to the person to whom he delivers it. Similarly, the indorsement and delivery of order paper imposes certain liabilities upon the indorsee. The liabilities differ according to the form of indorsement used. It is because of the warranties that arise automatically in favor of a transferee of a negotiable instrument as against his transferor and other indorsees in the chain of title that negotiable instruments approximate money.

A. Liabilities of Primary Parties

1. Maker

The maker of a promissory note, by making it, engages that he will pay it according to its tenor, and admits the existence of the payee and his then capacity to endorse (N.I.L. 60). This does not mean that maker cannot set up appropriate personal defenses against holders not in due course, or appropriate real defenses against holders in due course, but a maker is absolutely liable to any holder according to the tenor of the instrument except for these defenses, and further cannot use the defense of the incapacity of the payee.

2. Acceptor

No one is primarily liable on a bill of exchange until it has been accepted by the drawee. Once the drawee accepts he becomes primarily liable and thereafter he is known as the acceptor. The acceptor, by accepting the instrument, engages that he will pay it according to the tenor of his acceptance and admits the existence of the drawer, the genuineness of his signature, and his capacity and authority to draw the instrument; and the existence of the payee and his then capacity to endorse. (N.I.L. 62). Thus, primary liability on a bill of exchange resolves into the question of whether such a bill has been accepted.

The acceptance must be in writing and signed by the drawee.

It must not express that the drawee will perform his promise by any other means than the payment of money (N.I.L. 32). The normal method of accepting is for the drawee to write "accepted" and the date across the face of the instrument and then sign his name below.

An unconditional promise in writing to accept a bill before it is drawn or an acceptance on paper other than the bill are both valid and binding as to every person to whom these are shown and who, on the faith thereof, receive the bill for value. Thus, if *A* offers to give *B* a draft on the *C* Bank and *B* wires *C* Bank fully describing the draft (drawn or to be drawn) and *C* Bank unequivocally notifies *B* in writing that they accept such —or will accept the draft *A* is to draw on them—*C* Bank is liable on such draft as to all persons to whom the telegram of acceptance is shown and who, on the faith thereof, receives the bill for value (N.I.L. 134 & 135). If the holder of the bill does not know of the promise at the time he receives the bill, he may not hold the drawee upon the written promise of acceptance. N.I.L. 132, 133, 134, and 135 all require the acceptance or the unconditional promise to accept a bill to be in writing. Thus, when a person called the drawee Bank and inquired if certain checks given him were good and the Bank responded in the affirmative, it has been held that such oral statements did not constitute an acceptance as required by the N.I.L.

The holder of a bill presenting the same for acceptance may require that the acceptance be written on the bill and if such request is refused, may treat the bill as dishonored (N.I.L. 133).

The drawee may be estopped to deny his acceptance if he fails to promptly return a bill presented to him for acceptance. The drawee is allowed 24 hours or such other time as the holder allows after presentment, in which to decide whether or not he will accept. Should he destroy the bill or refuse to return it within 24 hours after such delivery, or within such other time as the holder may allow to return the bill accepted or non-accepted, he will be deemed to have accepted the same as of the day of presentment. If he accepts, his acceptance dates as of the day of presentment (N.I.L. 136 & 137).

An acceptance by a drawee may be general or qualified. An acceptance is general when the drawee accepts without qualification to the order of the drawer; it is qualified if the acceptance varies the effect of the bill as drawn (N.I.L. 138) or is conditional, partial, local, qualified as to time, or if accepted by some but not all of the several drawers named therein (N.I.L. 141). A conditional acceptance is an acceptance to pay only part of the amount for which the bill is drawn. A local acceptance is an acceptance to pay only at a particular place which is not the place designated in the instrument. It is qualified as to time when the acceptance states payment will be made at a later time than the instrument requires.

The holder may refuse to take a qualified acceptance (return the instrument to the drawer as being dishonored) if he does not obtain a general acceptance. Should he take a qualified acceptance, the drawer and indorsers are discharged from liability on the bill unless they expressly or impliedly authorize the holder to take a qualified acceptance or subsequently assent thereto. When the drawer or an indorser receives notice of a qualified acceptance, he must, within a reasonable time, express his dissent to the holder, or he will be deemed to have assented thereto (N.I.L. 142).

B. Liabilities of Secondary Parties

1. Qualified Indorsement

N.I.L. 65 provides: "Every person negotiating an instrument by delivery or by a qualified indorsement, warrants

(1) That the instrument is genuine and in all respects what it purports to be.
(2) That he has good title to it.
(3) That all prior parties had capacity to contract.
(4) That he has no knowledge of any fact which would impair the validity of the instrument or render it valueless. But when the negotiation is by delivery only, the warranty extends in favor of no holder other than the immediate transferee."

Examples:

(1) *D* indorses a $100 negotiable order to *P* "without recourse" or transfers a $100 negotiable bearer instrument to *P* by delivery alone. The note was originally drawn for $10 and had been raised to $100, but this was not known to *D* or to *P*. If *P* is a holder in due course, he can recover $10 from the maker (N.I.L. 124) and $90 from *D*. *D* breached the first warranty above and this is true irrespective of whether *D* knew or did not know of the alteration.

(2) *D* transfers a bearer negotiable note in the amount

of $100 to *P* by delivery alone. Upon maturity, *P* cannot collect as the maker pleads and proves he is an infant. *P* can collect from *D* under the third warranty above.

(3) *D* negotiates an order promissory note in amount of $100 to *P* by a qualified indorsement ("without recourse"). *D* knew at the time of sale that the maker was insolvent. *D* is liable to *P* for the full amount of the note as he has breached the fourth warranty.

NOTE: The above warranties run only to the transferor's immediate transferee when bearer paper is negotiated by delivery alone. If either bearer or order paper is endorsed and delivered, the warranties extend to all subsequent holders.

2. UNQUALIFIED INDORSEMENT

N.I.L. 66 provides that every indorser who indorses without qualification, warrants to all subsequent holders in due course:

(1) The matters and things mentioned in subdivision 1, 2, and 3 of the next preceding section (N.I.L. 65); and

(2) That the instrument is at the time of his indorsement valid and subsisting.

And, in addition, he engages that on due presentment, it shall be accepted or paid, or both, as the case may be, according to its tenor, and that if it be dishonored and the necessary proceeding or dishonor be duly taken, he will pay the amount thereof to the holder, or to any subsequent indorsee who may be compelled to pay it.

The first two illustrations under N.I.L. 65 above would be applicable under N.I.L. 66, but in the third illustration *D* would be liable to *P* even if *D* did not know at the time of the sale that the maker was insolvent. Further, N.I.L. 66 imposes on an unqualified indorser an absolute guaranty of validity instead of merely a warranty that the indorsee knows of no facts that would impair the validity of the instrument.

Finally, N.I.L. 66 imposes what is known as the conditional liability on an indorser who indorses without qualification. To hold an indorser liable requires (1) due presentment of the instrument and (2) the necessary proceedings on dishonor be duly taken. The general indorser is not liable under this paragraph unless these conditions are satisfied. The details of "due presentment" and "notice of dishonor" will be postponed to a later chapter.

3. DRAWER

The drawer by drawing the instrument admits the existence of the payee and his then capacity to indorse. Even though the drawer of a bill is not subject to N.I.L. 65 or 66 (he is not an indorser), his liability on the instrument is the same as an indorser unless he inserts in the instrument an express stipulation negativing or limiting his liability to the holder. This liability of the drawer is set out in N.I.L. 61: "The drawer by drawing the instrument admits the existence of the payee and his then capacity to indorse; and engages that on due presentment the instrument will be accepted or paid, or both, according to its tenor, and that if it be dishonored, and the necessary proceedings on dishonor be duly taken, he will pay the amount thereon to the holder, or to any subsequent indorser who may be compelled to pay it. But the drawer may insert on the instrument an express stipulation negativing or limiting his own liability to the holder."

4. LIMITED INDORSEMENTS

There are five kinds of indorsement. "An indorsement may be either special or in blank; and it may be either restrictive or qualified, or conditional." (N.I.L. 33)

An indorsement must be written on the instrument itself or upon a paper attached thereto. Following are illustrations of the type of indorsements:

TYPE OF INDORSEMENT	ILLUSTRATION
(1) Special indorsement	Pay to Richard Roe /s/ John Doe
(2) Blank indorsement	/s/ John Doe
(3) Qualified indorsement	Without Recourse /s/ John Doe
(4) Restrictive indorsement	For Deposit Only /s/ John Doe
	Pay to Richard Roe Only /s/ John Doe
	Pay to First Bank for Collection Only /s/ John Doe

	Pay to Richard Roe in Trust for Jack Smith /s/ John Doe
(5) Conditional indorsement	Pay to Richard Roe Upon His Completing the Erection of Garage at My Residence /s/ John Doe

N.I.L. 34 provides: "A special indorsement specifies the person to whom, or to whose order, the instrument is to be payable; and the indorsement of such indorsee is necessary to the further negotiation of the instrument." Thus, in our first illustration, the instrument remains order paper and may be further negotiated only by the indorsement of Richard Roe. An instrument initially issued as bearer paper cannot be converted to order paper by special indorsement; the rule being that paper originally issued as bearer paper is always bearer paper which may be negotiated by delivery alone, even if a holder does specially indorse.

N.I.L. 34 further provides: "An indorsement in blank specifies no indorsee, and an instrument so indorsed is payable to bearer, and may be negotiated by delivery." Thus, a blank indorsement converts order paper to bearer paper.

Whereas all authorities agree that bearer paper cannot be converted to order paper through a special indorsement, there is a split in opinion as to whether order paper once indorsed in blank so as to become bearer paper can be converted back to order paper by a subsequent special indorsement. The better view is that it can and this seems to be the intent of N.I.L. 9(5) which provides "The instrument is payable to bearer when the only or last indorsement is an indorsement in blank."

Example: *A Co.* cashes payroll checks (order paper) for its customers who indorsed in blank. Thus, the checks have become bearer paper and may be further negotiated by delivery alone. To prevent a thief from doing this, *A Co.* converts the blank indorsement to a special indorsement or puts a subsequent restrictive indorsement: "For deposit only to *A Co.*'s account with First Bank /s/ *A Co.*"

N.I.L. 38 provides: "A qualified indorsement constitutes the indorser a mere assignor of the title to the instrument. It may be made by adding to the indorser's signature the words 'without recourse,' or any words of similar import. Such an indorsement does not impair the negotiable character of the instrument." We have seen that a qualified indorsement limits the indorser's liability on the instrument to the warranties given under N.I.L. 65 and that this section does not make the indorser a guarantor of payment of the instrument. A qualified indorsement may be either special or blank. As a practical matter, most transferees will not accept a qualified indorsement.

N.I.L. 36 "An indorsement is restrictive, which either:

"(1) Prohibits further negotiation of the instrument." Illustrations: "Pay to Richard Roe only. /s/ *A*." The word "only" gives notice to all who may be concerned that the instrument is collectible only by Richard Roe. When one wants to mail a deposit to his bank, a restrictive endorsement, "For Deposit Only," and then signed by the indorser will prevent the instrument from being collected by a thief as this indorsement also prohibits further negotiation of the instrument.

"(2) Constitutes the indorsee the agent of the indorser." Illustrations: "Pay to First Bank for collection for my account /s/ *A*"; and "Pay to Bill Green as attorney for Jack Smith /s/ *A*."

"(3) Vests title in the indorsee in trust for or to the care of some other person."
Illustrations: "Pay to *X* in trust for *Y* /s/ *A*" and "Pay to *X* for my use /s/ *A*."

N.I.L. 37 provides that a restrictive indorsement confers upon the indorsee the right to (1) receive payment of the instrument, (2) bring any action thereon the indorsee could bring, and (3) to transfer his right where the form of indorsement authorizes him to do so. Thus, an indorsement, "Pay to *X* in trust for *Y* /s/ *A*" notifies all subsequent transferees of *X*'s limited interest in the instrument and prevents the obligor from "setting-off" any claim he has against *X* which he might have done had *X* been the outright owner of the instrument. Similarly, "Pay to First Bank for Collection for My Account, /s/ *A*" informs all subsequent indorsees that First Bank is not the beneficial owner of the instrument but is merely an agent of *A*'s for collection of the instrument.

N.I.L. 39 provides that where an indorsement is conditional, a party required to pay the instrument may disregard the condition, and make payment to the indorsee or his transferee, whether the condition has been fulfilled or not. But any person to whom an instrument so indorsed is negotiated, will hold the same, or the proceeds thereof, subject to the rights of the person indorsing conditionally.

An indorsement such as "Pay to Richard Roe upon his completing the erection of a garage at my residence /s/ John Doe" illustrates a special conditional indorsement. The condition (erection of the garage) must happen before the special indorsee (Richard Roe) is entitled to payment. A conditional indorsement creates a condition with reference to the instrument and the proceeds therefrom, binding in favor of the indorser as regards the indorsee and all subsequent holders through the indorsee. A party required to pay, however, may disregard the condition and pay irrespective of the fulfillment or nonfulfillment of the condition. If the instrument is paid in disregard of the condition, the person receiving payment thereof receives the payment subject to the rights of the conditional indorser, and may be forced to account to him for that amount. A conditional indorsement may be either special or blank.

Finally, we have a special breed of indorsers not heretofore mentioned—namely, an irregular indorser. An irregular indorser is one who signs in blank an instrument before delivery, and is not otherwise a party to the instrument. For example, he might be signing as an accommodation indorser to one of the parties to an instrument. Such an accommodation indorser is a person who indorses without receiving value but rather for the purpose of lending his name to some other person. An irregular indorser is liable in accordance with the following rules (N.I.L. 64):

(1) If the instrument is payable to the order of a third person, he is liable to the payee and to all the subsequent parties.
(2) If the instrument is payable to the order of the maker or drawer, or is payable to bearer, he is liable to all parties subsequent to the maker or drawer.
(3) If he signs for the accommodation of the payee, he is liable to all parties subsequent to the payee.

One final note as to limited indorsements. A negotiable instrument must be indorsed in its entirety—it cannot be partially indorsed. For example, if *A* holds a demand note for $1,000, he cannot indorse $500 of it to *B* and retain the right to collect the other $500. Of course, if it is a note payable in installments, and $500 has already been paid, *A* may indorse the remaining $500 to *B* for he would be indorsing the note in its entirety at the time of indorsement.

5. Order of Liability Between Parties Secondarily Liable

N.I.L. 68 provides: "As respects one another, indorsers are liable *prima facie* in the order in which they indorse, but evidence is admissible to show that as between or among themselves they have agreed otherwise." Thus, where *A* indorses to *B, B* to *C,* and *C* to *D,* on non-payment by the party primarily liable, *D* may collect from *C, C* from *B,* and *B* from *A,* unless they had agreed upon a different order of liability.

C. Agents' Liability on a Negotiable Instrument

When agents are given authority to make negotiable instruments for their principal, it is important that they properly sign the instrument in such a manner as to properly disclose the principal. One recommended form is "John Jones, by Wm. Smith, Agent." N.I.L. 1 requires the instrument to be signed by the maker or drawer. Sec. 18 provides no one is liable on an instrument whose name does not appear thereon, but Sec. 19 provides that the signature of the maker or drawer may be made by a duly authorized agent, and Sec. 20 states if the agent signs properly and within his authority the principal alone will be bound. If the agent merely signs his name alone, or adds the word describing him as agent without disclosing the principal, the agent will be personally liable on the instrument and not the principal. Sec. 21 provides that even if the agent properly signs for his principal, the principal is bound only if the agent had authority and acted within the actual limits of his authority. Thus, as in all dealings with agents, it is up to the third party to determine the extent of the agent's authority.

VIII. PRESENTMENT, ACCEPTANCE AND NOTICE OF DISHONOR

The drawer and general indorsers guarantee payment of the instrument. Their obligation, however, is not absolute. Certain steps must be taken before they become liable. Thus, the drawer's and general indorser's liability (parties secondarily liable) is said to be conditional. In order to charge them with liability; the holder must

1. duly present the instrument for payment to the party primarily liable;
2. such primary party must dishonor the instrument (fail to pay); and
3. the holder must take the necessary proceedings of giving notice to the secondary parties.

Thus, the drawer and indorsers of a negotiable instrument incur no liability (assuming no breach of warranty) unless these conditions are met by the holder. Presentment is not necessary to charge the person primarily liable on the instrument.

A. Presentment

The holder must make a proper presentment of the instrument if he is to hold the secondary parties (drawer and indorsers) liable on their conditional liability under N.I.L. 66 unless the holder is excused from presentment of the instrument. Presentment for payment is dispensed with and excused:

"1. Where after the exercise of reasonable diligence presentment as required by this act cannot be made.
"2. Where the drawee is a fictitious person.
"3. By waiver of presentment, express or implied." (N.I.L. 82).

Presentment is also excused where there is no right to expect that the instrument will be paid (e.g., a drawer of a check cannot expect or demand presentment to the drawee bank when he knows he has insufficient funds therein).

There are myriad details in the N.I.L. regarding time for presentment, manner of presentment, place for presentment, and the person to make the presentment. These details are best to be consulted directly from the N.I.L. when needed, for generally the commercial practice waives presentment, and setting forth herein the details of requirements rarely used would unduly lengthen this book.

B. Presentment for Acceptance

Presentment for acceptance applies only to drafts (bills of exchange) and is not applicable to promissory notes. Promissory notes require only presentment for payment. Since the drawee of a bill of exchange does not become liable on the instrument until he has accepted it, presentment for acceptance is very important to the holder. Some bills require presentment for acceptance in addition to presentment for payment, whereas others require only presentment for payment. Where only presentment for payment is required, the holder may at his option present it for acceptance.

Presentment for acceptance is required:

"1. Where the bill is payable after sight, or in any other case, where presentment is necessary in order to fix the maturity of the instrument; or

"2. Where the bill expressly stipulates that it shall be presented for acceptance; or

"3. Where the bill is drawn payable elsewhere than at the residence or place of business of the drawee." (N.I.L. 143).

In no other case is presentment for acceptance necessary.

Under 1 above, an instrument payable a certain number of days after "sight" does not become payable until the number of required days have elapsed after it has been presented to the "sight" of the drawee for acceptance. The reason for 3 above is that the drawee of a bill so drawn would not know when and how the instrument will be presented for payment unless it is first presented for acceptance.

Should a bill drawn requiring presentment for acceptance not be presented or negotiated within a reasonable time, and presentment for acceptance is not excused, the drawer and all indorsers are discharged. Where only presentment for payment is required, the holder may wait until maturity and present the instrument for payment only, but it is nevertheless usually advantageous to present the bill for acceptance as soon as possible in order to make the drawer liable thereon. The proper place, time, and person to present a bill for acceptance are set out in detail in the N.I.L.

Presentment for acceptance is excused and the bill may be treated as dishonored by non-acceptance:

1. Where the drawer is dead, or has absconded, or is a fictitious person, or a person not having capacity to contract;

2. Where, after the exercise of reasonable diligence, presentment cannot be made; and
3. Where presentment has been irregular but acceptance has been refused on some other ground (N.I.L. 48).

Where presentment is excused or where a bill is duly presented and its acceptance is refused (bill is dishonored) or its acceptance is not made within the prescribed time, an immediate right of recourse against the drawer and indorsers accrues to the holder, and no presentment for payment is necessary (N.I.L. 149, 150 and 151). However, the right of recourse against the drawer and indorsers is conditional upon the holder giving due notice of dishonor or protest as explained in the next section.

C. Notice of Dishonor and Protest

Section 83 of the N.I.L. provides that the instrument is dishonored when it is duly presented for payment and payment is refused or cannot be obtained. Section 150 of the N.I.L. provides that where a bill is duly presented for acceptance and is not accepted within the prescribed time, the person presenting it must treat the bill as dishonored or he loses his right of recourse against the drawer and indorser. Dishonor by non-acceptance entitles the holder to immediate payment from the drawer or indorsers even though the bill, if accepted, would not have been due for several weeks or months.

The liabilities of the secondary parties to a negotiable instrument is conditional upon a due presentment and the taking of the necessary proceedings on dishonor. We have considered due presentment and shall now discuss the necessary proceedings of giving notice of dishonor (in the case of an inland bill) and protest (mandatory in case of a foreign bill and optional, in lieu of notice, in case of an inland bill or promissory note).

"An inland bill of exchange is a bill which is, or on its face purports to be, both drawn and payable within this state. Any other bill is a foreign bill. Unless the contrary appears on the face of the bill, the holder may treat it as an inland bill." (N.I.L. 129).

Thus, to hold the secondary parties on their conditional liability under N.I.L. 66 when the primary party fails to accept or pay the instrument, the holder must (1) make a due presentment of the instrument for payment, (2) protest the instrument, if necessary, and (3) give the proper notice of dishonor to the drawer and indorsers. Failure to meet these requirements will discharge the secondary parties from liability on the instrument.

Notice may be given orally or in writing, even by a telephone call, so long as it sufficiently identifies the instrument and indicates that it was duly presented and dishonored by non-acceptance or non-payment. Notice must be given to the party sought to be bound, and within the time fixed by the N.I.L., which is generally one day (either to give the notice direct or place it in the mails). Notice of dishonor to a party secondarily liable does not have to be given by all parties who seek to bind him, for notice from one serves for all.

Notice of dishonor is not required to be given to the drawer, (1) where the drawer and drawee are the same person, (2) where the drawee is a fictitious person or a person not having capacity to contract, (3) when the drawer is the person to whom the instrument is presented for payment, (4) where the drawer has no right to expect or require that the drawer or acceptor will honor the instrument, or (5) where the drawer has countermanded payment. (N.I.L. 114).

Notice of dishonor is not required to be given to an indorser (1) where the drawee is a fictitious person or a person not having capacity to contract, (2) where the indorser is the person to whom the instrument is presented for payment, or (3) where the instrument was made or accepted for his accommodation. (N.I.L. 115). Notice of dishonor is also not required where it has been waived or, for one reason or another but after the exercise of reasonable diligence, it is impossible to give.

Notice of dishonor to the secondary parties is all that is required when an inland bill is dishonored, but where the instrument dishonored is a foreign bill, it must also be protested in a statement by a person other than the holder. This statement is in the form of a certificate and is to be made by a notary public over his seal or by a resident of the place of dishonor in the presence of two or more witnesses. If protest is made on the same day of dishonor, notice of dishonor is not required.

The certificate must specify:

1. The time and place of presentment;
2. The fact that presentment was made and the manner thereof;
3. The cause or reason for protesting the bill;
4. The demand made and the answer given, if any, or the

fact that the drawee or acceptor could not be found. (N.I.L. 153)

The certificate of protest is admissible in evidence as to the truth of the recitals contained therein and this facilitates the suit against secondary parties who are in another jurisdiction. Of course, protest can be and generally is waived.

IX. CHECKS

There are some sections of the N.I.L. that only apply to checks. These sections, and their applications, are now discussed.

A check is a bill of exchange drawn on a bank and payable on demand (N.I.L. 185). In other words, it is like any draft except that the drawee is always a bank. A check is drawn against funds which the drawer has placed on deposit with the drawee bank. The drawee bank has contracted with the drawer (depositor) to honor properly drawn checks to the extent that drawer has funds deposited. Thus, the drawee bank is acting as an agent for the depositor, and must accept and pay according to his instructions or not do so if he orders a "stop payment."

"A check must be presented for payment within a reasonable time after its issue or the drawee will be discharged from liability thereon to the extent of the loss caused by the delay." (N.I.L. 186) A check is payable on demand, and should a holder delay too long in presenting it for payment and during such lapse of time the drawee bank becomes insolvent, the holder must bear the loss, for without his delay the check would have been paid in full. Further, a check is not an assignment of the depositor's funds in the bank to his credit, nor is the bank liable on a check until and unless it accepts or certifies it. (N.I.L. 189) Thus, in the above situation where the holder delayed too long, if the bank had some funds to pay pro rata, the depositor would be paid, not the holder. Then, of course, the holder could seek recovery from the depositor (drawer) on the secondary liability of drawer but would recover only a pro rata amount, for as mentioned, his delay caused the check not to be paid in full.

Another effect of these rules to be kept in mind is that a bank is under no duty to a holder to honor a check presented for payment. The bank is under a duty to the depositor (drawer) by the contract they entered into, but a holder must seek recourse against the drawer for non-payment by the bank, and can do nothing against the bank. However, the depositor can go against the bank for a breach of its duty to him.

A certification of a check by a drawee bank is equivalent to an acceptance (N.I.L. 187), and the bank becomes primarily liable thereon. If a payee or indorsee has the check certified, the drawer and all indorsers are discharged from liability thereon. This is because the payee or indorsee could have demanded payment, and if he elects only to have it accepted he must shoulder the risk from then on.

If a drawee bank pays or certifies a check upon which the drawer's signature is forged, the bank cannot charge the drawer's account nor can the bank recover from the person for whom they cashed the check if such person qualifies as a holder in due course. This is because the drawee bank is conclusively presumed with knowing the signature of the drawer (their depositor). However, since a bank is not charged with knowing anybody else's signature, this rule does not apply to forged indorsements.

X. DISCHARGE OF NEGOTIABLE INSTRUMENTS

A. Discharge of Persons Secondarily Liable

A person secondarily liable on the instrument is discharged by any act which discharges the instrument. In other words, when the instrument is discharged, all parties, both primary and secondary, are discharged. On the other hand, a secondary party may be discharged without discharging the instrument. N.I.L. 120 provides: A person secondarily liable on the instrument is discharged:

1. By any act which discharges the instrument (discussed below).
2. By the intentional cancellation of his signature by the holder.

   Example: The holder of an instrument indorsed by *A, B,* and *C* intentionally cancels *A*'s signature. *A, B,* and *C* are discharged, *A* under the rule given, and *B* and *C* under the next rule.
3. By the discharge of a prior party.
4. By a valid tender of payment by a prior party.

5. By a release of the principal debtor, unless the holder's right of recourse against the party secondarily liable is expressly reserved.
6. By any agreement binding upon the holder to extend the time of payment, or to postpone the holder's right to enforce the instrument, unless made with the assent of the party secondarily liable, or unless the right of recourse against such party is expressly reserved.

Numbers 5 and 6 are merely the general law of suretyship (as applied to negotiable instruments) whereby the surety (secondary party) is discharged by actions of the creditor (holder), in which he has not consented, which change the terms of the original debt. The law will not force the secondary party to carry the risk of the instrument for a period longer than he agreed to. Should the holder so extend the time of payment or release the principal debtor and reserve his right of recourse against the secondary party, the latter can, if he so desires to protect himself, immediately pay the holder and thereby acquire the right to proceed against the primary party at once. (N.I.L. 121).

B. Discharge of the Instrument

A negotiable instrument is discharged:

1. By payment in due course by or on behalf of the principal debtor. Payment in due course is defined in N.I.L. 88 as "payment at or after maturity of the instrument to the holder thereof in good faith and without notice that his title is defective." Payment in due course to the holder of "bearer paper" discharges the instrument, whereas payment to the payee of such paper who is not the holder (he, having negotiated the instrument to a holder in due course) will not discharge the instrument. It is always best for the person paying the instrument to demand surrender of the instrument simultaneously with his payment. Payment must be in money. The giving of a new note is not payment unless the parties intend it as such.

2. By payment in due course by the party accommodated, where the instrument is made or accepted for accommodation.

3. By the intentional cancellation thereof by the holder (e.g., destruction, mutilation, marking it paid or cancelled with the intent to discharge the instrument).

"A cancellation made unintentionally, or under a mistake, or without authority of the holder, is inoperative, but when an instrument or any signature thereon appears to have been cancelled the burden of proof lies on the party who alleges that the cancellation was made unintentionally, or under a mistake or without authority." (N.I.L. 123)

4. By any other act which will discharge a simple contract for the payment of money (e.g., running of the statute of limitations, bankruptcy of principal debtor, accord and satisfaction, etc. (see Contracts)).

But the giving of a new note in place of the old will not pay or extinguish the original note whether the new note is made by the same person or another. The new note is only an accord, and until the new note is paid (satisfaction) the original note is not discharged. Of course, if the parties intend the new note to discharge the original note, as would be evidenced by the surrendering of the old note for the new, such intent would govern and the original note would be discharged.

5. When the principal debtor becomes the holder of the instrument at or after maturity in his own right. This helps explain the last illustration above. Also, it should be noted that if the principal debtor acquires the instrument before maturity and elects to further negotiate it, it is not discharged. Then too, mere possession obtained through fraud or theft by the principal debtor would not discharge the instrument.

6. Renunciation. "The holder may expressly renounce his rights against any party to the instrument, before, at, or after its maturity. An absolute and unconditional renunciation of his rights against the principal debtor made at or after maturity of the instrument discharges the instrument. But a renunciation does not affect the rights of a holder in due course without notice. A renunciation must be in writing, unless the instrument is delivered up to the person primarily liable thereon." (N.I.L. 122)

7. Material Alteration: N.I.L. 125 provides any alterations which change the date, the sum payable (either for principal or interest), the time or place of payment, the number or the relations of the parties, the medium or currency in which payment is to be made, or which adds a place of payment where none is specified, or any other change or addition which alters the effect of the instrument in any respect, is a material alteration.

N.I.L. 124 provides: "Where a negotiable instrument is materially altered without the assent of all parties liable thereon, it is avoided, except as against a party who has himself made, authorized, or assented to the alteration, and subsequent indorsers.

"But when an instrument has been materially altered and is in the hands of a holder in due course, not a party to the alteration, he may enforce payment thereof according to its original tenor." The details of material alterations were previously discussed under "Real Defenses," but it might be added that even an innocent material alteration discharges the instrument. If done fraudulently, not only the instrument, but also the debt, is extinguished. But even in the latter case, a holder in due course, not a party to the alteration, may enforce the instrument according to its original tenor.

INDEX